Textbook on Jurisprudence

The daring publisher, Universal Law Publishing Company, among the foremost in the law publishing field and progressive in venturing to bring out rare legal literature of avant garde *character has rightly enriched the* corpus juris *of India*

Justice V R Krishna Iyer
Random Reflections, page 14

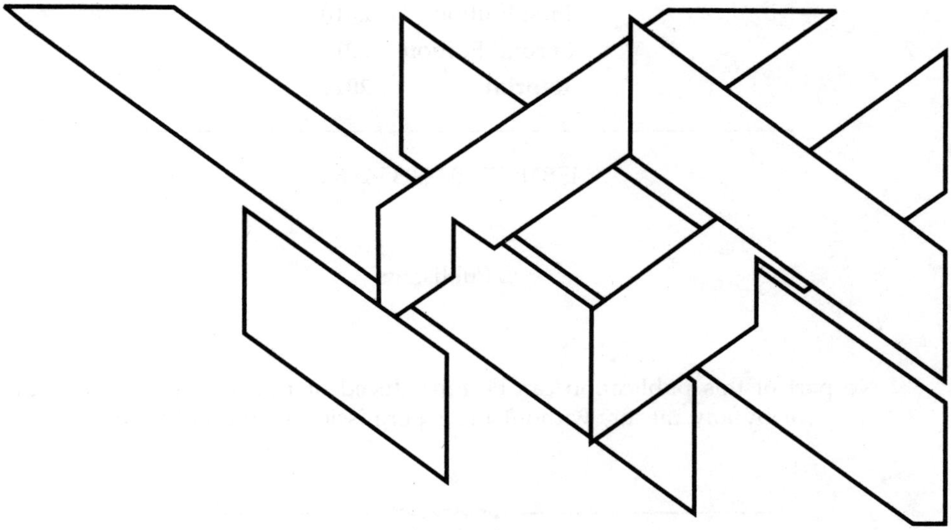

Textbook on Jurisprudence

SECOND EDITION

Dr. Veena Madhav Tonapi

B.Sc. (Hons.); LL.M.; Ph.D. (Law)
Principal, J.S.S. Sakri Law College,
Hubli, Karnataka

Universal
Law Publishing Co. Pvt. Ltd.
NEW DELHI - INDIA

First Edition : 2010
Second Edition : 2013
Reprint : 2014

ISBN: 978-93-5035-296-0

Published by

Universal
Law Publishing Co. Pvt. Ltd.
NEW DELHI - INDIA

A-58, G.T. Karnal Road Industrial Area,
(Near Azadpur Metro Station), Delhi-110033
Tel. : 011-47082254, 27458529, 27215334 Fax : 011-27458529
e-mail: unilaw@vsnl.com

- Showroom : C-27, Connaught Place, New Delhi-110001
- Sales : sales@unilawbooks.com
- Editorial : edit@unilawbooks.com
- Website : **www.unilawbooks.com**

Join us on Facebook
www.facebook.com/unilawbooks

Recommended citation: Dr. Veena Madhav Tonapi, *Textbook on Jurisprudence* 2nd Edn. (New Delhi: Universal Law Publishing Co. Pvt. Ltd., 2013).

Computer Typeset at Aesthetic and *Printed* at Sita Fine Arts Pvt. Ltd., New Delhi.

This book is dedicated
to the memory of
my mother-in-law
Late Indirabai Laxmikant Tonapi

PREFACE TO THE SECOND EDITION

With my experience as a law teacher for more than two decades I have seen that, by and large Jurisprudence is considered as a difficult subject in the law curricula as it deals with the abstract concepts and theories. The subject becomes all the more difficult for comprehension and understanding when the language used by jurists is a bit more sophisticated. All along I had a feeling that with a simpler language and an explanation with Indian examples and case law, may be, the students would develop more interest in this very important subject. I have made a conscious attempt to keep the language simple and meanings of the difficult words/phrases/legal maxims and concepts are explained in the glossary. The book is student-centric. It covers the topics prescribed by the Bar Council of India for law curriculum.

Every chapter begins with a detailed synopsis which nearly sums up the salient points in the chapter which can be easily remembered by the student. Wherever the concepts are complicated they are made simple through proper illustrations. Many examples have been given from Indian Laws and Judgments which make it easier for an Indian student of jurisprudence to appreciate and enjoy "Jurisprudence". A grasp of the basic principles of jurisprudence would surely help to understand the essence of the legal system.

February 2013 **Dr. Veena Madhav Tonapi**

WORD OF THANKS

I owe a 'word of thanks' to all the persons who have directly or indirectly assisted and motivated me to undertake the writing of this book. I specially remember my mother in law – Late Smt. Indirabai Laxmikant Tonapi – herself a traditional house-wife – but without whose presence and encouragement I could never have taken up my law education after my marriage and with two kids to be looked after. My husband Madhav has ever been a source of inspiration in all my academic ventures.

I am grateful to Dr. Manish Arora and his team at Universal for their consistent support and guidance in the publishing of this work.

CONTENTS

CHAPTER 3

THEORIES OF LAW: COMMAND OF THE SOVEREIGN: POSITIVE THEORY

CHAPTER 4

LEGAL THEORIES: LAW AS THE PRACTICE OF THE COURT: LEGAL REALISM

CHAPTER 5

THEORIES OF LAW: LAW AS A SYSTEM OF RULES

CHAPTER 6

INTERNATIONAL LAW

CHAPTER 7

THE FUNCTION AND PURPOSE OF LAW

CHAPTER 8

LAW AND FACT

CHAPTER 9

THE TERRITORIAL NATURE OF LAW

CHAPTER 10

CONSTITUTIONAL LAW

CHAPTER 11

THE ADMINISTRATION OF JUSTICE

CHAPTER 12

SOURCES OF LAW: LEGAL AND HISTORICAL SOURCES

CHAPTER 13

SOURCES OF LAW: LEGISLATION

CHAPTER 14
PRECEDENT AS A SOURCE OF LAW

CHAPTER 15
CUSTOM AS A SOURCE OF LAW

CHAPTER 16
CONCEPTS: LEGAL RIGHTS

CHAPTER 17

CONCEPTS: OWNERSHIP

CHAPTER 18

POSSESSION

CHAPTER 19
CONCEPTS: LEGAL PERSON

CHAPTER 20
TITLES

CHAPTER 21
PRINCIPLES OF LIABILITY

CHAPTER 22
THE LAW OF PROPERTY

CHAPTER 23
OBLIGATIONS

CHAPTER 24
PROCEDURE

CHAPTER 25
THE EVOLUTION OF LAW

TABLE OF CASES

CHAPTER 1
INTRODUCTION

SYNOPSIS

I. What is Jurisprudence?
- **1. Investigation into 'Law' and not 'the Law'**
- **2. Two Meanings of Jurisprudence: 'The Science of Civil Law' and 'The Science of the First Principles of Law'**

II. Nature and Value of Jurisprudence
- **1. Philosphical Aspect of Law**
- **2. No Immediate Practical Application**
- **3. Investigation into Abstract Principles of Law**
- **4. Analysis of Legal Concepts**
- **5. Link Law with Other Disciplines**

III. Advantages of Studying Jurisprudence
- **1. Intrinsic Interest**
- **2. Helps in Refining the Rules**
- **3. Helps in Generalizing the Legal Principles**
- **4. Concrete Laws Provide No Answer**
- **5. Sharpens the Lawyer's Skills**
- **6. Helps in Appreciating Social Functions of Law and Social Realities**

IV. Purpose of Legal Theory

V. What is Law?
- **Holland; Aristotle; Salmond; Goodhart; Blackstone; Holmes; Kelson; Roscoe Pound**

VI. Schools of Jurisprudence
- **Historical School; Analytical School; Ethical School**

VII. Historical Development of Different Schools of Jurisprudence
- **1. Jeremy Bentham**
- **2. John Austin**
- **3. Hans Kelson's Pure Science of Law**
- **4. Historical School**
- **5. Functional School**
- **6. Sociology of Law**
- **7. Teleological School**
- **8. Scandinavian Realist**
- **9. Ancient Hindu School of Thought**

I. What is Jurisprudence?

1. Investigation into 'Law' and not 'the Law'

Jurisprudence is the name given to a systematic and scientific investigation into law. Jurisprudence is derived from two Latin words: *jus* or *juris i.e.* law and *prudentia i.e.* knowledge. It is *jurisprudentia – the knowledge of law.* Here we must distinguish between 'law' and 'the law'. When we speak of *'the law'* we are speaking of the concrete or specific law of a particular legal system which is to be applied to solve a given legal problem. It may be different for different legal systems. For example, under our Indian law, to find out whether past consideration is a valid consideration for an enforceable contract we refer to Section 25 of the Indian Contract Act, 1872 and find out *'the law'* on the point and conclude that past consideration is a valid consideration. Whereas past consideration is not a valid consideration under English law. But when we take an investigation into why is past consideration a valid consideration; or why some legal systems like the English legal system have not considered it a valid consideration; or why did they subsequently consider it to be a valid consideration etc., we are making an investigation into the philosophical aspect of 'law'. *Thus one finds that Jurisprudence is different from the other subjects prescribed for the Law course.* The other subjects by and large tell us what is 'the law' whereas Jurisprudence tells us what is 'law'.

"Jurisprudence was the first of the social sciences born", said Wurzel[1]. Its province has been determined and re-determined and there is no finality to it. Any book on Indian Penal Code or Contract will give much the same idea regarding the subject unlike books on Jurisprudence. This is because Jurisprudential writings deal with thought about law on the broadest possible basis. It deals with structure, uses and functioning of law and legal concepts. The word *'Jurisprudence'* is also used to describe the legal connections of any body of knowledge like Medical Jurisprudence; Dental Jurisprudence etc,. This would indicate such aspects of Medicine or Dentistry as is important in law. The question that arises is – does the word *'Jurisprudence'* have any 'proper meaning' as such? But no word – least of all 'Jurisprudence' has a proper meaning. Reason for avoiding a term like Medical Jurisprudence is that this kind of expression is no longer currently in use in English speaking countries. It has been largely superceded by the term 'forensic medicine' to mean application of law for purposes of medicine.

In French law, Jurisprudence is the term applied to the body of law built up by decisions of particular courts. In England, the word was in use throughout the early formative periods of common law, but it meant a little more than the study of law or skill in law.

The word began acquiring a technical significance among English lawyers only during Bentham and his disciple Austin's time. Bentham distinguished between 'law as it is' (expositorial) and 'law as it ought to be' (censorial). He was also concerned with law reform (deontology). Austin[2] concerned himself with expository Jurisprudence *i.e.* law as it is. His work consisted in the formal analysis of the structure of English law.

Analytical exposition of the type Bentham pioneered and Austin developed, has dominated English legal thought almost to the present. Hence in England, Jurisprudence came to mean – analysis of the formal structure of laws and its concepts.

1. "Methods of Juridical Thinking" in Science of Legal Methods: Select Essays, quoted in R.W.M. Dias: Jurisprudence, 4th Edn., p. 1.
2. First Professor of Jurisprudence in University of London.

The end of nineteenth century witnessed conflicting ideologies, troubled social conditions and hence there was a change in the outlook. Jurisprudence today is viewed in an immeasurably broader and more sweeping sense.

As Julius Stone puts it- Jurisprudence is 'The lawyer's extraversion. It is the lawyer's examination of the precepts, ideals, techniques of the law in the light derived from present knowledge in disciplines other than law"[1]. It is thus a study of law in action and not just in law books.

Thus study of Jurisprudence concerns thought about law on the broadest possible basis. This needs an analysis of the term – 'thought' 'about law' and the 'basis of approach'. Thought is linked with language and use of the words. Thought involves communicating or conversing or reasoning out or arguing with one self and also with the other persons. L. Macmillan said, "The lawyer's business is with words". 'Words control thought and also' the logic.

2. *Two Meanings of Jurisprudence: "The Science of Civil Law'; and 'The Science of the First Principles of Law'*

Salmond gives two meanings of Jurisprudence – a broad sense and a narrow sense. In its *broad and generic sense,* Jurisprudence includes the entire body of legal doctrine. In this sense, all law books are books of Jurisprudence. It is a synonym for law. In its widest sense, Jurisprudence is *'the science of civil law'*. In this sense, it is an intellectual investigation of law, done in a systematic manner.

Investigation of law in a systematic manner means investigation into:

1. The *legal exposition i.e.* to set forth the contents of an actual legal system as existing at any time – whether past or present,
2. The *legal history i.e.* to set forth the historical process whereby any legal system came to be what it is or what it was, and
3. The *science of legislation i.e.* to set forth the law as it ought to be.

But this is not the sense in which the term Jurisprudence is used here. The term Jurisprudence is used in a narrow sense to mean: *'the science of the first principles of law'*.

Jurisprudence deals with the ultimate principles of law underlying a legal system. It is an investigation of an abstract, general and theoretical nature which seeks to lay bare the essential principles of law and legal system. Jurisprudence thus deals with knowledge of 'law' and not 'the law'.

II. Nature and Value of Jurisprudence

1. *Philosophical aspect of law:* Study of Jurisprudence consists of finding out the 'rationale' or the 'reasoning' behind such laws. In the study of Jurisprudence we go deeper and find out why is it that a particular rule or a regulation or a particular mode or manner of behaviour has taken the status of 'law'; what distinguishes a legal rule from a moral rule or etiquettes, manners, a social rule or a custom; what makes a rule enduring or lasting; why people obey or disobey laws, etc. We thus reflect on the rules already known and not look for new rules. Thus when we speak of *'law'*, we speak of the philosophical aspect of law. When we speak of *'the law'* we are referring to a definite or a concrete law laid down by a specific legal system, say the English or the Indian legal system.

1. Stone, Legal System and Lawyers Reasonings, p.16, quoted in Dias: Jurisprudence.

2. *No immediate practical application:* Jurisprudence is not created by legislation or by a Statute. It is not a law laid down by any authoritative source like a legislation, precedent or a recognized custom. It does not consist of a set of rules to be applied to given legal problems. Therefore, it is without 'immediate' practical application. It is the result of the thinking process of jurists and philosophers who have reflected on the working of the legal system. They have full freedom to speculate, assess, and analyze the legal system. Hence, Jurisprudence allows greater scope for the author's imaginative analysis and thinking. Therefore, one finds less agreement in different Jurisprudence text books than in text books of other legal subjects. For example, in all the text books on Indian Penal Code you find the same definition of murder and the same punishment mentioned. But in Jurisprudence books one jurist may lay down the deterrent theory and another may emphasise the reformative theory of punishment. One jurist may criticise the views of the other. And his analysis is neither binding on the Government nor the court nor the party to the case. It is an intellectual exercise without immediate practical application. However, *it can set the tone for reforming and reshaping the law.*
3. *Investigation into abstract principles of law*: Jurisprudence is, therefore, an investigation into an abstract, general and theoretical nature which seeks to find out the essential principles of law and legal systems. It is a second order subject whose object is to reflect and analyze on the rule already known and investigate into the working or non-working of certain rules and not to discover the rule. In the process it may lay down the seeds for a new rule.
4. *Analysis of legal concepts*: Likewise, Jurisprudence also deals with analysis of legal concepts. 'Concept' means thought, or an idea or a hypothesis. We have laws speaking of rights, duties, powers, immunities, obligations, liabilities, intention, interest, ownership, negligence etc. In Jurisprudence we study the conceptual meaning of these terms; the ultimate meaning – the philosophical aspect of these terms. For example, does *A* have the right to transfer a particular land? We refer to the Transfer of Property Act, 1882 to find out whether he has a subsisting marketable title to the property, does he have the capacity to transfer etc. In Jurisprudence we try to find the ultimate—*viz.* what is a right? So, we say that it is a recognised and a protected interest? Who protects it and how is it protected? How many kinds of rights are there? What is being transferred? What is meant by interest, can you transfer a part of the interest etc. Thus, legal concepts and legal ideas are analysed.
5. *Link law with other disciplines*: Another task of Jurisprudence is to link law with other disciplines like sociology, psychology etc. Therefore, Jurisprudence should not confine itself only to logic. Legal theory is concerned with law as it exists and functions in society. Therefore, concepts are analyzed against the background of social developments, changing political and economic attitudes, changing aspirations of the people. For example, why does man commit crime? Should crime be punished or should the criminal be reformed? What is the purpose of punishment? etc.

III. Advantages of Studying Jurisprudence

Though Jurisprudence is without immediate practical application following are the advantages of studying Jurisprudence:

1. *Intrinsic interest:* Scholarly treatment of any concept or any subject has its own intrinsic interest and fascination. When the concept is one which is connected with life and living; rights and duties; ownership and possession etc. it becomes all the more fascinating as law is a phenomenon which makes its presence felt in every field–name any field and you have a law governing it. Speculation and theory have a natural appeal. Concept of zero is an important mathematical concept where Indians have played a pioneering role. Today zero is a concept extensively used in computers. Likewise Jurisprudential concepts are fascinating.
2. *Helps in refining the rules:* It has repercussions on the whole of legal, political & sociological thought which could find a practical application in refining the rules in their day-to-day operations and applications in the society.
3. *Helps in generalizing the legal principles:* Jurisprudence aims at generalizing the legal principles. Generality can mean improvement. It may unify various concepts underlying various facts, situations and pave the way for solution of various problems by one technique. Thus complexities of law can become manageable.
4. *Concrete laws provide no answer:* Jurisprudence is an instrument through which a concrete subject like Torts, Contracts, Indian Penal Code etc. can be put to more effective practical use specially when such concrete laws do not provide a direct answer to the question involved or where the facts are such that one has to rely on the logical analysis and argumentative skill to make a point. This is specially so in the higher courts like the Supreme Court and the High Courts. It is the jurisprudential knowledge and intelligent analysis that comes in handy. It would not be a case of a *straight jacket* formula. For example, under Article 32 of our Constitution it nowhere says that letters can be treated as writs by courts. All that Article 32 says is that "the Supreme Court may be moved by an appropriate proceeding for the enforcement of writs". The court and the lawyers concerned conducted a jurisprudential analysis of the Article; took note of the social set up in the country; the length and breadth of poverty and illiteracy in the country which led to social injustice in the country and gave a new meaning to the term 'appropriate proceeding' in Article 32 and made way for epistolary jurisdiction of the courts—*i.e.* jurisdiction invoked just by writing letter to the court or the judge.
5. *Sharpens the lawyer's skill:* Logical analysis of legal concepts sharpens the lawyer's own logical technique. The mind gets trained to read in between the lines and to see beyond and behind the words.
6. *Helps in appreciating social functions of law and the social realities:* Lawyers are in the habit of looking either to the statutes or precedents for an answer to the legal problem. In other words, they suffer from the occupational vice of formalism. Study of Jurisprudence would make them appreciate the social function of law and social realities. This is because

Jurisprudence helps to link law with other disciplines like Sociology, Psychology, Economics etc and thus helps to appreciate the law in its wider social context. Jurisprudence helps to debate over the changing needs and aspirations of the people; the evolving developments and analyses the prospects and consequences of bringing them within the fold of the legal system. In short, as P.B. Mukherjee points out, Jurisprudence includes whatever law thinks, says and does in any field of human society. "Law and jurisprudence have a universal quality. It also has a timeless element. They are Ihering's 'Alphabets of Law'. It is, therefore, inevitable in every civilized Jurisprudence in the world to find some common basic elements. But subject to the demands of universality, the Jurisprudence of a country cannot afford to be entirely exotic, for the simple reason that law in the ultimate analysis, remains the relative expression of the life and spirit of the land and the community it serves."[1]

IV. Purpose of Legal Theory

If Jurisprudence is knowledge of law, legal theory is an attempt to answer the question 'what is law'? Attempts to define law are not just ornamental. It may be questioned that while learning chemistry we do not dedicate a vast literature to answer a similar question—what is chemistry? Why then take an investigation into 'what is law?' rather than begin with the study of the contents of law? Likewise it is argued that just as geometry is not a geometrical concept, law is not a legal concept. In geometry, the mathematician simply works with geometric concepts like triangle, and circle. Similarly, in law we have concepts of consideration – property, right, person etc. to be analysed and debated, and applied in practice. Court decisions do not depend on the answer to the question 'what is law?'. Hence it is only a thecretical question with no practical application, rather *no immediate practical* application.

Yet there is a need to define law because of the following reasons:—

1. Jurisprudence is an investigation into *legal* concepts', *'Law'* is the basic of all legal concepts.
2. Questions like whether international law is 'true law' and whether unjust law is 'law' can be answered only with reference to the definition of law. But the counter argument is that in such a case the court enquires whether there exists any such rule as is claimed within the framework of international law and does not deal with the question 'what is law'?[2] Likewise it finds out whether the injustice urged contravenes any fundamental principle under the legal system. They don't begin by defining law to find out if unjust law is law.
3. Law is a basic concept of Jurisprudence. Legal notions like possession and right can be explored without reference to the definition of law but in the end, completeness involves reference to a definition of law.
4. Desire to define law.

---

1. Mukherjee P.B.: The New Jurisprudence, Calcutta Eastern Law House, p. 1.
2. Today in the 21st Century, after Liberalisation, Privatisation, Globalization this question is hardly of any significance. International law has all the trappings of law.

V. What is Law?

It is a very difficult question to answer. The term 'law' has been variously defined. A definition must ideally fix the boundaries and fix the limits of the term with precision. Law in fact is not capable of being defined. It can only be explained and hence there is a lot of literature on law. Several authors and jurists have attempted to give their version of the term 'law'. And for every version you find that there is a criticism or a counter argument. Following are some of the definitions:—

Holland

A law is a general rule of external human action enforced by a sovereign political authority.

Defects: There is a confusion between rule and a law: it does not account for the internal element in the law *viz.*, the intention, the motive which is so essential for an act to become a crime or not to become a crime.

Aristotle

Law is reason without desire.

Defect: The dividing line between reason and desire is confusing. In almost every desire there is a reason and behind every reason there lurks a desire.

Salmond

Law means the rules recognized and acted on by courts of justice.

Defects: It does not account for those laws which are not justiciable at all *i.e.* those which cannot be questioned in the courts of law– as in the case of the Directive Principles of State Policy of the Indian Constitution; in addition what about the laws which do not come up before the court at all for being recognized and acted upon? Are they not laws at all?

Goodhart

A law is any rule of human conduct which is recognized as being obligatory.

Defects: Who owes the obligation and to whom? Who should recognize it as obligatory? *E.g.* when *X* commits theft – he violates Section 378 of Indian Penal Code which says: 'Don't steal or else you will be punished'. Does the section lose its obligatoriness because *X*, by committing theft, has refused to recognize the obligatory nature of law?

Blackstone

Municipal law is the rule of civil conduct prescribed by the supreme power in a State commanding what is right and prohibiting what is wrong.

Defects: Modern States know of several laws not prescribed by the supreme power. What about customs having the force of law, which are commanded not by the supreme power but have their source in practices followed from time immemorial.

Holmes

Law is a prediction of what will be done by judges or officials.

Defects: The definition is by symptoms and not by its basic foundations; it does not take into account a majority of the laws where such prediction is not at all involved as the law is fairly certain. It also does not account for the customary laws and conventional laws.

Kelson

Law is the basic norm which gives validity to the Constitution of the State and to all subordinate legal norms.

Defects: It is a logical fiction. A basic norm needs to have a standard or frame of reference.

Roscoe Pound

He formulated the social control concept in jurisprudence and provided an edge for sociological jurisprudence. He coined the phrase 'social engineering' to describe the problems of the legal order in balancing individual wants and social interests. Justice, according to law, was his dominant idea. He distinguished between divine justice, moral justice, natural justice and justice according to law. Justice 'according to law' is not a new concept. That was Austin's and Hegal's doctrine also. Under Indian jurisprudence after the decision in *Maneka Gandhi* v. *Union of India*[1], law must be just, fair and reasonable. In this sense, it is not only justice according to law, but law also has to be in accordance with justice.[2]

He points out that there are 6 advantages when justice is according to law:

1. Predictability of the course of administration of justice.
2. Appeals and revisions secure against errors of individual judgment.
3. Law secures against the improper motives on the part of those administering justice.
4. Ethical ideas of the community are formulated in the laws. Hence the judges also get an insight into the standards on which the ethical ideas of the community are formulated.
5. Law prevents the sacrifice of the ultimate interests – social and individual for the more obvious and pressing, but less weighty and immediate interests.

What is justice? It is a complex question involving divine or God revealed laws; natural laws; ethical laws and political laws or State made laws. Judicial decisions like *Maneka Gandhi's*[3] case and the new doctrine in *Ajay Hasia* v. *Khalid Mujib*,[4] case where it was held that if a law is arbitrary and capricious it would be struck down as being opposed to Article 14 of our Constitution have minimized the difference between statute law or the positive laws on one hand and the divine ethical or natural laws on the other hand. In addition under the rules of interpretation which are again the creation of the Judiciary that interpretation which would cause injustice is to be avoided. When they do so they do not invoke the divine or the ethical laws but they invoke the acceptable rules of common sense, equality and good conscience.[2]

VI. Schools of Jurisprudence

As seen earlier, Jurisprudence gives lot of freedom to the jurists to play with their imagination and thought process and gives an account of what is law and

1. AIR 1978 SC 597.
2. Mukherjee P.B.: The New Jurisprudence, p. 38.
3. AIR 1978 SC 597.
4. AIR 1981 SC 487.

what are the first principles of law. This has given rise to various Schools of Jurisprudence. They can be broadly classified[1] into:

1. Analytical
2. Historical
3. Ethical.

Analytical School

1. It analyzes the first principles of law 'as it exists in the legal system' and does not investigate into what the law 'ought to be'.
2. They also do not refer to the historical origin of law.
3. They are concerned mainly with the analysis of the concept of civil law. It analyses the essential ingredients of the fabric of law. For *e.g.* the sovereignty of law and administration of justice.
4. It analyses the relation between the State and the law.
5. It analyses the legal sources of law *i.e.* the legislation the judicial precedents and customary laws.
6. It favours codification of law. The works of Bentham, Austin and Salmond are based on analytical school of Jurisprudence.

Historical School

1. It deals with the general principles governing the origin and development of law and with the influences that effect the law. It makes history an important reason in the development of law.
2. According to Sir Henry Maine, Montesque was the first jurist of this school. His work is contained in *Esprit des Lois* (Spirit of the Laws). He emphasized more on the external causes in the framing of the laws. He did not see the qualities of human nature which go to make and develop the law.
3. For Hugo, law is the result of the habits and ways of the people themselves acquired because of necessity or accident. When the community accepts a rule for a long period it becomes a law.
4. For Savigny, the organic evolution of law with the life and character of people develops with the ages. Law grows with the nation, increases with it and dies at its dissolution and is a characteristic of it.

Ethical School

1. It investigates the purpose of a particular law. It considers the reasonableness and soundness of law. It concerns with the theory of justice in its relation with law. It considers questions like is the law just and reasonable; is it in accordance with natural justice etc.
2. It is not concerned with detailed criticism of actual legal system.
3. It deals with the difference between law and morality and how each can contribute to the ends of justice.
4. The greatest contributors of this theory are Bacon, Grotius, Spinoza and Kant.

---

1. Salmond: Jurisprudence, 10th Edn., p. 3.

5. Ethical School of Jurisprudence is prevalent in Europe; in England it is the Analytical School that predominates.

Salmond, the proponent of Analytical Jurisprudence, says that Analytical Jurisprudence does not totally disregard the ethical implication or the historical origin of law. If ethical implication is disregarded law would be reduced to a system of arid dry formalism. If historical origins are neglected we would not arrive at an adequate explanation of principles and concepts involved in the formation of law.

The other Schools are Sociological School, Synthetic School and Comparative School.

Sociological School deals with the study of law as a social phenomenon. It is the study of man in society. The study deals with synthetic how law governs the behaviour of man in the society.

Comparative School of jurisprudence deals with the comparative study of the systems of Jurisprudence in different countries.

Ultimately, Jurisprudence has to be a combination of several schools like that of analytical, historical, comparative, philosophical and sociological.

VII. Historical Developments of Different Schools of Jurisprudence

Historical Development of Different Schools of Jurisprudence[1]

1. Jeremy Bentham (1748-1832)

Bentham is the founder of the English analytical school and had interest in the mechanics of legal system. Not being interested in publicity his treatise 'Limits of Jurisprudence Defined' written in 1782 was published in 1945 when it was found by Prof. Everett at University College, London. His desire for reform was based on the doctrine of utility, his desire for codification was based on the hatred of judge-made law; his definition of law was wide enough to include subordinate legislation and administrative regulation; his analysis of rights and duties puts in an embryo (seed) what was once thought to be a discovery of the 20th Century.

Concept of utility was his gospel. He wished to test every law to see if it led to the greatest happiness of the greatest number. His attempt was to examine the structure, concepts and functioning of the legal system in order that the out-worn abuses be swept away.

Bentham's each work created a separate school–the pure analyst in the law as such; and the teleological writer interested in the ends of law.

2. John Austin

In 1832 Austin published his *Province of Jurisprudence Determined.* He became popular after his death and his School was known as Analytical School. He believed that analysis is the chief tool of Jurisprudence. Allen calls it the Imperative School because analysis is a method used throughout Jurisprudence. Though an analyst – analyzing law as it is – he has devoted several lectures to the role of ethics and utility in the evolution of law but finding works on Jurisprudence confusing, Austin confines himself to the study of law 'as it is.'

1. G.W. Paton, A Text Book of Jurisprudence.

3. *Hans Kelson's Pure Science of Law*

A century separates the work of Kelson from the work of Austin. Kelson reacted to the Modern Schools which widened the boundaries of Jurisprudence to such an extent that it overlapped with those of social sciences.

Kelson wanted to create a pure science of law stripped of irrelevant material. He argued that just like a mathematician is not interested in the way in which men think nor is he directly concerned whether his work is used to build a bridge or to break a bank, so also a jurist must study the legal rules in isolation from all social conditions. He argued that law does not attempt to describe what occurs but it prescribes rules to lay down standards of action which man ought to follow. He attempted to trace every legal act back to a law which imputes legal validity to certain human behaviour.

4. *Historical School*

Historical School antedates the work of Kelson. It considered law in direct relationship to the life of the community and laid the foundation on which modern Sociological School is built. Writers began emphasizing the spirit of the people rather than of the individual. They argued that law evolved like a language- by a slow process. Just as language is a peculiar product of Nation's genius – so is law. Source of law lies in the instinctive sense of right possessed by every race; law cannot be understood without an appreciation of the social milieu in which it has developed. Legislation can succeed only if it is in harmony with the internal conviction of law to which it is addressed. The prominent jurists of this School are Savigny, Maine, Vinogradoff.

5. *Functional School*

The fundamental tenet of this School is that we cannot understand what a thing is unless we study what it does. To Dean Pound, law is more than a set of abstract norms or legal order. It is also a process of balancing conflicting interests and securing the satisfaction of maximum wants with minimum friction. He believes that a jurist can only effect compromises valid for his time and generation. Hence they are not absolute ideals but views held by that particular community at the moment. Functional School is identified with School of Sociological Jurisprudence.

6. *Sociology of Law*

Pound's Sociological Jurisprudence must be distinguished from sociology of law. To avoid confusion between the terminologies, Pound's Sociological Jurisprudence is referred to as functional school.

Emphasis of the study of sociology of law is on science of social life as a whole. It covers a great deal of general sociology and political science. Study is on the society and law is a mere manifestation. Pound concentrated on law and considered society in relation to it.

Ehrlich (1862-1920) lays down a broad theory that law depends on popular acceptance and that each group creates its own living law which alone has a creative force. The judge merely makes precise and definite the raw material furnished by the community. Many criticize this school on the ground that they desire to teach a little of everything except the law. However study of law and social interests is useful in Jurisprudence in three aspects:

1. For better understanding of the evolution of law
2. Though man's views on his needs and ethics change over a passage of time, two legal theories of two systems may be miles apart, yet each system may be forced to modify its theory so that the practical results are not far removed from the theory.
3. Functional school infuses new life into both the study and the development of law. Attempt is made to teach law as a function of society instead of as a mere abstract set of rules and the courts freely support the reasons of social policy which lie behind the rules of law.

7. Teleological School

There are two fundamental points in this approach.

1. Proper answer must be given to the problem of validity of law *i.e.*, what is it that makes the law valid? This question must be answered.
2. Law is intimately related to justice. Hence we need to discover the yardstick by which to judge the law. This school asks the question – what is the ideal end (goal) of law? This school mainly concerns philosophy and hence it is known as Philosophical Jurisprudence.

8. Scandinavian Realist

The Scandinavian Realists are influenced by the philosophical works of Hagerstrom. He attempted to destroy the notion that right-duty relations and legal obligations have any objective existence. He asserted that the ideal of duty had no logical meaning. It was just an expression of a feeling which could be explained psychologically but had no place in the logic of a legal system. They are not the reasons for enforcing a legal system. They are the consequences of operation of law. He insisted that arguments from justice and such general notions were merely emotional and were neither scientific nor of objective or logical value. They attempted to see what law was and how it worked as a social fact divorced from value judgment and emotional attitudes.

Olivecrona, Lundstedt and Ross are the popular Scandinavian Realists. Lundsedt was the most extreme of the writers. He laughed at the traditional English theory of law. He rejected the method of justice and introduced his own 'method of social welfare'.

9. Ancient Hindu School of Thought

As far as Ancient India is concerned, under the laws applicable to Hindus law was intermingled with religion. Our scriptures and texts formulated the Ancient Indian Wisdom in the form of 'Dharma' and was evolved as the panacea for all human problems and is acknowledged as such by great modern thinkers of the West. Dharma cannot be defined. It can only be explained. It is that which helps the upliftment of living beings. That which ensures the welfare of living beings is surely Dharma.[1] Dharma sustains the society; it maintains social order; it ensures well being and progress of Humanity; it is that which fulfills these objectives.[2] Dharma is that which sustains and ensures progress and welfare of

1. Shantiparva 109-9-11 quoted in Justice M.Rama Jois: Dharma – the Global Ethic.
2. Karna Parva Ch. 59 verse 58

all in this world and eternal bliss in the other world. Dharma is promulgated in the form of commands (positive and negative, *vidhi* and *nishedha*).[1]

Dharma or rules of righteous conduct was evolved as a solution to the eternal problem arising out of the natural instinct of man. In Shantiparva of the Mahabharat[2] after explaining that an ideal state of affairs did exist when people protected each other acting according to *Dharma*, Bhishma proceeded to state that when a few persons began to deflect from the path of Dharma being overpowered by sensual desires, passion and greed for wealth and material pleasure and being physically stronger began to harass the weaker ones as a remedy to this situation the three-fold ideals called *Dharma, Artha* and *Kama* were laid down for the welfare and happiness of the people and the State was established with a King as its head. He was empowered to ensure the implementation of the Trivarga Doctrine.

After an in-depth study and meditation the great seers declared that unless *Kama* (desire) for material pleasure (Artha) and those proceeding from anger, greed, passion, infatuation and enmity of every individual is controlled by rules and not by the strength or weakness of individual human beings, incessant conflict, fight, loss of happiness, peace and loss of material pleasure itself would be the inevitable consequences. Hence rules of Dharma were expanded to cover all aspects of life. 'Dharma' is thus a collective term for the entire code of righteous conduct covering every sphere of human activity, and in every capacity or role of an individual, in relation to other individuals.

In ancient India, societies were governed by moral law. Law as we understand today is identified by a command issued by a sovereign and sanction imposed for non-compliance. In ancient India law was that which was believed to have been ordained by a Divine Author. It was more like what the Romans called *jus receptum* – that is law by acceptance. The principle sources of law were Vedas coming from divine origin, Shrutis – that which was heard and Smritis – that which was remembered. Smritis are the recollections of the precepts of God handed down by the Rishis. However in the process they did not exercise any sovereign powers. Smritis derived legal authority due to the respectable position held by the Rishis and because of the belief that what they laid down was agreeable to good conscience. The Smritikars also did not consider themselves to be law makers. They only claimed to be the compilers of the traditions handed down over generations. The Smritis also known as *Dharmashastras* (that is the strings of the rules of Dharma) were a compendium of principles for regulating human conduct. They were a blend of religious, moral and social duties.

There were three Principal Smritis. Foremost in rank of authority was Manusmriti (between 200 BC and AD 100). Then came Yajnavalkya Smritis (between 200 AD and 300 AD). Mitakshara is a leading commentary on this Smriti. Then came the Narada Smriti. If Smritis constituted the foundation of the written text of 'law', the 'Sadachar' (approved usage) supplied the unwritten customary practices of the people of Bharat.

Manusmriti is considered to be an authoritative reservoir of law and a systematic and cogent collection of rules in simple language. All the

1. Parashara Smriti.
2. Karna Parva Ch. 59 verse 14.

Dharmashastras from Rig Vedic age onwards copiously refer to the opinions of Manu- the primeval legislator. Lord Hobhouse described Manu in 1899 as the 'most revered of all the sages'.

Manu's code is divided into twelve chapters. The eighth chapter deals with eighteen subjects of law including civil and criminal law. Sir William Jones, one of the first judges of the Judicature of Bengal,[1] observed 'the style of Manusmriti has a certain austere majesty that sounds like the language of legislation and exhorts a respectful awe...and the harsh admonitions even to Kings are truly noble...'.

Yajnavalkya Smriti is founded on Manusmriti but the treatment is more logical and synthesized, particularly on the question of women and their right to inheritance. Though a follower of conventional conservatism, he was more liberal than Manu. There are a number of verses in the code of Yajnavalkya which testify to the fact that the law of procedure and the law of evidence to be followed in civil disputes had made considerable progress.

The code of Narada deals with judicature in its first part and in the second discusses eighteen titles of legal subject contained in the Manusmriti. It states the law in a straightforward manner in a logical sequence and in a clear and attractive style. Some of the topics dealt with by Narada are inheritance, ownership, gift, property, partnership. Narada Smriti lays down a series of rules relating to pleading, evidence of witness and procedure. It is the first of the Dharmashastras to accept and record the principle that King made laws (legislation) override the rules of law laid down in the Smritis.

The Dharmashastras (Smritis) did not visualize an ordered legal system but they conceptualized an aspiration 'nyaya' – that is justice. Nyaya meaning natural equity or reason was applicable to cases not covered by the written law and where two Smritis differed.

In the Smriti of Brahaspati it is stated that no decision should be based exclusively on the letter of Dharmashastra because where a decision is devoid of 'yukti' that is reason, there is failure of justice. Brahaspati perfected the doctrine of invoking equity even against written law. He describes the concept of justice as:

> *'justice being violated, destroys*
> justice being preserved, preserves;
> therefore justice must not be violated;
> *lest violated justice destroy us'*

It is uncertain whether *this* concept of justice was applied while administering the law. European scholars claim that the law of Dharmashastras did not represent a fixed set of rules. It was a stage when 'rule of law was not yet separated from the rule of religion' as expressed by Sir Henry Maine in his classic work *Ancient Law*. But John Mayne, another Oriental scholar, propounded the theory that the law of Dharmashastras was based upon an immemorial custom and had an existence prior to and independent of Brahminism and that it got altered by Brahmin writers so as to favour the then prevailing policies of Brahminism.

1. After coming to India in 1774, he learnt Sanskrit and translated Manusmriti

Kautilya's Arthashastra[1] predated the Manusmriti (around 300 BC) and it was written at the time of powerful warrior emperors like Chandragupta Maurya. It embodies the imperial code of law of Maurya Kings. Arthashastra dealt with secular law. Whereas Dharmashastra considered the same problems from an ethical, moral or religious viewpoint and gave effect to the notions on which the Hindu social structure was based, it was widely believed that Arthashastra had progressed independently of Dharmashastras until the Manusmriti was composed. Subsequent to Manusmriti Arthashastra ceased to function separately. Hindus in ancient India began taking their laws from Smritis and the commentaries on them. Kautilya gives a vivid description of the King's courts of justice:

a court for the 'Sangraha'- a group of 10 villages;

a court for 'Dronamukha' – a group of 400 villages;

a court for 'Sthaniya' – a group of 800 villages;

Above all of these a court presided by 'King's Judges'(the King was only the Head of an autonomous clan).

In ancient India the bulk of the administration of justice was carried out in popular assemblies known as Sabha or Samiti. They discussed public business and served as a forum for judging the cases brought before them.

---

1. It was a chance discovery in 1909.

CHAPTER 2

THEORIES OF LAW: LAW AS THE DICTATE OF REASON: NATURAL LAW THEORY

SYNOPSIS

INTRODUCTION

As Jurisprudence gives ample scope for creative and innovative thinking different theories have been developed based on the writers' attitude and imaginative and logical skill. We will study 4 main theories of law dealing with:

1. Content of law: Natural law theory
2. Form of law: Command of the Sovereign
3. In terms of actual functioning: Realist theory.
4. Law as a system of rules

I. Law as a Dictate of Reason: Natural Law Theory

Essence: Man-made laws to be tested with reference to the divine natural law to ascertain its validity.

The theory addresses the question what is the permanent basis of law and what is its relationship to justice.

In the primitive society, law was found mingled with religion and morality. For example, under the Hindu law the 18 branches of law are found intermingled and scattered in different sources of Hindu law like Vedas, Smriti and Shruti. According to Vinogradaff, all earlier societies place at the centre of their concept of human world, an idea that there is an all pervading, all knowing, all seeing God, the Almighty, who regulates life at every juncture. Every religion believes in the divine origin of their religious and moral tenets. God is infallible. God makes no mistakes. Therefore, laws made by God are ideal. Hence, man made laws must be tested with reference to the divine natural law to ascertain its validity. This is the essence of the Natural law theory.

Today our legal rules are separated from religion. Yet our rules are based on our concept of morality. There is a belief that there is a divine law to which human law should conform. This belief has given rise to a concept of law of nature which is superior to man made law. In England, it also gave rise to a separate system of justice known as courts of equity based on the principle of justice, equity and good conscience. Cases which did not have a legal solution came before the courts of equity. In India we have a merger of courts of equity and courts of law.

II. What is Natural Law? Man Made Law to be Tested with Reference to the Divine Natural Law

The central notion of this theory is that:

- There exist objective actual or tangible principles as distinguished from subjective (personal or individual) moral principles
- They depend on the essential nature of the universe
- Those principles can be discovered by natural reason
- They are necessarily valid because they are logically connected
- Ordinary human law is truly law only to the extent it conforms to these principles of natural law
- Man made law contrary to natural law, is no law. It is an abuse of law.

The term natural law has been understood to mean a variety of things to different people at different times.[1]

Natural law thinking is all inclusive and is encountered in various contexts. In other words, natural law deals with values. Values are an indispensable part of day-to-day administration of law. It is used either to support power or to

1. R.W.M. Dias: Jurisprudence, 4th Edn., p. 653.

ensure freedom from power according to the social needs of the times. For example, in *Addl. Distt. Magistrate, Jabalpur* v. *Shivakant Shukla*,[1] J. Khanna observes that even in the absence of Article 21 of the Constitution, the State has got no power to deprive a person of his life or liberty without the authority of law; that sanctity for life and liberty represented a facet of higher values which mankind began to cherish in its evolution from a state of tooth and claw to a civilized existence.

III. Two Kinds of Natural Law Thought

1. *Natural law of method*—It is an attempt to discover the method by which just rules may be devised. *i.e.* a prescription for rule making. For example, one of the principles of natural justice is to give a fair hearing. Methods of arriving at fair hearing are opportunity to examine, cross examine, assign a competent advocate etc.
2. *Natural law of content*—Attempt to deduce entire body of rules from some absolute first principle. The high aim was to arrive at perpetual peace. It was this 'Natural law of content' which came under damaging criticism. Natural law thinking, therefore, started fading and it reached its nadir (all time low) in the 19th century and was superceded by Positivism. Positivism (man made laws) flourished under stable social conditions. But when accepted social and moral beliefs were challenged Positivism gave no guidance; Positivism failed when it could not tackle monstrous abuses of power and liberty. There was then a new concept of social justice which included revival of Natural law doctrine.

IV. Merits/Attractions of the Natural Law Theory

1. *Appeal to a higher standard*: When ordinary laws fall short of an ideal, man has felt the need for an appeal from the positive law to some higher standard. *'Lex injusta non est lex* – unjust law is no law' has served to criticize and restrict unjust positive law.

   For example, setting up of the International Military Tribunal in Nuremburg was justified on the moral basis that war crimes were essentially immoral in character. Its basis was really the general anger of mankind against brutalities of the Nazi regime in waging an aggressive war. It did not fit into the Positivist theory. When the *Habeas Corpus* case was decided by the Supreme Court of India stating that when emergency was in operation and Presidential proclamation was in force, a writ for *Habeas Corpus* did not lie even if there were *mala fides*, the Western World wrote that the World's largest democracy has gone to sleep.[2]

   The whole concept of PIL under which the *locus standi* rule was liberalized; procedures relaxed; letters treated as writs can be said to be based on the dictate of reason *viz.* that procedure is the handmaiden of justice.
2. *Defense against ethical relativism*: Natural law served as a defense against ethical relativism. Ethical relativism attacked the very binding basis of law. The Greek philosophers drew a distinction between laws of nature

1. AIR 1976 SC 1207 (1255-56).
2. James Cameron: India goes back to sleep – A contemporary view of the Emergency from the West. Published in the Guardian on June 30, 1975.

(growth of plants, movement of the heavenly bodies, etc.) and conventional phenomenon (laws arising out of custom or practice) depending on human choice, for example, human customs, fashions and manners. Rules of law were like rules of language and etiquette *i.e.* being man-made, laws had arisen out of historical accident or convention. They were not naturally necessary or obligatory. In other words, laws of nature like rising of the sun, falling of an apple or a stone are obligatory because there is no choice for the sun but to rise and set and for an apple to fall. These are factual realities based on the law of nature *i.e.* an 'is' proposition. But laws being manmade are not obligatory (*i.e.* the Governments have the option to alter the laws) hence they are arbitrary and contingent *i.e.* contingent on the political will of the party in power. Man-made laws may be made and unmade to suit the political philosophy of the party in power. A classic example is where 'internal disturbance' as a ground for imposing President's rule under Article 356 was altered to 'armed rebellion' going by the experience of our country during the internal emergency. Likewise, MISA brought under the 9th Schedule during Emergency by the Congress Government was deleted by the 44th Constitutional amendment after Janata Party came to power.

3. *Some laws purely conventional while others common to all States*: In order to prevent laws from being classified as non-obligatory, for that could create disorder in the society, Aristotle pointed out that while some laws were purely conventional, others were common to all States. For example, that murder or theft is an offence is common to the whole civilization but one State may prescribe death penalty and another may prescribe life imprisonment. To this limited extent law may be said to be conventional.
4. *It was the Stoic philosophers who have the true construction of natural law theory*: Their philosophy was that man was endowed with reason; reasoning power was the distinguishing feature of man's nature and so man must live according to dictates of reason.
5. *'Dictate of reason'—Secular in its content*

   The distinguishing element of (concept of) 'dictate of reason' was secularism in its content. Hence, it provided a common moral ground for different religions and different outlooks.
6. *Reasons for development of natural law:* During the medieval period,[1] natural law developed because of the—
   - need for preserving not freedom, but the newly born stability in the medieval period
   - need to establish authority of the Church by reason and argument and not by force
   - need for a unifying Christian philosophy. Law of Nature was identified with Law of God by the 'Decretum Gratianum'.
7. *St. Thomas Aquinas: Means and ends connection*: St. Thomas Aquinas said that there is a natural connection between means and ends. Natural phenomenon has certain inevitable consequences. For example, fire burns,

1. R.W.M. Dias: Jurisprudence, 4th Edn., p. 655.

it does not freeze. Tendency to develop in a certain way is naturally inherent/ordained in things *e.g.* a corn will develop only into an oak and not a pine. A mango tree will give rise to a mango tree only and not an apple tree. Thus, there is a relation between means and end. This is appreciated only by man because man alone can reason out but a corn or a mango cannot. Hence law is an ordinance or a dictate of reason for common good made and promulgated by him who has the care of the community. Man identifies the end and then uses appropriate means to achieve the end. For example, the Government decides that health is an end worth achieving and then thinks of means to attain this end. This thinking process is unique to man. Through this thinking process man can control his destiny to a large extent. Yet he too is subject to certain basic impulses which can be perceived by observing human nature. At the *lowest level* there is the impulse of self-preservation; at the *next level* there is the impulse to reproduce the species and rear children and at the *highest level* the impulse to improve and take decisions for attainment of higher and better things. The third is peculiar to man by virtue of his reason. But the first two are shared with other things like a corn or a mango. Hence this means-end relationship could only have originated in the reason of some superhuman legislator. This is eternal law. Eternal law is the plan of the divine wisdom in directing all the acts and motions to attainment of the ends.

- Thus, according to St. Thomas Aquinas all things are governed by God's eternal law. But man unlike the rest of the creation can act contrary to that part of the eternal law which applies to him. This law (wherein he acts contrary to the eternal law) has to be promulgated to him through reason. This is Natural law. In addition to eternal law and natural law there is divine law which is 'eternal law revealed through the Scriptures' and lastly there is human or manmade law. The latter should conform to reason and thus to the law of God. (This does not mean that order in nature was guided by reason. It is only the faculty of appreciating order, implanted in the mind, that should be ascribed to the Deity).[1] According to Aquinas, this discretionary part of eternal law is the natural law discoverable by reason and quite distinct from revealed portion of divine law. For example, say the eternal law lays down that women shall have only limited rights in property or prohibits chanting of Vedic mantras by women, man may apply his reason to say that the rule does not fit into the present time frame having regard to the egalitarian society that we have moved into.

8. *Universal principles:* Another advantage of natural law is that it does not depend on the human belief on any particular deity or divine being but only on human reasoning. Hence, the whole humanity cutting across all religions would arrive at the same universal principles.
9. Medievalists had viewed natural law from the standpoint of man's function and duties. Later philosophers like Hobbes and Locke were

1. This is similar to the Hindu philosophy of *'datta swatantra'* under which, though by and large everything is destined by God, it is believed that man is gifted with an area of discretion which is to be exercised according to reason and judicious discretion.

concerned with man's rights and sought to derive certain natural rights from characteristics of human nature.

V. Criticisms

Natural law theory faces formidable difficulties.

1. *'Ought' cannot be deduced from 'is'*: Bentham argues that natural law theory is the result of confusion between moral/legal laws on one hand and scientific laws on the other. Scientific laws prescribe what generally occurs and moral or legal rules prescribe how men should behave. Moral proposition 'ought' is not always deducible from or conformable with the factual proposition *i.e.* 'ought' cannot always be deduced from 'is'. Factual propositions can be established as true and are therefore less open to disagreement than moral propositions. For example, whether euthanasia (mercy killing) is justifiable or whether prostitution should be legalized is a moral question; hence we find that in our country we have not recognized either of them but there are countries like. The Netherlands where euthanasia is legally permissible and prostitution is legalized. But the statement that arsenic is poisonous is a factual statement, a scientific statement and hence it can be established as true. But then, it is not possible to derive a moral proposition from a factual proposition.
2. *From 'is' to 'ought' is not strictly necessary:* The inference of a moral proposition from a factual proposition is not one of strict logical necessity. In a strict logical inference it is impossible to affirm the premise (starting point or root or source) and deny the conclusion. For example, it is impossible to say that the object is red and at the same time deny that it is coloured. But when a factual proposition is used as a premise for an ethical conclusion the premise can be affirmed and the conclusion denied without producing a self-contradiction. *E.g.* "if anyone shows you kindness, you ought to repay it with kindness" is the statement, where conclusion flows naturally from the premise. But it would not be illogical to say that "one need not always repay kindness with kindness". The statement sounds odd but not illogical. This is because deriving a moral proposition from a factual proposition is not one of strict logical necessity. It was Hume (1711-1776) who argued that there is no causal connection between ideas and facts. Causal connection is found on physical sciences. Concepts like good and evil are subjective emotional reactions. Values are not inherent in nature nor is justice.[1]
3. *Proper function argument fails:* Natural law arguments that everything has a proper function and so to be good of its kind it must fulfill this function, breaks down in case of man. For example, the function of a good watch is to show correct timing. But this comparison cannot be applied to man. Watch has a definite purpose given to it by the maker of the watch. But is a man given a definite purpose by his maker? This question raises innumerable problems starting with the need to prove the existence of the maker *i.e.* God which is impossible.

1. R.W.M. Dias: Jurisprudence, 4th Edn., p. 662.

4. *'Nonsense on stilts':* Bentham regarded natural law as *'nonsense on stilts'.* He said that the natural law reasoning was the result of confusion between scientific laws on the one hand and moral and legal laws on the other. Scientific laws describe what occurs; moral/legal laws prescribe how men should behave. For example, under the law of gravity a stone when thrown in the air must fall down. But suppose it does not fall down. It does not mean that the law of gravity is broken. It only means that law of gravity must be revised/qualified to fit in the facts. Hence it is wrong to argue from 'natural laws of scientific type' to 'natural laws of moral type'. To say that it is natural for men to have children only shows the tendency but does not lay it down as a moral duty to conform to the tendency. For example, population control is a State Policy in India; people are encouraged to have small families by freeships and subsidies offered for families with only two children and incentives for undergoing family planning operations.
5. *Criticism is not totally correct*: Scientific laws describe not merely how things behave but also the manner in which they are designed to behave. That is, the creator has imposed a law on things to which they are in perfect obedience unlike men. Discrepancy between observed phenomenon and the law of gravity means that we had not succeeded in discovering the law that was actually designed. Hence, naturalists conclude there is no confusion between scientific and moral laws.
6. *Moral principles: varying principles*: Moral principles vary from person to person; and from society to society and from time to time. Hence in morals logical validity may not be of universal acceptance. That killing is wrong is an attractive proposition. Yet slavery was justified under Greek, Roman and American laws. Attitude towards colour, religion, caste etc. dilute the universality of natural law. We find that one legal system allows monogamy and another allows polygamy showing that natural law theory is not universally common.
7. *Difference between legal and moral rules:* To describe moral laws as natural law is to get the best of both the worlds. The term 'law' gives additional prestige arising from the emotive power of the word; the term 'natural' suggests that these laws are in some way superior to ordinary positive law which owes its origin to some historical accident. This temptation must be resisted because there is a difference between legal and moral rules. Legal rules can be changed, amended, added or even abrogated by the legislature. Moral rules are not amenable to such a change. Legal disputes can be finally settled by the courts unlike moral disputes because moral correctness of the judge's verdict can be always questioned.
8. *Unjust law has to be obeyed:* If a law is unjust, the naturalists would say that it is no law at all. But the positivists would say that it is law but it is liable to be criticized. In actual practice, even an unjust law has to be obeyed.

Truth lies somewhere in between both the theories. An ordinary positive law which is against the moral principles is still a law, but moral principles serve as an antidote to legal rigidity. They serve as some set of standards which the legislature must follow.

Law must be evaluated not in terms of one rigid platform but in terms of simplicity, efficacy meeting social justice and also morality.

VI. Principles of Natural Law and Natural Justice Followed in India

The concept of natural justice is invoked in cases where statute law is silent as in the case where there is no statute laying down minimum procedure which administrative agencies must follow while exercising decision making powers.[1]

Maneka Gandhi's[2] case gave wide ambit for the use of the natural law theory that law is the dictate of reason.

Natural justice means different things to different writers, lawyers, judges and different systems of law. It is used nearly as a synonym for divine law or moral law. It has changed its concept depending on the needs and problems to be addressed by the society. Yet taken at any point of time a set of principles of natural justice can be identified.

In India, we have ample cases where courts have relied upon the dictates of reason and applied the principles of natural justice whenever the State made law was found insufficient to do justice. Following are some of the examples:

1. The most innovative and imaginative use of the principles of natural justice was in *Maneka Gandhi* v. *Union of India,*[2] where J.P.N. Bhagwati and J.V.R. Krishna Iyer read 'the due process' clause into the otherwise blandly worded expression in Article 21 of the Constitution which lays down that 'no person shall be deprived of his life and personal liberty except by a procedure established by law'. On the face of it the Article means that as long as life or personal liberty is taken away by the procedure laid down by law it is legitimate and the contents of law cannot be looked into. But then the Supreme Court held that the law which deprives a person of life and personal liberty must be just, fair and reasonable. Likewise, the procedure by which life is taken away or liberty curtailed also must be just fair and reasonable. Thus, both the substantive law and the procedural law must answer the test of reasonableness. This interpretation gave wide powers to the judiciary to judge the reasonableness of legislative and executive action. In other words, it expanded the judicial powers of the judiciary. It lays down the foundation on which the concept of natural justice and the dictates of reason are being applied to judge the validity and legality of the statute and the executive power and the action taken.
2. It was held in *Mohinder Singh Gill* v. *Chief Election Commissioner,*[3] that natural justice has many colours and shades and except when excluded by law, it applies when people are affected by acts of authority. Exceptions to the rules of natural justice are a misnomer. It only means that in those exclusionary cases nothing unfair can be inferred by not affording an opportunity to be heard.

---

1. I.P. Massay, p. 161.
2. AIR 1978 SC 597.
3. AIR 1978 SC 851.

3. Following rulings are the result of reasonableness being read into Article 21, and therefore, in a sense application of the natural law theory:
   - Non-payment of minimum wages to workers employed in Asiad projects in Delhi was a denial of right to live with human dignity. Peoples'[1]? This decision has clothed millions of workers in factories etc, with human dignity.
   - Holding of beauty contest is repugnant to decency and dignity of women. Hence it offends Article 21.
   - Right to life also includes right to livelihood.[2] Sections 313, 313A, 314, and 497 of the Bombay Municipal Corporation Act, 1888 which empowered removal of huts and pavements was challenged as violative of Aricle 21. They were held constitutional as they imposed a reasonable restriction, yet, taking a humanistic approach it was directed that the huts could be removed only after the ensuing monsoon season and directions were given to create hawking zones.
   - Right to health and medical care has been held to be a fundamental right.[3]
   - Right to clean and unpolluted environment is a fundamental right. Lime stone quarries were ordered to be closed down;[4] a Chemical factory with chlorine leakage directed to be closed down;[5] the Government was directed to perform its functions under various Environment related Acts and was held liable for all the damage caused to the soil, to the underground water, to the village in general on the principle of 'polluter pays.'[6]
   - In *Vellore Citizen* v. *Welfare Forum Union of India*,[7] pollution was caused by enormous discharge of untreated effluent by the tanneries and other industries in Tamil Nadu. Supreme Court held that principle of sustainable development is a balancing concept between ecology and development. Precautionary principle and polluter pays principle are essential features of sustainable development. These are important principles which have been evolved by the judiciary by testing the laws with the yardstick of reason.
   - Likewise, the prisoners' rights to free legal aid,[8] right against solitary confinement,[9] right to speedy trial,[10] right against inhuman treatment are practical applications of the natural law theory.

---

1. *Democratic Rights* v. *Union of India*, AIR 1982 SC 1473.
2. *Olga Tellis* v. *Bombay Municipal Corporation*, AIR 1986 SC 180.
3. *Parmananda Katara* v. *Union of India*, AIR 1989 SC 2039; *Paschim Bang Khet Mazdoor Samiti* v. *State of West Bengal*, (1996) 4 SCC 37; *Consumer Education and Research Centre* v. *Union of India*, (1995) 3 SCC 42.
4. *Rural Litigation and Entitlement Kendra* v. *State of Uttar Pradesh*, (1985) 2 SCC 431.
5. *M.C. Mehta* v. *Union of India*, AIR 1987 SC 1086
6. *Indian Council for Enviro-Legal Action* v. *Union of India*, (1996) 5 SCC 647.
7. (1996) 5 SCC 650.
8. *M.H. Hoskot* v. *State of Maharashtra*, AIR 1978 SC 527.
9. *Sunil Batra* v. *Delhi Administration*, AIR 1978 SC 1575.
10. *Hussainara Khatoon* v. *Home Secretary, Bihar*, AIR 1979 SC 1360.

VII. History of the Theories of Natural Law[1]

1. Developments in Greece

The story of Natural Law begins with the philosophers of ancient Greece. The theory ponders over the questions of what is the permanent basis of the law and its relationship to justice.

Natural Law has exercised a great influence on legal developments. To take only one example – no other philosophy has shaped American thinking and American Institutions as Natural Law theory in the form given to it in the Seventeenth and Eighteenth Century.

What is common to all the Natural Law theory is that law is an essential foundation for life of man in society and is based on his needs as a reasonable man. It is not based on whims of the ruler.

The Greeks traditionally regarded law as being closely related to justice and ethics. Yet the million dollar question to this date is – where is the permanent element of justice to be found? Plato's *Republic* is a constructive attempt and discusses the basis of justice. But in the end, he under emphasizes the importance of justice with the observation that execution of justice was to be left to the philosopher Kings – whose education and wisdom needed no shakles by higher laws. (It follows closely the Hindu theory – *Raja – pratyaksha devata)*

Aristotle formulated more carefully the theory of justice. He regarded justice as meaning what is lawful or what is fair and equal. He divided justice into distributive and remedial justice; he also distinguished between Natural justice which is universal and Natural justice which is conventional.

To the Greeks, nature of a King was discoverable not by studying its primitive form but its highest development.

Stoics popularized the maxim: *live according to nature.* A thing was in accordance with nature when it was governed by its own leading principle and in the case of man – the governing principle was reason. He who based his life on a rule of reason could face the world more confidently. Therefore a universe based on reason could not be hostile to him.

2. Developments in Rome

Roman classical writers used the Stoic theory as an ornament for their texts-without weaving its implications into the theory of law. Roman texts provided the basis for legal study for many centuries. Hence Natural Law got established as a theory.

What did the Romans mean by 'nature' and 'reason'? Sometimes the jurists tried to draw rules from human nature itself. There were contradictions which puzzled the jurists. For example if Natural Law prescribes that all men should be free and if Jurisprudence was a base for every positive law- how could the practice of slavery be recognized? As civilization grows – respect for human personality grows and rules of law correspondingly develops. Hence a search for unchangeable universal rules of law is futile.

---

1. G.W. Paton: A Text book of Jurisprudence, 3rd Ed., pg. 94 -100. Ideally this should come in the beginning of the Chapter itself. But it is believed that the students will appreciate the history better after a full discussion on the Natural Law theory. Hence it is placed at the end of the Chapter.

As the Roman view got further away from deeper elements of Greek philosophy – it became superficial.

3. Christian Fathers

Christian Fathers extended the authority of Natural Law by ascribing divine origin to it. Aristotle had treated State as a natural result of the social tendencies in man's nature but early Christian Fathers treated the State as unnatural and believed that before men committed sin, they lived together in peace and no Government was needed to restrain and control. With the fall of man, God created the State as a means to correct new tendencies of evil. Thus a great gulf was created which separates the theory of Christian Fathers from that of Aristotle who treated State as natural result of social tendencies in man's nature.

4. Middle Ages

Natural Law theory was very popular in the Middle Ages due to reasons of conservatism and liberalism, religion and practical convenience. Law is also defined as the Will of the Sovereign or the Will of the community. During Middle Ages law was defined differently. Since the fall of Rome, Europe was steering uneasily between the two dangers – tyranny and anarchy. Austinian theory- where law is the command of the Sovereign might lean to tyranny of the ruler and without a cohesive community- the doctrine of general Will of the community may lead to anarchy, chaos and disorder. Men therefore sought for a law based on something more lasting and enduring than the Wills of men.

Natural Law satisfied the interests of conservatism because it was ancient in origin; it could be made to satisfy the demands of liberalism as no one knew exactly what it was and many propositions could be drawn from the needs of man as a reasonable being. The King also was subject to the higher law.

St. Thomas Aquinas is the most famous representative of the Natural Law theory. He emphasizes that man's intellect and free Will are the closest images of God in the material universe.

5. Development in the 17th Century

Grotius (1583-1645) is the most famous representative of the rationalist school. To discover the rules of natural law we must see if what is in accordance with the rational and social nature of man and then test our conclusions by seeing whether the rules have been adopted by all nations or at least by the most civilized ones.

His most significant contribution is in the area of International law. Moved by the savagery of wars, he attempted to build rules of Natural Law to restrain the cruelty of States.

6. Natural Rights

Many theories of Natural Law still have a religious base, but 18th century was a witness to secular approach to legal and political questions. Hence identifying the binding force of Natural Law became difficult. Therefore the easier answer that it was based on the Will of God was not acceptable to all men. Yet this period was the "golden century of human reason".

In the 18th century theory of natural rights became the spearhead of revolutionary activity. Virginian Declaration of Rights declared "all men are by nature equally free and independent and have certain inherent natural rights" which even the future generation cannot be deprived of by the present generation. Today we find that preserving or conserving the nature and the natural resources, sustaining environment for the future generation represent this viewpoint. Thus for example, the doctrine of sustainable development goes ahead of the right to development of the present generation and recognizes the rights of future generation. Stressing on the need for sustainable development and on the right of every human being to live decently the World Commission on Environment and Development observes:

> "what is required is a new approach in which all nations aim at a type of development that integrates production with resource conservation and enhancement and that links both to the provision for all of an adequate livelihood base and equitable access to resources".[1]

In the 20th century we see the beginning of a functional and relativist approach. Theories of Law became secularized - that is, detached from religion and concept of God. Pragmatism emerged as a legal philosophy and the advance of science turns the mind of the men into materialistic channels.

---

1. World Commission on Environment and Development, *Our Common Future,* (1987) at pg. 39-40 quoted in Leelakrishnan P: Environmental Law in India.

CHAPTER 3

THEORIES OF LAW: COMMAND OF THE SOVEREIGN: POSITIVE THEORY

INTRODUCTION

Imperative theory or the Positivist theory of law is almost diametrically opposed to the Natural Law theory. Under the Natural law theory, laws were explained, tested and either criticized or justified with the yardstick of 'dictates of reason' which in turn were believed to have universal validity. But these were unverified hypothesis which did not satisfy the critical temper of the new scientific learning. As a reaction to the Natural theory, there emerged the Positivist theory.

I. Positive Theory: What is Law ? Command by the Political Sovereign, Enforceable by Sanction

It seeks to define law from the view point of 'what *is* law' rather than 'what *ought* to be law'. This theory seeks to define law not with reference to its content but in relation to its form. Austin is the main proponent of this theory. According to him, positive law has three characteristics:

1. It is a type of *command*
2. The command is laid down *by the political sovereign* and
3. The command is *enforceable by sanction*. That is – if the command is not obeyed it is enforced by penalties and punishment. For example, the Indian Penal Code is a command and also lays down penalties, the Motor Vehicles Act is **a command** to do or not to do something; it is laid down by the sovereign authority (the Parliament in case of the Motor Vehicles Act and Article 371 of the Constitution under which laws enacted before the independence continue to be valid until altered or abrogated by law) and the violation of it is **punishable by sanction.**

1. *Command: From Superior to Inferior*

The nature of command is an important element; command must be distinguished from request. Requests are expressions of desires pure and simple. Commands also are expressions of desire but they are given by the superiors to the inferiors. This relationship of superior and inferior speaks of the power which the superior has over the inferior. This power is manifest by the ability to punish the inferior for disobedience. Hence the idea of sanction is built into the Austinian nature of command.

- *All commands are not laws*. For example, a monarch or an absolute ruler orders his servants to close the door or to make preparations for a meeting etc. It would not qualify as law as we cannot relegate law to such isolated, random commands even though the monarch may punish him for disobedience. Austin defends his theory by saying that laws are general commands unlike other commands which are transitory in nature like the command given by the military officer to his troops. But then generality alone is not a sufficient distinguishing feature of law. For example, laws abolishing privy purse are directed to particular persons yet they are laws though there is no generality.

One problem is: how do we distinguish commands which are laws from commands which are not laws? Every day life is sprinkled with commands given by the teachers to the students; by the parents to the children; there may be unlawful commands like that of a bank robber who commands the clerk to hand over cash to him. Dr. Goodhart criticizes the Positivist theory as the 'Gunman Theory' as there is no distinction between a law and the command of a bank robber. This criticism is answered by the second requirement of law: *viz.* that the command must emanate from the Sovereign. A bank robber is not the sovereign.

2. *Political Sovereign Commands Obedience*

To qualify as law it must emanate from a political superior. Sovereign is any person, or body of persons, whom the bulk of the political society habitually obeys and who himself does not habitually obey some other person or persons. Law would be effective only if it commands general obedience. Perfect obedience is neither feasible nor necessary because disobedience is bound to be there. For example, the year 2006 recorded 2,60,000 cases of crime against women. But this does not mean that laws prohibiting crime against women are not laws at all. Laws may be obeyed out of respect, fear or habit or love of order etc. For the legal theorist, it is enough that laws are generally obeyed.

3. *Sanction: Penalties for Violation of Laws*

For the positivists law, is a command which must be obeyed whether one likes it or not. This is ensured by some method of sanction. Sanctions are a logical part of the concept of law. They are penalties inflicted for violations of law.

II. Criticisms Against the Positivist Theory

1. *Lack of Moral and Ethical Content*

Naturalists attack the positivist theory on the ground that it lacks moral and ethical content. Mere positive law can seldom be equated with good law because it would not be tested with the higher ideals of Natural Law theory. The positivist theory does not consider whether the command given by the sovereign is just or unjust.

To this the counter argument is that exponents of positivist theory like Austin never intended to exclude the problem of evaluating law. In Austin's view law must be critically assessed to find out its utility level.

Whether the separation between 'is' and 'ought' is tenable or not is a debatable issue. 'Is' indicates factual content and 'ought' indicates moral content. The jurisprudential context of the issue has been attempted to be clarified as described below:[1]

2. *'Is' Propositions are Largely Composed of 'Ought' Propositions*

Analysis of the concept of duty shows that a large part of law consists of prescriptive patterns of behavior prescribing 'do's' and 'don't's'. For example, Don't steal; Don't kill or hurt or else you will be punished; or say you can transfer the immovable property beyond value of Rs. 100 only by registration; or you must stop at the red signal or you must submit your tax returns by a particular date etc. These laws lay down the models of conduct to which people ought to conform and by which their actual behavior is judged. Hence the 'is' which the positivists want to preserve is largely composed of 'ought' propositions. The positivists say that only those 'ought' propositions which have been filtered through Legislation, Precedent and Custom acquire the character of law. In other words, only those 'oughts' which pass through the medium of Legislature, Precedent and Custom are recognized as laws. This means that even an unjust or an immoral proposition becomes law automatically once embodied in the Legislation or Precedent or Custom. The modern Natural law theorists do not accept this contention. They say that in addition to the formal requirement (*i.e.* in form it is law because all the 3 requirements of command, political sovereign and sanction are present) there must be a minimum moral content. According to them, an immoral rule would not be law however much it may satisfy the formal requirement.[2] It is submitted that taken in this sense in India it is the Modern Natural Law theory which is most prevalent. After the due process clause was read into *Maneka Gandhi* v. *Union of India*[3] substantive and procedural laws; and administrative actions which are unjust, unreasonable and unfair and hence lack the minimum necessary moral content are struck down as

---

1. R.W.M. Dias: Jurisprudence, 4th Edn., p. 452-453.
2. J. Sajjad Ahmad in *Jilani* v. *Govt. of Punjab, Pak L.D.*, (1972) SC 139 (261) quoted in Dias: Jurisprudence, p. 453.
3. AIR 1978 SC 597.

being violative of Articles 21 and 14 of the Constitution. Hence it can be said that in India law is one that satisfies the formal requirement and also has the minimum moral content. But then until the court strikes it down it remains valid and binding- however unjust it may be.

3. *Customary Laws, International Law, Constitutional Law in England do not Fit into Positivist Theory*

The positive theory denies the name 'law' to rules which are generally recognized as legal. The rules of *customary laws, International law and even the Constitutional law in England* (England has an unwritten Constitution) are habitually obeyed but do not fall within the Austinian definition. The origin of customary law is habitual behavior; of International law is State practices and Constitutional law in England are the Constitutional conventions. The positivist theory raises questions like is International law a true law.

In India we have a written Constitution hence by and large, it can be said that our Constitution can come within the purview of the Positivist definition of law. However we do have Constitutional conventions which are followed routinely. And so the question arises whether they are laws within the Austinian definition? Such a question arose in *Union of India* v. *Sankalchand Himatlal Sheth*[1] where the High Court judges were transferred during internal emergency in 1976 without their consent, whereas it was an unwritten convention to transfer them with their consent though our Constitution does not require consent before transferring the judges.

4. *Power Conferring Rules*

There are laws which are not commands but only power conferring rules which do not fit into Austinian definition. For example, election laws, law of property, law of contract etc. These laws confer rights on the citizens to vote, to hold and dispose of property, etc. Answer to this criticism is that right given to one citizen is a command to another citizen. For example, right to vote to a citizen is a command given to the Returning Officer to register the vote. But then, this counter argument distorts the true nature of power conferring laws and is a play with the words.

5. *Command Suggests a Personal Commander*

The term command suggests a personal commander. But law making is so complex under the modern legal system that it is impossible to identify any commander.

6. *Extinction of the Law Maker*

Law continues in existence even after the extinction of the law giver. To this the counter argument is that what the Sovereign permits he commands. The later Sovereign by not repealing the laws enacted by the earlier Sovereign impliedly commands the subjects to abide by those laws. A statute may be either perpetual or temporary. When no duration is fixed it is perpetual. It remains in operation until repealed. In India it has been held that a cessation of transitional legislative power has no effect on the continuance of a perpetual Act enacted during the continuance of that power.[2] In simple words a perpetual Act passed by the Law

1. AIR 1977 SC 2328.
2. *Ishwardas* v. *Union of India*, AIR 1972 SC 1193.

making body (Parliament or the Legislature of the State) continues to remain in operation even after the Legislative Body has ceased to exist.

7. Judicial Decisions do not Fit into the Positivist Theory

Bulk of the English law is the result of judicial decisions. So they do not fit into the positivist theory. The Austinians argue that since judges are appointed by the Government and removable by parliamentary procedures, they are really delegates of the Parliament. But to describe judges as delegates is wholly misleading. It obscures the fact that their law making powers are co-extensive with that of the Parliament.

Under our Indian Constitution, executive powers are co-extensive with the legislative powers. The doctrine of separation of powers is recognized under our Constitution. Judges can never be considered as delegates of the Parliament. They are constitutional authorities appointed under the constitutional provisions. They have the powers of judicial review over the legislative and executive actions of the State. Constitution mandates that steps shall be taken to keep the judiciary independent from the Executive. They do not have law making powers as such. By and large we recognize the doctrine of separation of powers under which Legislature legislates; the executive executes and the judiciary interprets the law. In the course of interpreting the laws it makes laws only incidentally and to the extent necessary for resolving the case in hand.

Under Article 141 law declared by the Supreme Court is binding on all the subordinate courts and is the law of the land until overruled by a later law enacted by the Parliament. For example, in *Mohd. Ahmed Khan* v. *Shah Bano Begum*[1], the Supreme Court ruled that a Muslim woman divorced is entitled to maintenance from her husband as long as she remains unmarried and is not able to maintain herself. The Parliament passed the Muslim Women's (Protection of Rights on Divorce) Act, 1986 which overruled the judgment.

> "in this sense, it can be said that – in respect of the limited cases which reach the court and the court pronounces a judgment – it is a command given by the judge to the party to the case to obey the command and if not obeyed, law provides for execution proceedings in the form of arrest/ detention/attachment etc"

8. Identifies the Sovereign before he Issues the Command

Ruls of succession in England prescribe who shall inherit the throne and identify the Sovereign even before he issues the command.

Under our Indian Constitution, We the People of India have given the Constitution to ourselves. The people are supreme. It is like people giving laws unto themselves. There is no question of succession to the throne etc.

9. Basic Rules not Created by Sovereign

In every legal system, there are some basic rules that define sovereignty but these rules are not themselves created by the Sovereign. Nevertheless they are rules of law. Here again Austin's definition fails. Where is the Sovereign and where is the Supreme power is the question.

---

1. AIR 1985 SC 945.

10. Statutes Passed Due to Reasons other than Sovereign Will

Sovereignty consists not in having power but in having authority. Legal sovereign and political sovereign may be different. The former may have ultimate authority to make laws but the latter has the ability to enforce obedience and even lobby for law-making. Statutes may be passed due to lobbying by interested groups. For example, the Muslim Women's (Protection of Rights on Divorce) Act, 1986 was passed due to lobbying by the fundamentalist Muslims; if we still have the right to get information of file notings under the Right to Information Act, 2005, it is because Anna Hazare went on strike against the move of the Government to take away this right by an Amendment. Thus laws are passed or retained not always because the sovereign wants them but because the section of the people want it.

11. Sanction – Logically not a Must

Institutional sanctions may be necessary for human nature being what it is. But it is only for a small section of the society which disobeys the laws. Bulk of the society obey the laws for whatever reasons. Sanctions are required for preventing a selfish minority from gaining an unfair advantage and not to coerce the law abiding majority. Therefore, element of sanction is logically not necessary.

12. Austin Considered Sanctions as a Necessary Element

Austin described international law as positive morality instead of law. International lawyers do not consider sanctions as a necessary element of law.

> "For details on whether International law is truly a law or just positive morality, refer Chapter 6".

CHAPTER 4

LEGAL THEORIES: LAW AS THE PRACTICE OF THE COURT: LEGAL REALISM

SYNOPSIS

INTRODUCTION

Under the Natural Law theory we have seen that law is the dictate of reason; and under positive theory we have seen that law is the command of the sovereign. Legal realism regards law as being made through the medium of the Courts.

To the realist (as for the positivist) law is the command of the Sovereign but the Sovereign is not the Parliament but the Court. Under this theory laws are rules recognized and acted upon by the Courts of Justice. The two important realist movements in this area are that of American and Scandinavian Realist.

I. Salmond's Version of Legal Realism

He argued that all law was not made by the Legislature. In England much of it is made by the law Courts. But all law however made, is recognized and administered by the Courts. The Courts do not recognize those rules which are not rules of law. Hence for Salmond it is the courts which determine the true nature of law. Salmond defined law as rules of law recognized and applied by the Courts in the administration of justice.

1. Criticism

a. *Meaning of Court:* The critics question whether courts include Tribunals & Commissioners & whether rules made by them are law. To this Salmond replies that all words have a core meaning and a hazy marginal meaning and that the word 'law' is no exception and the criticism regarding the meaning of 'court' falls under the exception.

b. *Statutes are laws before Court recognition:* Statute law is law as soon as it is passed. It does not require judicial recognition before it can be termed as law. The fact is that the statutes are recognized by the courts because they are law. They are not law because the courts recognize them. There are persons and administrators other than the courts who enforce rules of conduct. Are they included within the meaning of 'Court'? Does it include Administrative Tribunals or the Commissioners under the National Insurance Act, 1946? For example, in *Sheriff of Middlesex's case*[1] the Sheriff was imprisoned by the order of the House of Commons for attempting to enforce the judgment of the court. It was an act done by the Sheriff in accordance with law enforced by the law courts. So the criticism is that the word 'court' does not include such other bodies or persons who enforce rules of conduct.

We have similar situations in India also. For example under Article 105 of the Constitution the House of Commons has the power to punish a person whether a member or a stranger for its contempt or for breach of Parliamentary privilege. The House is the sole and exclusive judge provided such privilege falls under Article 194(3) of the Constitution. Eenadu Privilege issue provides an example where Court order is not obeyed and it has the backing of the House. The Chief Editor of a Telegu Newspaper 'Eenadu' was found guilty by the Andhra Pradesh Legislative Council for publishing an item- 'Elder's commotion' in his newspaper and was ordered by the House to appear before it for admonition. The Supreme Court had issued an order to the Secretary of the House not to arrest him. He refused to appear in the House unless 'arrested and taken.' In spite of the Court's stay order the Council expressed the view that the House was supreme and sovereign in the matter of privileges and the Court had no place in the matter and it should not surrender to the Supreme Court and the Editor should be arrested and brought before the House for admonition. In order to avoid a conflict between the Judiciary and the Legislature the Chief Minister intervened and got the deliberations postponed. This puts a question mark over the meaning of 'court' in the Realist theory that law is what the 'court' decides.

Re under Article 143[2] is a classic example of a question mark on the legal Realism Theory with reference to their ideology that – 'law is what the Court decides' with special reference to the meaning of 'Court'. In this case, U.P. Assembly held Keshav Singh – a non MLA, guilty of contempt of the House because he had published certain remarks which were expunged by the House. He was sentenced to imprisonment for 7 days. A Bench of two judges of the Allahabad High Court granted interim bail. UP Assembly passed a resolution that the two judges and the Advocate of Keshav Singh be brought into custody before the House. Petition under Article 226 was moved by the two judges and the Advocate contending that the resolution amounted to contempt of Court and that it be set aside. The implementation of the Resolution was stayed by the High Court. The judges were now asked to appear before the House and explain their conduct. High Court again granted a stay. At this stage the President referred the matter under Article 143 of the Constitution. The case goes to show that some of

1. (1840) 11 A&E 273 quoted in Fitzgerald P.J.: Salmond on Jurisprudence (New Delhi, Universal Law Publishing Co. Pvt. Ltd.) at pg. 36.
2. AIR 1965 SC 745

the critical questions which arise in the theory of Legal Realism put a question mark on the theory. To this Salmond replies that as long as the courts and the legislature work in harmony it does not matter whether the statute is law because courts recognize it or whether courts recognize it because it is law. Problem arises only in marginal cases where law made by the legislature is declared to be void by the court.

In India, (unlike in England where much of the law is judge-made) it is the Parliament/State which is assigned the task of making laws for the whole of India or the State concerned under the provisions of our written Constitution.[1] Parliament can by law increase the number of courts in the interest of justice. The judges interpret the laws, exercise judicial review over the acts of the Legislature and the Executive. They can declare legislative and executive acts as void. However the Parliament may by amendment supercede the judgment and render it infructuous. In India an example of this tug of war between the Parliament and the Judiciary has been seen in relation to the Zamindari Abolition Laws; the Muslim Women's (Protection of Rights on Divorce) Act, 1986 and when the Constitution was amended to provide for reservations in promotions in order to supercede *Indira Sawhney* v. *Union of India*[2] by the 77th Constitutional Amendment. Likewise since 1960's from *Balaji* v. *State of Mysore,*[3] it was consistently held by the Courts up to *Indira Sawhney's* case that reservations for Scheduled Castes, Scheduled Tribes and the Backward Classes shall not exceed 50%; the 81st Amendment in the year 2000 laid down that while computing the 50% limit the unfilled vacancies during the previous years due to non-availability of eligible SC-ST candidates shall not be taken into consideration. Thus the consistent judicial rulings which was the law of the land for 40 years and which was based on sound reasoning was made infructuous after 40 years.

II. Holmes' Version: 'A Bad Man's Version'

Oliver Holmes' version (American realist) – A bad man's version sowed the seeds of the realist movement in 1897. He considered all law as judge made. He viewed the question from the position of a bad man – the man who is anxious to secure his own selfish interests. Such a man is not interested in finding out what the Statutes or the text books say. A bad man would try to find out what the court would do in fact. Holmes' theory distinguishes law in action and law in books/statutes. What the court will do cannot be accurately predicted from the wordings of the statute because the words can have different interpretations. It is for the court to give the authoritative interpretation. Holmes has remarked that life of law is not logic but experience. As Gray puts it "Courts put life in the dead words of the statute".

III. Days of Judge-made Law are not Over

Even in modern days, with so many statutory laws, days of judge-made law are not over. This is because Legislature is concerned with the general classes of persons, objects and actions and must necessarily use words of general application which are not precise. The legislator is not in a position to forsee

1. Articles 245, 246.
2. AIR 1993 SC 477.
3. AIR 1963 SC 649.

every possible situation that may arise in future. Hence he has to use words of general application and leave it to the judges to use their imagination and intelligence in solving actual and specific cases that come up before them. In a way, legislative uncertainty is counter balanced by judicial flexibility. Precise and rigid words used by the legislature would make it difficult for the judges to tailor-make justice in individual cases. Hence the realists argue that the creative days of the judges are not over because of a plethora of statutory laws. For example notional extension of employers premises under the Workmen's Compensation Act, 1923 is the creation of the judiciary. The Act lays down that the employer's liability extends to accidents arising out of and in the course of employment. Ordinarily, employment does not begin until he has reached the place of work and after he has left that place. It has been time and again held that employers premise is not necessarily always limited to the place of work. In *Vardarajulu* v. *Masaya Boyan,*[1] the workman, a coolie employed by the contractor for road formation was injured when the lorry which was conveying him to the work spot capsized. Applying the doctrine of notional extension of the employers premises it was held that as it was the only mode of transport to reach the hilly tract and it was reasonable means of transport hence it was an accident arising in the course of employment. Likewise the whole concept of public interest litigation has been evolved by our Supreme Court by giving specific meaning to the general word 'appropriate proceeding' used by the framers of our Constitution in Article 32 of our Constitution; That judicial review is the basic structure of the Indian Constitution is the creature of the judiciary. In England the Road Traffic Act, 1930 makes it an offence to drive a motor vehicle in a manner dangerous to the public. Does 'steering a broken down vehicle on tow' amount to driving? Parliament has not defined the word 'driving' hence it has to be given its ordinary meaning. But ordinary meaning of driving does not provide an answer to the problem. The court had to draw an arbitrary line and further define the term. It was held not to amount to driving.[2]

Take another example – in England (as in India) the unlawful and intentional killing of another amounts to the crime of murder. But if *A* intentionally inflicts on *B* a fatal wound and then thinking him to be dead – throws his body into a lake, and *B* dies by drowning. Is it murder? Certainly *A* intended to murder *B* who would have died from the wound if he was not thrown into the lake. Wounding was intentional but actual killing was not. In 1954 the existing law had no answer to this problem which arose in the case of *Thabo Meli* v. *R.*[3] and so the court had to tackle the problem.

Since law in practice differs from law in Statutes American Jurisprudence developed considerable skepticism (questioning the correctness) about legal rules. They argued that when the courts have to choose between alternatives much depends on the upbringing and the temperament etc. of the judges. For example, whether he is conservative (old fashioned) minded or from an aristocratic background, it will affect not only his decisions on law but also on facts. For example law says that contributory negligence is a complete defence to

1. AIR 1954 Mad 1113.
2. *Wallace* v. *Major*, (1946) KB 473.
3. (1954) 1 All ER 373.

an action for negligence. But courts may be so sympathetic to the plaintiff or so antipathic to the insurance companies as rarely to find any plaintiff guilty of contributory negligence. Thus the law of contributory negligence would remain in paper only.

The proponents of the Realist School therefore conclude that a statement of law is nothing more than a prediction of what the Courts will decide.

IV. Merits of the Theory

The theory does have an element of truth. The distinction between law in practice and the law in books is a valid one. It highlights and acknowledges the creative nature of judicial role and discards the slot machine deduction role of the judiciary in providing solutions to the legal problems. It shows that legal decisions must often involve value judgments on questions of policy.

V. Following are the Plus Points in a Statute which Legal Realism Fails to take into Consideration

1. *Statute is not a prediction*: The idea that law is prediction of how the judges will react undermines (weakens) certainty and definiteness of law. The statute is definitely not a prediction. In passing a statute the Legislature lays down what shall be done. It does not predict what will be done by the judges.
2. *The advocate's submission not a prediction (guess):* The advocate's submission on a point of law is not a prediction (guess). He argues about what the judge 'should' decide based on Statute law or other forms of law like customary laws etc. A judicial decision lays down what the law 'is'.
3. *Litigations form a small fraction:* It is only a fraction of the law suits which create a new law. In addition, law is so certain that a great number of disputes never reach the courts and even where they reach the courts major part of the law being certain, the law is automatically applied. For example, rules regarding how the property is to be transferred, what documents need to be registered, what is the court fee to be paid etc. are fairly clear and certain.
4. *Uncertainty of language is marginal:* Uncertainty of the language is not universal. It is only marginal.
5. *Litigations cover a minor area:* Majority of the human situations governed by law produce no litigation. People act in accordance with the law as they understand it.

CHAPTER 5
THEORIES OF LAW: LAW AS A SYSTEM OF RULES

SYNOPSIS

INTRODUCTION

Natural law theorists regard law as consisting of rules dictated by reason. Positivists regard law as command of the Sovereign and Realists regard law as the practice of the Court.

One more way of looking at law is to analyse law in terms of legal rules. The theory was proposed by Prof. H.L.A. Hart in his book 'Concept of Law.' He was a linguistic philosopher, a Barrister and a jurist.

I. What is a Rule

1. *Idea of obligation:* Prof. Hart says that where there is law, human conduct is made in some sense non-optional or obligatory & binding. The idea of obligation is at the core of the rule.
2. *Imperative and prescriptive*: Rules are concerned with what ought to be done and not with what happens. They are imperative (essential and must be followed) and prescriptive (regulatory) rather than indicative or descriptive. This imperative nature of rules is common to commands. Yet there are differences between a rule and a command.
3. *General application & repeated activity:* Rules are of general application and demand repeated activity. A command normally calls for a unique performance.
4. *Some rules – constitutive in nature*: Some rules may be **constitutive in nature** and define the activity in question. For example, rules of chess, table-tennis, badminton etc. when the player complies with the rules, he is not just using a particular method to achieve the objective of playing the game but following the rules is partly what chess playing is. That is, some rules constitute activity itself. In other words, without the rules the activity is no chess or badminton at all.
5. *Some rules may be regulatory:* Some rules may **regulate the activities.** That is the activity would in any case take place whether there were rules or not. For example, rules of grammar and spelling, etiquette of morals and law etc. The rules of grammar are followed not as a means to an end but as a part of the correct usage of the language, *i.e.* even before the rules of grammar were framed, people did use some language for communication. Rules of morals are followed not as a means to being polite but as a part of being polite. So also law is observed as a part of what constitutes an ordered tolerable society.

II. Views of Scandinavian and American Realists

American realists identify rules with regularities in judicial behaviour. Scandinavian Realists say that there are no such thing as rules. Conformity with a rule consist in habitual behaviour accompanied by a feeling of being bound to act in this habitual way.

III. Hart's Views

1. 'Rules' is not Mere Acting Out of Habit

Hart says compliance with *rules differs from mere acting out of habit.* For example, consider the case of a man who habitually cleans his car every Sunday without fail. It can be said of him that 'he always behaves like this'. But take the case of a driver who regularly stops at the red signal. To say that he always stops at red signals would be insufficient/incomplete description. Why does he stop is an important question to be addressed or answered. He stops because there is a traffic regulation to that effect. If this aspect is known or at least realized by the narrator, by the driver then it would be compliance with the rule and not mere acting out of habit.

2. *Compliance with the Rule Involves Two Aspects: External Behaviour and Internal Attitude*

- External behaviour – such as stopping at the traffic signal and
- Internal attitude that such behaviour is obligatory/compulsory

From where does this feeling of obligatoriness arise? Hart's analysis is that when a man considers his own conduct to conform to a certain pattern he will expect others also to conform to the same pattern of behaviour. Applying this test we must see to the general reaction of the society to a particular rule. For example, a driver does not stop at the red traffic signal; or say a person does not wait at the queue for getting a train ticket you find others in the queue or other drivers grumbling and objecting and criticizing such violation, it is an indication of the internal attitude of the people which regards following the rule as mandatory. This marks the important difference between Scandinavian realists and Hart. For the Scandinavian realists it is an unanalysable feeling of being bound by the rule.

For Hart – it is **conduct coupled with attitude of mind** that the conduct in question is obligatory because a particular rule requires him to act in a certain way. With this mental attitude he considers that his conduct must conform to the particular rule and he also expects that others will follow the rule. Hence he criticizes when others do not follow the rule. To find out whether a person accepts the rule we have to see how he reacts to the violation or non-conformity with the rule.

Hence, generalizing the situation, we must look for society's reaction to the rule to find out whether it has accepted the rule. For example, take the case of Sati system in Rajasthan – a custom wherein the widow burns herself in the pyre of her dead husband. When Roop Kanwar went on Sati in Rajasthan there were wide spread protests which ultimately led to the passing of Prevention of Sati Act. This shows that the custom was not acceptable to the society as a rule and the Government reacted by derecognizing the custom (though stray cases of following of the custom were found even afterwards).

a. Compliance – for Hart and for Austin

For Austin – compliance is through sanction by the sovereign authority *i.e.* a coercive process.

For Hart – compliance with laws arises out of an internal sense of obligation and hence, more lasting and more efficient. Even a person who cannot be compelled by law to obey the rule is still considered as having an obligation to obey as in the case where a driver does not wait at the red traffic signal and speeds away: no case is booked against him by the police because he cannot be caught yet other bystanders object to his attitude. Many a times it is this reaction of the public which would make him feel like obeying the rule at the next signal point.

IV. Legal Rules and Rules of Game, Club, and Societies

They resemble each other in some aspects and differ in others.

1. Both are formal in nature, they can be amended, they are binding on the members. There can be adjudication in case of disputes also. For example, – Rules of Cricket. This differentiates them from rules of morality.

V. Legal Rules and Moral Rules

1. *Differences*

Moral rules cannot be amended by legislations unlike legal rules. It cannot be a subject of adjudication. This is not because of the non-existence of legislators and judges of morality but because of the very nature of morality. However by a passage of time moral rules do undergo a change due to change in the values, priorities of the people, changing aspirations and also because of technological developments like easy communication of views, ideas and happenings around them leading to debates on the worth of such a rule in the relevant time frame. For example, abortion which was illegal and immoral at one time is now no longer considered immoral. In some countries even prostitution and mercy killing are no more immoral. In some countries even gays/lesbians getting married to each other is recognized.

2. *Similarities*

a. *Both are in invitum (non-optional)*: Both legal and moral rules are in invitum *i.e.* obedience to them is non-optional.

b. *Both deal with broader aspects of life*: Rules of games are applicable only to the players and only for the duration of the game. Likewise rules of club apply only to members and membership is a narrow segment of the members' lives. But law and morals are concerned with much broader aspects of life. Morality applies to every aspect of life and human act. Law is narrower but still extends to a great number of such acts.

c. *Compulsory application*: Games and clubs are not compulsory. All need not be members. Even members can withdraw and resign at will. Moral and legal rules are applicable whether one likes it or not and whatever be the individual views about them. For example, one may have reservations, say-laws pertaining to reservation policy of the Government; or may be opposed to the Government signing the General Agreement on Trade and Tariff; may be opposed to the Government signing the Nuclear Deal with America, etc. but nonetheless the rules and the laws are binding. In exceptional cases one may withdraw from one legal system and take to another one. For example, he may renounce the citizenship of India and acquire the citizenship of America.

Law, therefore, consists of rules which are of broad application and are non-optional in character. They are amenable to formalization, legislation and adjudication.

VI. The Unifying Element for the Legal System

The next question is: what is it that unites these rules into a legal system?

1. *For Austin*

The uniting element is the command from the same sovereign. That is several rules all emanating from the same sovereign unifies the rules into a legal system.

2. *For Kelson*

The uniting factor is that all the rules or norms are derived from the same basic rule or rules known as grundnorm. Where there *is* a *written Constitution* the grundnorm is the Constitution itself as the basic rule is that the Constitution must be obeyed and all laws and rules derive their validity from the

Constitution, as in India. In India under Article 13 of the Constitution any law that violates or abridges the Fundamental Rights is void to that extent; in addition, the judiciary has the power of judicial review over legislative and executive actions and declares them to be void if they have violated any provisions of the Constitution. Power of judicial review is held to be the basic structure of the Constitution. Hence Constitution can be said to be the unifying element.

Where there is *no written Constitution,* as in England, we must look to the social behaviour for the basic rule. English legal system is based on several different basic rules like rules concerning Parliamentary legislation; rules concerning binding force of the precedents. These basic rules are like Geometrical axioms *i.e.* they are initial hypothesis from which other propositions are derived.

3. *For Hart*

- Legal system arises from a combination of **primary and secondary rules.**
- Primary rules are duty imposing rules.
- **Secondary** rules are power conferring rules. They confer power to make and unmake other rules of legal system and are called **Rules of Recognition**. They are rules of a higher order.
- These rules of recognition transform a static (motionless or inert) set of unrelated rules into a uniform, dynamic legal system capable of adaptation to social change.
- They serve two purposes. One, they prescribe the method of procedure for creating, annulling, altering rules. Secondly, they also serve as test to discover whether a given rule is one belonging to a legal system. For example, **in England,** rule of parliamentary sovereignty is the secondary rule. It lays down the procedure for creating, annulling etc. a rule of law. It is also a touchstone with which to test a given rule to find out whether it belongs to the English legal system.

Under the **Indian Constitution,** Article 246 gives the powers to make the laws to the Parliament and the Legislature and Article 368 confers power to amend the Constitution and also lays down the procedure to be followed. They are secondary powers or rules of recognition. For us, the touchstone to find out whether the rule properly belongs to the legal system is to find out whether it is in conformity with the Constitution and not the rule of parliamentary sovereignty as in England.

- It is these secondary rules of recognition which transform a static set of unrelated rules into a unified dynamic legal system
- For Hart, these basic rules are not just hypothesis to be assumed. It is itself a rule accepted and observed by the society. It is found in social practice and general attitude of the society. It cannot be derived from any more basic rule.

VII. Criticisms Against Hart's Theory

1. *Sovereign Forcibly Replaced but Legal System Remains the Same*

Where a legislative sovereign is forcibly replaced by a new body, according to Hart the legal system should change but when law remains the same, legal system also remains the same. Hart's theory is questioned because it is only the Constitution of the State which is changed and not the legal system.

2. Other Factors which Weld the Legal System not Addressed

There may be other factors to weld the legal system. For example, there may be fundamental principles which lie behind rules of the system. For example, it may be said that even behind the fundamental rules laid down in our Indian Constitution it is the basic rules laid down in the Indian Value system that are a unifying factor.

3. Limitations of External and Internal Behaviour

Hart says that rules are obeyed because of internal attitude and external behaviour and that there is an expectation that others will follow rules and their non-observance will be criticized. But this is not true in all the cases. Many a times people follow the rules (say-stopping at the red traffic signal or driving on the left side of the road) for whatever reasons without bothering to ascertain whether others are following or are not following the rule. The lack of internal attitude will not make the 'rule' a 'no rule'.

4. Position of 'Ought' not Settled in Secondary Rules

The position of 'ought' or its status in a basic secondary rule is not settled in Hart's analysis. Truth seems to be that behind all basic rules lies a moral principle that social life is desired and is necessary and that to attain a social life some basic rule is necessary.

CHAPTER 6

INTERNATIONAL LAW

SYNOPSIS

Introduction

- **I. Is International Law a True Law?**
  - **1. Positivist View that it is not Law**
  - **2. International Lawyers Reject Austin's Definition**
  - **3. The Question is only a Verbal Question**
  - **4. All Verbal Questions are not Trivial**
  - **5. For Hart, International Law is only a Set of Rules and not a Legal System**
  - **6. International Law: A Borderline Case**
  - **7. The Question is only of Academic Interest Today**
- **II. Factors Indicating that International Law is True Law**
  - **1. Codification of International Law**
  - **2. Codification under the League of Nations**
  - **3. Codification of International Law under the United Nations**
  - **4. UNCITRAL**
  - **5. General Assembly**
  - **6. Specialised Agencies**
- **III. Settlement of International Disputes**
  - **1. Amicable means of Settlement**
  - **2. Judicial Settlement**
  - **3. Compulsive or Coercive Means**
    - **Retortion**
    - **Reprisal**
    - **Embargo**
- **IV. Authority of International Law/Binding Force of International Law**
  - **1. International Law Derives its Binding Force from Natural Law**
  - **2. Binding Force Rests on the Consent of States**

INTRODUCTION

International law may be either Public or Private International Law. Here we deal with Public International Law. It is also known as the Law of Nations. It consists of rules governing sovereign states in their relation with each other. According to Salmond, it is essentially a species of conventional law and has its source in International Agreements and Treaties. International agreements consist of rules which sovereign States have agreed to observe in their dealings with each other. International agreements are of two kinds – express and implied. Express agreements are contained in Treaties and Conventions. Implied Agreements are evidenced in the customs and practices of the States. These rules have developed as a result of International Conferences, opinions and writings of the jurists.

I. Is International Law a True Law?

This is a popular debate amongst jurists. The problem whether International law is a true law is a difficult question. We have hitherto studied the Natural law theory, the Positivist theory, Hart's theory and Kelson's theory. It is now to be seen whether International law is law within the meaning of these theories.

Following are the observations under different theories:

1. ***Positivist view that it is not Law***: Positivists say that International law cannot qualify as true law because it lacks sovereign authority. It does not possess any institutional method of sanction.

This stand is countered by an argument that there is legislation in the form of multi-lateral treaties and there is sanction in the form of self-help and war. But here again the diluting point is that treaties bind only the consenting States and method of self-help or war can hardly be said to be the institutional method of positivist thinking.

2. ***International lawyers reject Austin's definition of law & define law as a body of rules for human conduct:*** International lawyers reject the Austinian definition of law. They say that ingredients of Sovereignty and sanctions are not necessary to define law. They propose a definition which would be wide enough to include International law. Oppenheim defines law as a body of rules for human conduct within a community which is enforced by external power by common consent. International law fits into this definition. There is common consent in the form of agreement; there are rules of conduct; there is enforcement by external power. But still the question remains: which of the two versions- whether Austin's or Oppenheim's version, is correct?
3. ***The question is only a verbal question:*** According to some writers- whether international law is law proper is only a verbal question. They say that there is no such thing as the proper sense of the word. Words have no God given meaning but only those which we choose to bestow upon them. The facts remain the same however one may define International law. Hence, whether International law is or is not law is a trivial and empty verbal question.
4. ***All verbal questions are not trivial***: All verbal questions are not trivial. Some verbal questions can be answered by just a reference to dictionary definition. But questions like – does steering a car on tow amount to driving cannot be so answered. It has some similarities and some dissimilarities with normal driving. Whether we will term it as driving or not will depend upon whether we are impressed with the similarities or the dissimilarities. International law falls within the non-trivial question.
5. ***For hart, international law is only a set of rules and not a legal system***: Hart's analysis of law requires primary rules and secondary basic rules of recognition for the set of rules to be transformed into a system of rules. But in International law there are no rules of recognition. Hence for Hart International law is only a set of rules and not a legal system. To regard International law as simply a set of unconnected rules would be erring in the opposite direction. In fact they are knit together by a cluster of basic principles and organizing concepts rendering the set of rules into a coherent network.

6. ***International law: A borderline case:*** International law is clearly a borderline case. It lacks certain important features of a standard legal system such as legislative organ, Courts with compulsory jurisdiction and institutional method of law enforcement. However it is something more than a species of international morality, though it may lack the rigid features of law.
7. ***Whether International Law is a true law or not is today only of academic interest***: Yet its discussion is important to understand the true nature of international law. The observation that International law is not true law was propounded by jurists like Austin, Pufendorf, Hobbes, Holland, Jethrow Brown who were groomed under Municipal law. They were under a fallacy that there was no system of law other than the municipal law and municipal jurisdiction. They failed to realize that while the Municipal laws operate in centralized system, international law operates in decentralized system and hence comparison is not proper. International law and municipal law operates under different set of circumstances. International law is as good and strong as it can be under the system and circumstances it operates. Its significance and efficacy are constantly increasing. It deals with varying matters like Nuclear weapons, Environment, International Pressures and compulsion works. For example, we amended our Patent law and introduced product patent inspite of opposition within India in order to keep our laws in tune with TRIPS and GATT which itself was signed under compulsions. Can we still say that international law is not true law. Likewise many developing countries including India signed GATT as there was no way out if they were to survive in the international market.

II. Factors Indicating that International Law is True Law

1. Codification of International Law[1]

There has been codification of International Law which has taken it nearer to it being accepted as law. Codification of International Law was attempted initially on a private basis. The first private codification was rendered by Bentham in 1789 in the treaties entitled "The Principles of Morals and Legislation". In 1873 the Institute of International Law was founded at Ghent in Belgium & an Association for the Reform and Codification of the Law of Nations was founded – now known as International Law Association.

2. Codification under the League of Nations

After the First World War, partial codification took place in the field of the law of peace through general instruments like the Covenant of the League of Nations, the Statute of the Permanent Court of International Justice and the General Act for the Pacific Settlement of International Disputes of 1928 and the General Treaty for the Renunciation of War. It was only the League of Nations which handled the problem of codification properly.

At the Hague Conference in 1930 conventions on topics of Nationality were like those pertaining to Conflict of Nationality Laws; Military Obligations in

1. H.O. Agarval: International Law & Human Rights, p. 54-60.

certain cases of Double Nationality; Statelessness. But they were adopted only by a few countries.

3. Codification of International Law under the United Nations

Codification of International Law is done by various agencies of the United Nations: International Law Commission (ILC), United Nations Commission for International Trade Law (UNCITRAL), General Assembly and specialized Agencies.

ILC: The object of the International Law Commission is to promote progressive development of International Law and its codification. Some important conventions are the Geneva Conventions on the Law of the Sea; Vienna Convention on Diplomatic Relations (1961); Conventions on

- Consular Relations (1963),
- Special Mission (1969),
- Law of Treaties (1969)
- Prevention and Punishment of Crimes Against Internationally Protected Persons Including Diplomatic Agents (1973)
- Vienna Convention of Succession of States in respect of State Properties Archives and Debts (1983)
- Law of Non-Navigational Use of International Water Courses (adopted by the General Assembly in 1997)

Thus, a great deal of customary International Law has been transformed into treaty rules. Its outstanding contribution is the preparation of the draft Statute of the International Criminal Court. On the basis of the draft, Rome Statute of the International Criminal Court has been adopted on July 17th 1998.

In the year 2002 it discussed the topics of State Responsibility, Reservations to Treaties; Diplomatic Protection, International Liability for Injurious consequences arising out of acts not prohibited by International Law (Prevention of Trans-boundary Damage from Hazardous Activities).

4. UNCITRAL

It was established by the General Assembly on 17th December, 1966. It was a vehicle through which the United Nations could remove the obstacles created by disparities in national laws governing International trade which in turn prevented a free flow of trade. The UNCITRAL has since come to be the 'core legal body' of the United Nations' system of International Trade Law. Conventions drafted by it and adopted in diplomatic conferences are United Nations Conventions on

- Limitation Period in the International Sale of Goods (1976);
- Carriage of Goods by Sea (Hamburg Rules, 1978);
- Contract on the Sale of Goods
- Liability of Operators or Transport Terminals in International Trade
- International Bills of Exchange and International Promissory Notes (1988);
- Independent Guarantees and Stand-by Letters of Credit
- Assignment of Receivables in International trade.

UNCITRAL has also adopted Model Laws on important topics like International Commercial Arbitration (1985), Procurement of Goods and

Construction (1993), Procurement of Goods Construction and Services (1994), International Commercial Conciliation (2001).

5. General Assembly

General Assembly has entrusted the work of codification to its different bodies. Conventions are framed by the General Assembly on adopting resolutions on their recommendations. E.g., International Covenants on:

- Civil and Political Rights (1966)
- Economic Social and Cultural Rights (1966)

Protocol of 1989 called upon the State Parties to take measures to abolish death penalty within their jurisdiction. The adoption of a convention by the assembly on the Right of the Child in November 1989 created a new international norm.

6. Specialised Agencies

Specialised agencies of United Nations are engaged in codifying International laws in different fields. E.g., International Civil Aviation Organisation; World Health Organization are constantly engaged in formulating new conventions and revising old ones. International Labour Organization and International Postal Union are bodies older than United Nations and have proved to be useful agencies for the codification of International Law.

III. Settlement of International Disputes

Under International Law procedure for settlement of disputes has been laid down only for legal disputes and not for political disputes. This means that a dispute must be capable of being settled by the application of principles and rules of International Law.[1] However when there is a dispute between two States on the question whether a particular dispute is or is not a dispute, it is settled by the decision of the International Court of Justice in accordance with Article 36 para 6 of the Statute. International Law lays down the procedure for the settlement of those disputes which arise when a party presents to another a specific claim based upon an alleged breach of the law and the latter rejects it. Legal disputes may be settled in two ways. They are amicable means (pacific means) of settlement and compulsive or coercive means of settlement.

1. Amicable Means of Settlement

Peaceful settlement of disputes is one of the principles of the Charter of United Nations. Article 33 para 1 of the Charter says that parties to any dispute shall seek a solution by negotiation, enquiry, mediation, conciliation, arbitration, judicial settlement or other peaceful means of their choice. The various peaceful means of settlement may be broadly divided into two categories *viz.*, extra-judicial mode and judicial mode of settlement. In extra-judicial settlement dispute is settled by an agreement between the disputant States. They are also known as political means or diplomatic procedures. The judicial settlement is a legal process where settlement is according to International Law by an impartial third party. The two processes are not completely divorced from each other. The General Assembly and the Security Council of the United Nations are concerned with evidence and legal arguments though they are political organs and their

1. *Nicaragua* v. *Honduras*.

basis of action remains primarily political. For example, in 1976, India and Pakistan settled their outstanding differences in the Shimla conference; India and Srilanka settled their boundary differences in 1974; The Farraka Barrage issue was settled through negotiation between India & Bangladesh. In all these cases negotiations resulted in conclusion of agreements.

At times disputes are settled through Good Offices and Mediation. E.g., McNaughton in 1949, Dickson in 1950, Graham in 1951 and Jarring in 1957 were appointed by the Security Council as the United Nations' representative to settle the Kashmir issue between India and Pakistan.

Disputes may be settled through mediation, that is, where a third party participates in the discussion with the disputant States and also gives its own suggestions in resolving the dispute. E.g., mediation of Soviet premier Kosygin in the dispute between India and Pakistan concluded in Tashkent agreement in 1966.

When a dispute is referred to a Commission or a Committee to investigate the basis of the dispute and to make a report containing proposals for settlement after finding out the facts is known as Conciliation. At present conciliation is used by States when the treaties provide it as a means to settle the dispute.

The two organs of the United Nations – General Assembly and the Security Council are empowered to discharge certain functions towards settlement of disputes by peaceful means.

2. Judicial Settlement

When a dispute is settled by the International Tribunal in accordance with the rules of International Law, the process is called Judicial Settlement. At present International Court of Justice is the most important International Tribunal. *Ad-hoc* arbitral tribunals and *specialized* tribunals of a semi-permanent nature are other judicial tribunals. Consent of the parties is essential before a case is heard by an International Court of Justice. Judgment of the court is binding on the parties. Judges of the court are elected by the General Assembly and the Security Council of the United Nations. They represent the main forms of civilization and of the legal systems of the world. They are persons who are qualified to occupy the highest judicial office in their own countries. The court has a permanent registry and performs all necessary functions of receiving documents for filing and recording. It also acts as a channel of communication with States and other bodies. All members of the United Nations are *ipso facto* parties to the court. Non-members also can become parties subject to fulfillment of certain conditions laid down by the General Assembly.

3. Compulsive or Coercive Means

Coercive means for settlement of disputes are non-peaceful methods. They involve a pressure or force on a State to settle the dispute. But it does not mean use of armed forces in all cases. Normally they include measures falling short of war. They are

- *Retortion:* It means retaliation – tit-for-tat. Acts done in retortion are not illegal; they are permitted under International Law. They are unfriendly acts and in given circumstances they may be effective tools for law enforcement. In retortion those actions cannot legitimately be taken which are likely to endanger International peace and security. Such actions if taken are illegal. E.g., in December 1992, when two Pakistani High Commission officials were declared *persona non grata* by India, Pakistan also expelled three Indian officials declaring them *persona non grata*. When India expelled Nasiruddin Ahmed, a Pakistani diplomat, for indulging in espionage activities, Pakistan also expelled an Indian diplomat on similar grounds.

- *Reprisal:* It includes employing any coercive measure by a State for securing redress. The main purpose is to compel the delinquent State to discontinue the wrong doing. Formerly reprisals were restricted to seizure of property or persons. Later it included bombardment, occupation of territories of a State, seizure of ships, freezing of assets of its citizens. State is at liberty to take any action in reprisal. But certain conditions must be satisfied in order to make it lawful. Reprisals are limited in time. They are legitimate only after a claim to perform the obligation arising from State responsibility has been unsuccessful and must not be continued when the claim is honoured. For example, U.S. forces launched 23 cruise missiles against Iraqi Intelligence Headquarters. It resulted in killing and injuring several persons. U.S. took this decision after it was confirmed that Iraq had sponsored a plot to kill the Former President Bush. U.S. defended the attack by describing it as proportionate to the attempted assassination of its Former President. But the action was not justified because use of force by a State against the territorial integrity or political independence of a State under Article 2 para 4 of the UN Charter.[1]
- *Embargo:* It means detention of ships in port. Embargo may be applied by the State in respect of its own vessels (civil embargo) or vessels of the other State (hostile embargo). The purpose of an embargo is to exert financial or economic pressures on the other States and compel them to settle disputes. At present embargo may be applied by a State individually or collectively under the authority of the United Nations. It should not endanger International peace and security.

It is submitted that going by the latest developments there is a "Rise of International Law" and whether or not International Law fits into the framework of any Theories of Law – International Law is being enforced.

The latest news item[2] speaks of the rise of International Law.

This week's opening of a special U.N. Tribunal to investigate the 2005 assassination of Lebanon's former Prime Minister, Rafiq al-Hariri, is the latest bit of evidence suggesting that the boom times are here for international justice. ....The modern-day system of dispensing international criminal justice takes as a starting point the establishment by the U.N. Security Council in 1993 of the criminal tribunal for former Yugoslavia in The Hague. That was followed by a comparable tribunal charged with investigating the 1994 Rwanda genocide. U.N. backed special or hybrid courts have since been created for Sierra Leone and Cambodia and there has been pressure for similar tribunals in East Timor and Iraq.

1. Security Council failed to condemn U.S. may be due to political reasons.
2. The Hindu 04-03-2009.

The International Criminal Court (ICC), its founding treaty underwritten by 108 states including Britain but not the U.S., has increasingly taken the lead since 2002. It is pursuing investigations into genocide, war crimes and crimes against humanity allegedly committed in northern Uganda, the Democratic Republic of Congo, the Central African Republic and in Darfur, western Sudan.

Confirming this activist trend, the ICC's most ambitious step yet is likely to come on Wednesday, when it is widely expected to order an arrest warrant for Sudan's president, Omar al-Bashir, for crimes allegedly committed in Darfur. If so, Bashir will be the first sitting head of state to be indicted.

While the Bashir case marks a watershed for the ICC and, more broadly, for international criminal justice, it also dramatizes the many unresolved problems facing attempts to enforce global accountability. One is the central issue of political support.

Nick Donovan of the Aegis Trust said recent years had seen a successful effort to develop the "architecture" of international law, meaning treaties, tribunals, conventions and courts.... The result is a reasonably comprehensive set of international penal codes, a nascent system of courts and tribunals, but relatively few convictions."

The argument promulgated by rightwing American nationalists, that international criminal law is irrelevant, unenforceable, and undesirable, is less often heard these days. But it's clear, if the system is to flourish, that "wanted posters" are not enough. Expanded judicial powers and jurisdiction are needed. © Guardian Newspapers Limited, 2009.

IV. Authority of International Law/Binding Force of International Law

1. ***International law derives its binding force from Natural law:*** Some writers opine that International law derives its binding force from Natural law. But then Natural law is nothing more than morality. But then this overlooks the fact that International law has clippings of an ordinary law which distinguishes it from morality. Thus like ordinary law and unlike rules of morality International law can be formalized, in principle-legislated and adjudicated upon.
2. ***Binding force rests on the consent of States:*** Some believe (Like Hugo Grotius) that *the binding force rests on the consent of States.* But from where does this principle itself derive its validity? But then this problem is not peculiar to International law. The problem lies in showing authority for any system of law. For example, how do we show authority for the Constitution of India or other basic laws of different legal systems. But it is not feasible and practical to go on an endless search to trace a rule which is 'basic to the basic rule' in which case the prior rule cannot be termed as 'basic' at all.

This would mean that basic rules of a system of law are mere rules of practice and that they involve a mixture of moral, legal and other 'ought' propositions.

CHAPTER 7

THE FUNCTION AND PURPOSE OF LAW

SYNOPSIS

I. Functions and Purpose of Law: Justice, Stability and Peaceful Change

Law is not an end in itself. It is a means to an end. And the 'end' here is 'justice, stability, peaceful change, orderly society'. Society already exists. Law is a means or an instrument to secure justice.

Theorists differ in their views of justice:

- Thomas Aquinas and Salmond claim that justice is the goal of law. For Aquinas unjust law is no law.
- For Salmond law means a body of principles recognized and applied by the State in the administration of justice.
- For the Positivists who concern themselves with what law 'is' and not what the law 'ought' to be 'Justice' is relevant for the critical evaluation of law though they do not see any logical or necessary connection between the two.

II. Analysis of the Jurisprudential Concept of Justice

1. Justice: Wide and Restricted Sense

In its wide sense unjust law is no law (Aquinas). Here justice is roughly synonymous with morality.

Justice has a narrow sense as used in the expressions 'court of justice'; 'natural justice' 'denial of justice'. Here the expressions refer to only one area of morality. The narrow sense of justice can be understood by examining the reverse concept of injustice. Discrimination or 'like not being treated alike' is injustice. It may be a father who favours one child against the other or the Government policy which does not treat like alike, it is a case of injustice. Hence justice means 'treating like alike, whether in terms of conferring benefits like allotment of Government sites or say equality in public employment; or in meting out penalties and punishments for wrong doing. In other words, justice is 'equal treatment to those who are equally placed'. For example, in India our Constitution guarantees equality before law and equal protection of the laws; no discrimination only on the ground of race, caste, sex, place of birth, religion; equality in Government employment. In the interest of justice to those who have been left behind in the race of life due to evil practices like untouchability etc. there is a provision for reservations, lowered recruitment standards, special concessions and privileges etc. to certain category of citizens. This is with a view to equalize the inequalities; to give a helping hand to the underprivileged so that they can raise themselves to the level of the better placed. This also would mean that justice demands that once they are on an equal footing as that of the General Merit Candidates they must compete on a level playing ground with others. This is what the latest Supreme Court 10th April, 2008 decision allowing quota for OBC's does by keeping the creamy layer out of the reservation scheme. In *Indira Sawhney* v. *Union of India,*[1] Kerala State Backward Classes (Reservation of Appointments and Posts in Services) Act, 1995 was held discriminatory and violative of Article 14 and 16(4) for not excluding creamy layer from reservation.

2. *Justice: Distributive and Corrective*

1. Distributive Justice – falls within the Legislative field
2. Corrective Justice – falls within the area of the courts

a. *Indian Constitution and Distributive Justice*: Falls within the area of the Legislation or delegated legislation because it is primarily their task to make laws and rules for division/distribution of social goods (*i.e.* benefits and burdens) amongst the members of the Society. The Indian Constitution lays down several provisions as to the manner in which to attain distributive justice. It lays down in Article 39 that the State must see that the material resources of the community are is equitably distributed and that there is no concentration of wealth; that there shall be equality before law and equal protection of the laws; that there shall be no discrimination only on the grounds of race, religion, caste, sex, place of birth.

While 'equality before the law' is a somewhat negative concept implying the absence of any special privilege in favour of any individual, 'equal protection of law' is a positive concept implying equality of treatment in equal circumstances[2]. However the dominant idea common to both the expressions is that of equal justice.[3] It means that all persons similarly situated shall be treated alike, both in privileges conferred and liabilities imposed by the laws. Equal law should be applied to all in the same situation and there should be no discrimination between one and another. This rule of law embodied in Article 14 is the 'basic feature' of Indian Constitution and hence it cannot be destroyed even by an amendment of the Constitution under Article 368.[4]

However the scope of Article 14 is watered down in the following cases:

1. Under Article 31C of the Constitution, laws made by the State for implementing the directive principles under Article 39(b) and (c) cannot be challenged on the ground that they are violative of Article 14. The Supreme Court has held that where Article 31C comes in, Article 14 goes out.[5] Yet, the purpose is to give effect to the theory of distributive justice under Article 39 of the Constitution.

---

1. AIR 2000 SC 498.
2. Dicey Law of Constitution, 10th Edn., (Universal Law Publishing Co. Pvt. Ltd.), p. 49.
3. *Sheo Shanker* v. *State of Madhya Pradesh,* AIR 1951 Nag 53.
4. *Indira Nehru Gandhi* v. *Raj Narayan,* AIR 1975 SC 2299.
5. *Sanjeev Coke Manufacturing Company* v. *Bharat Cooking Coal Ltd.,* (1983) 1 SCC 147.

2. When there is a proclamation of emergency and the President has issued an order under Article 359 (1), enforcement of Article 14 may be suspended during the period the Proclamation is in force.

(a) *Indian Constitution & distributive justice*

1. Article 38 (1) provides that the State shall strive to promote the welfare of the people by securing and protecting as effectively as it may, a social order in which justice- social, economic and political – shall inform all the institutions of national life. It also provides that the State shall strive to minimize inequalities in income and endeavour to eliminate inequalities in status, facilities and opportunities not only amongst individuals but also amongst groups of people residing in different areas or engaged in different vocations. The new clause aims at equality in all spheres of life. It would enable the State to have a national policy on wages and eliminate inequalities in various spheres of life.

2. Principles of policy to be followed by the State for securing economic justice. Article 39 requires the State to direct its policy towards securing the following principles:

(a) Equal rights of men and women to adequate means of livelihood.
(b) Distribution of ownership and control of the material resources of the community to the common good.
(c) To ensure that the economic system should not result in concentration of wealth and means of production to the common detriment.
(d) Equal pay for equal work for both men and women.
(e) To protect health and strength of workers and tender age of children and to ensure that they are not forced by economic necessity to enter avocations unsuited to their age or strength.
(f) That children are given opportunities and facilities to develop in a healthy manner and in conditions of freedom and dignity and that childhood and youth are protected against exploitation and against moral and material abandonment.

Article 38 and 39 of the Constitution embody the Jurisprudential doctrine of 'distributive justice'. The Constitution permits and even directs the State to administer what may be termed 'distributive justice'. The concept of distributive justice in the sphere of law-making connote, *inter alia,* the removal of economic inequalities rectifying the injustice resulting from dealings and transactions between unequals in the society.[1]

In *State of Tamil Nadu* v. *Abu Kavar Bai* the Court upheld the validity of a law enacted for the nationalization of transport services in the State on the ground that it was for giving effect to the directive principles contained in Article 39(b) and (c) and as such was meant for the purpose of distribution or preventing concentration of wealth; and hence towards securing distributive justice.

b. *Indian Constitution and Corrective justice*: It may so happen that the Legislature errs while making such distribution. Or though the Legislature has not made any error, the implementing authority makes an error or it is some other citizen who prevents another from exercising his right. It is here that corrective justice steps in to set right the wrong that is done. Corrective justice

1. *Central Inland Water Transport Corporation* v. *Brojo Nath Ganguly,* (1986) 3 SCC 156.

falls within the area of the courts. For example, if the legislature gives voting rights only to those above 5′ height – it would be unjust on the ground that distributive justice is not taken care of by the Legislature. Or if a person entitled to exercise the right to vote is illegally prevented by the Returning Officer as it happened in *Ashby* v. *White*, (1703) 2 LD Rays 398, corrective justice steps in and redresses/sets right the unjustness. This is done by the courts. Or if *A* wrongfully seizes *B's* property or if *A* without a reasonable cause leaves the consortium of his wife corrective justice acts to restore the property or to direct the erring spouse to join the consortium of her husband under the Hindu Marriage Act, 1955.

Corrective justice also includes fair rules of procedure like – right to be heard before any order is passed against a person; that no person shall be a judge in his own cause. Equal opportunity to every citizen to redress the wrong. For example, Article 39A of our Constitution lays down that the State shall take steps to ensure equal justice and free legal aid; that it shall provide free legal aid by suitable legislation or scheme to ensure that opportunities for securing justice are not denied to any citizen by reason of economic or other disabilities. The Indian Legislature and the Courts have laid down a number of schemes and judgments to ensure corrective justice. For example, the Legal Services Authority Act is an Act enacted *inter-alia* to ensure free legal aid to the specified category of persons like women, victims of disasters, persons below a certain income group etc.

Legal aid and speedy trial have now been held to be fundamental rights under Article 21 of the Constitution available to all prisoners and enforceable by the courts. The State is under a duty to provide a lawyer to a poor person and it must pay to the lawyer his fee as fixed by the Court.[1]

In *Centre of Legal Research* v. *State of Kerala*[2] it has been held that legal aid programme which is meant to bring social justice to the people cannot remain confined to traditional or litigation oriented programme, but it must take into account the socio-economic conditions prevailing in the country and adopt a more dynamic approach. The voluntary organizations must be involved and supported for implementing legal aid programme and it should be free from Government control.

In a notable case *State of Maharashtra* v. *Manubhai Bagaji Vashi*[3] the Supreme Court has held that Article 21 read with Article 39A casts a duty on the State to afford free legal aid and guarantee speedy trial, for which a vast number of persons trained in law are essential. Legal aid is required in many forms and at various stages for obtaining guidance, for resolving disputes in Courts, Tribunals or other authorities. It has manifold facets. The need for a *continuing and well organized legal education* is absolutely essential in view of new trends in the world order to meet the ever growing challenges. For this purpose a vast number of persons trained in different branches of law are needed every year. This is possible only when adequate number of law colleges with proper infrastructure including proper and expert law teachers and staff are established. As is in this case a sole Government Law College cannot cater to the needs of legal education or requirement in a city like Bombay. If the State is unable to start colleges on its

1. *H.M. Hoskot* v. *State of Maharashtra*, AIR 1978 SC 1548.
2. AIR 1986 SC 1322.
3. (1995) 5 SCC 730.

own it should allow private colleges duly recognized by the University or the Bar Council of India or other appropriate authorities and should be afforded reasonable facilities to function effectively and in a meaningful manner. This requires substantial funds. Under the label of self-financing institutions the College should not be allowed to hike their fees to any extent to meet their expenses. The private law colleges may not afford the huge cost required for this purpose. The standard of legal education and discipline is bound to suffer. The court said that if this is allowed, free legal aid will only be a farce and therefore it is necessary to afford them grant-in-aid by the State as it will facilitate and ensure the recognized private colleges to function effectively and in a meaningful manner and turn out sufficient number of well trained law graduates in all branches every year. This will enable the State to provide free legal aid and ensure that State opportunities for securing justice are not denied to any citizen on account of any disability. This decision goes towards building up of the infrastructure needed for ensuring efficient management of corrective justice.

There are any number of examples of corrective justice. All the cases where the action of the Legislature or the Executive is challenged on the ground of discrimination and it is upheld by the Courts are examples of corrective justice. To take just a few examples, in *John Vallamatton* v. *Union of India*[1] Petitioner challenged Section 118 of the Indian Succession Act. Section 118 imposes restriction on a Christian having a nephew or a niece or any other relative on his power to bequeath his property for religious or charitable purposes. The definition in the Act did not include wife of a testator as near relative while an adopted son was included as a relative. So a Christian testator having a nephew or a niece must execute the Will at least 12 months before his death and deposit it within 6 months otherwise the bequest for religious or charitable use would be void. This restriction did not apply to a person having a wife. The court held that Section 118 of the Succession Act is unconstitutional being violative of Article 14 of the Constitution.

In another landmark judgment in *Daniel Latif* v. *Union of India*[2] the Supreme Court held that a Muslim divorced woman has right to maintenance even after iddat period under the Muslim Women (Protection of Rights on Divorce) Act, 1986. The Court said that a Muslim husband is liable to make reasonable and fair provision for the future of the divorced wife which clearly extends beyond the iddat period in terms of Section 3(1)(a) of the Act. A divorced woman who has not remarried and who is unable to maintain herself after iddat period can proceed under Section 4 of the Act against her relations who are liable to maintain her in proportion to the properties which they may inherit on her death according to Muslim Law from such divorced woman including her children and parents. If the relatives are found unable to pay her maintenance the Magistrate may direct the State Wakf Board established under the Wakf Act to pay maintenance. This is a classic case of corrective justice as the Act containing only 7 Sections is loaded with infirmities and confusions.[3] Inspite of a conflict

1. AIR 2003 SC 2902.
2. AIR 2001 SC 3262.
3. Article titled Muslim Women (Protection of Rights on Divorce) Act, 1986 – An Illustration of Legislative Supremacy over the Judiciary, AIR 1995 JS 135

between Sections 3 and 4 of the Act, the judiciary has used the resourcefulness at its command to do justice to the Muslim divorcee wives.

The Supreme Court of India has adopted a unique method of doing corrective justice. Inspite of the Jurisprudential theory that legislating or not legislating on a particular area is a policy matter for the Government – in the interest of justice the courts have issued directions to the Government to pass certain laws. For example in *Sarala Mudgal* v. *Union of India*[1] – the question that came up for consideration was whether a Hindu husband married under the Hindu law, after conversion to Islam can solemnize a second marriage without dissolving the prior Hindu marriage. Court held that such a marriage is illegal and the husband can be prosecuted for bigamy. It also directed the Union Government to file an affidavit within the prescribed time indicating the steps taken and efforts made by the Government towards securing a Uniform Civil Code for the citizens of India.

In yet another landmark judgment- the Supreme Court has stepped into the shoes of the Legislature as never before to do corrective justice. Moved by the plight of the women fighting for their rights under marriage like maintenance and custody of their children- the Supreme Court directed the Centre and the State Governments to amend the law or frame rules and notify them within 3 months; to provide for consequences of non-registration of marriage; rules to be formalized after inviting public response; the rules to remain in operation until the respective governments frame proper legislations for compulsory registration of marriages. For the first time in the history of the judiciary, Justice Pasayat said that all new laws to be framed by the governments be placed for scrutiny before the Supreme Court.

Fair and equal dispensation of justice whether distributive or corrective must be attained at the individual level and also at the larger level where all are equal before law. This does not mean that the rich and the poor; the old and the young be all treated alike. It means that like should be treated alike. This explains why we have special laws favouring the women, the children, those below poverty line. This is what Articles 14 and 15 of the Indian Constitution lays down. Reasonable classification is allowed but class legislation is not allowed. Thus under Article 42 women workers can be given special maternity relief and a law to this effect will not infringe Article 15 (1). Likewise Article 15 is not violated if educational institutions are established by the State exclusively for women. The reservation of seats for women does not offend Article 15(1)[2]. Justice also requires that judges should mete out justice without fear or favour; and without distinction between rich and poor; influential and uninfluential etc.

Likewise, corrective justice is extended to the stage of the findings of the court. If today's plaintiff is awarded a certain amount of damage tomorrow's plaintiff under identical situation must be given the same damages.

The role of distributive and corrective justice is to strike a balance among different members of the society. Once general rules of substantive law are created by the legislature or by judicial decisions we no longer speak of *A's* rights

1. (1995) 3 SCC 635.
2. *Dattatraya* v. *State*, AIR 1953 Bom 311.

to reputation against that of *B's* right of speech but we consider rights in its abstract term *i.e.,* we speak of balancing Freedom of Speech and Expression with that of reputation of a person or the court (as in the case of contempt of court). This led the American writer Roscoe Pound to regard law as a species of social engineering. The purpose of social engineering is to maximize the fulfillment of the interests of the community and its members and to promote smooth running of the machinery of society. An interest is anything that is of general advantage to a person like physical security, protection of property, reputation, job etc. All these interests may not get legal recognition. What interests must be protected are questions partly for law, partly for sociology and partly for ethics. In short, reconciliation of conflicting interests is a part of problem of justice.

The other goal of law is uniformity. Laws must be definite, certain, known, permanent and predictable. This helps the citizen chalk out his line of action. At times fixed rules which cause some hardship are preferred to uncertain rules which are more certain. Fixed rules are better than the arbitrary opinions of the judges. Rule of law is to be preferred than the rule of men. They protect the administration of justice from allegations of improper motives.

Law also aims at stability and security of social order. But too much of rigidity would also be unjust. No rule howsoever well conceived and well drafted can provide an answer to every possible situation that may arise. In criminal matters as in the case of life imprisonment some amount of individualization is necessary. For example, the Indian Penal Code gives a wide range of prescribed punishment say for rape up to 10 years; for murder either imprisonment for life or capital punishment etc. This helps in individualising justice. However, to reconcile stability of law with flexibility of law is a tough job.

CHAPTER 8

LAW AND FACT

SYNOPSIS

I. Law and Fact

Questions which arise before the courts may be either questions of law or questions of fact or mixed questions of law and fact. These terms are used in three different senses:

1. First Sense: Predetermined and Authoritatively Answered Questions are Questions of Law

A question which the court is bound to answer in accordance with a rule of law is a question of law. All others are questions of fact. That is all **predetermined and authoritatively** answered questions are questions of law and remaining are questions of fact. Whether a child below 7 years can commit a wrong under the Indian Penal Code? Whether a person whose income is below 50,000 is entitled to free legal aid under the Legal Services Authority Act, 1986 is a question of law. But whether there is unreasonable delay in the performance of the contract? Whether the Scheduled Caste persons are adequately represented in the services of the State is a question of fact.

2. Second Sense: Questions of Law Arising for the First Time

Question as to what is the law to be applied in a particular case may arise for the first time before the court. Such a question arises because the law is uncertain or ambiguous or because the Statute is silent. In the first sense of the term this is a question of fact. But once it is judicially determined it becomes authoritative, and therefore, it becomes a question of law to be followed in all further similar cases. For example, the question whether reservations in promotions under Article 16 of the Constitution are permissible arose for the first time in *General Manager, S. Rlys.* v. *Rangachari,*[1] This was a question of law in the second sense of the term. It was held by the court that there can be reservations in promotions. This judicial determination puts the question into the first sense of the term (*i.e.* a predetermined question of law). Later the 77th Constitutional Amendment introduced Article 16(4A) to the Indian Constitution which expressly provided for reservations in promotions giving legislative approval to the judicial determination. Thus there is a continuous process wherein a question of law in the second sense of the term becomes a question of law in the first sense of the term *i.e.* from unsettled law to settled/pre-determined law.

3. *Third Sense: Jury System*

There are questions of law determined by the judges and questions of fact determined by the jury. This third sense has limitations because all the cases are not decided with the help of the jury. The Judge may withdraw questions of fact from the jury and decide them. In India there is no jury system. However, the court may appoint a Commission under Order 26 of the Civil Procedure Code which is a fact finding body.

4. *Question of Fact Generally Means those Questions which are not Question of Law*

It means:

- Questions not determined by rule of law
- Any question except the question as to what the law is
- Questions to be answered by the jury instead of by the judge

5. *Question of Fact is Opposed to a Question of Judicial Discretion and Judicial Opinion*

Judicial discretion includes all questions as to what is right, just, reasonable or equitable so far as not predetermined by authoritative rules. Judicial discretion pertains to 'what ought to be' rather than 'what is'. 'What is' are matters of fact. They are capable of proof and can be proved by evidence. But what is just, right or reasonable cannot be proved by evidence. They can be proved by reasoning and argument and by appealing to the conscience of the court Questions of fact attempt to discover the truth of the matter. Questions of judicial discretion attempt to discover what is right or proper or just under the circumstances. For example, whether. *A* has committed an act amounting to an offence is a question of fact determined by evidence. What particular offence is committed say - whether murder or murder and rape is determined by reference to the Penal laws like the Indian Penal Code. Hence it is a question of law. What punishment is to be imposed is for judicial discretion subject to the minimum and maximum laid down by the law.

Thus while trying offences under Indian Penal Code, the court exercises its discretion on whether to impose fine, simple imprisonment, rigorous imprisonment, death penalty or life imprisonment etc. In so exercising its discretion it is guided by the provisions under Indian Penal Code. For example for murder – death penalty or life imprisonment, for rape – imprisonment up to

1. AIR 1962 SC 36.

10 years. Here 10 years is the upper limit up to which the discretion can be exercised.

Under Section 74 of the Indian Contract Act, for breach of Contract, the parties may have stipulated a sum of money to be paid to the aggrieved party by way of penalty. The amount of penalty indicates the maximum penalty that can be awarded by the court. Here the court has the discretion to award such amount as it deems fit and just subject to the maximum penalty stipulated by the parties. For example, if Rs. 50000 is the penalty stipulated, court has the discretion to award penalty up to Rs. 50000. Court has to ascertain what is just and reasonable and award the penalty. Thus it can be less than but not more than Rs.50000. Court may grant divorce on any of the grounds under Section 13 of the Hindu Marriage Act and make such provisions as it deems just and proper regarding custody of the child. The question of grounds of divorce like adultery, cruelty and desertion are questions of fact. But the question of custody of child is one of right and discretion. Here the limitation on the judicial discretion is set by the rule that the interest of the child must be of paramount consideration. Discretion never means that the judge can act as he likes, according to his whims and fancies. He must act according to his dictates of reason. In every law which requires a person or authority to act in a *just and reasonable manner,* there is an element of discretion – not unfettered discretion but fettered by dictates of reason.

Of course in wider sense of the term 'fact', the question whether an act is just or right is also a question of fact. But it is not a question of demonstrable fact to be dealt with by a purely intellectual process: it involves a question of moral judgment and is therefore different from questions of pure fact. E.g., question whether Scheduled Caste or Scheduled Tribe women were exploited in the past is a question of fact: whether Govt. has taken steps to bring them into the mainfold is a question of law as it can be found out by referring to different provisions or enactments favouring Scheduled Castes and Scheduled Tribes. However whether Reservations should be continued: whether new areas of reservations should be opened up is a question of opinion.

6. Judicial Opinion and Judicial Discretion

There is a fine distinction between judicial opinion and judicial discretion. Judicial discretion involves value judgment. Judicial opinion involves assessment of the situation. For example, whether reasonable enquiries were made while purchasing the property; whether due care was exercised while driving the car are matters of judicial opinion.

The area of judicial discretion includes all questions as to what is right, just, equitable or reasonable – to the extent not already pre-determined by authoritative rules of law. Question of discretion pertains to *what ought to be* as opposed to *what is.* Matters of fact can be proved but matters of judicial discretion are not the subject of evidence and proof. They are matters of argument. They are to be determined exercising reason, conscience and humane considerations.

For example, past history of a company's business (profits/losses made, etc.) is a question of fact. But whether it will make profits in future is a matter of opinion. A prospectus which erroneously sets out the past history amounts to misrepresentation, but the one which contains prediction for future prosperity and growth is not misrepresentation, because it is a matter of opinion.

7. Primary and Secondary Facts

There is also a distinction between primary and secondary facts. Primary facts are proved by oral or documentary evidence. Secondary facts are inferred from primary facts. Trial court can use both but the appellate courts can use only the second. For example, wife lodges a complaint against the husband regarding harassment against beating is the primary fact. Secondary fact to be inferred is that the situation was so much unbearable for the wife that she took the ultimate step of lodging complaint, situation is unbearable is the secondary fact, lodging complaint is a primary fact.

Thus, there are three classes of questions that come up before the court:

(a) Questions of law *i.e.* all questions determined by authoritative legal principles. Court's duty is to find out the legal rule applicable.

(b) Questions of judicial discretion *i.e.* value judgments as to what is just and equitable. Duty of the court is to arrive at a moral judgment.

(c) Questions of fact *i.e.* all other matters and questions whatever. Duty of the court is to exercise its intellectual judgment based on evidence and arrive at the truth. It is based on this judgment that the other two duties are to be discharged.

8. Question of Fact Transformed into Question of Law

There are two ways in which questions of fact are transformed into questions of law:

(a) *by presumption of law* (*presumptio juris et de jure*): Presumption means a rule of law, courts shall draw a particular inference from a particular fact or from a particular evidence. Presumption are of two kinds: rebuttable presumption – a conclusion which the court draws unless there is contrary evidence to disprove the same. A person not heard of for 7 years is presumed to be dead; an accused is presumed to be guilty unless proved otherwise. Conclusive presumption – the courts have to infer one fact from the existence of another fact though this inference could be proved to be false. For example, certificate issued by the *Director of Central Food Laboratory* is the conclusive proof of facts stated therein. Examination of the Director as a witness is not permissible.[1] Under Section 25(6) of the Water Act, 1974 the conditions subject to which permission to discharge the effluents is given is mentioned in the Register kept for the purpose, they are conclusive proof that consent was granted subject to such conditions.

(b) *by fiction of law* (*fictio juris*): The fact is deemed to exist whether in fact it exists or not by the construction of law. For example, the doctrine of constructive notice under the Transfer of Property Act under which the buyer is deemed to have notice of the title under which another person is in occupation of the property he wants to buy. An adoptive child is deemed to be the child of the adoptive parents and has rights in the property of the adoptive parents as though it were their natural born

1. *K.V. Baby* v. *Food Inspector Waddakhan*, 1994 Cr LJ 3421 (Ker).

child. If a workman is dismissed he can raise an industrial dispute even if the Union does not espouse his cause under Section 2A of the Industrial Disputes Act, 1946. The deeming clause is an important clause in an agreement.

For example, as per the provision in an agreement with the Electricity Board if the electricity bill is not paid even after three months notice of non-payment, the agreement to supply power is *deemed* to be cancelled.

9. The Same Question may be Partly a Question of Law and Partly of Fact

This is in two senses:

(a) the question may be really a composite question consisting of two or more questions combined. For example, the question is whether there is a partnership between *X* and *Y*. It is partly a question of fact *i.e.* what is the agreement between them and partly of law *i.e.* whether the agreement is sufficient to constitute the legal relation of partnership.

(b) It is a case where there is a fixed rule of law, yet the judicial discretion is not taken away, but there is a limit within which to exercise the judicial discretion.

CHAPTER 9
THE TERRITORIAL NATURE OF LAW

SYNOPSIS

INTRODUCTION

Law consists of rules created by the Legislature and applied and developed by the courts. Both the Legislature and the Courts are the organs of the State. State is territorial in nature. Hence laws are said to be territorial in nature. The true significance of the territorial aspect of law is complex. We need to distinguish between territorial enforcement of law and the territoriality of law itself.

I. Territorial Enforcement of Law

In times of peace, State power is exercised only within the territories of the State and on its public ships and vessels and aircraft registered under its laws. No State allows other States to exercise power over person, events or things within its jurisdiction. This meaning flows from the political division of the world. As a general rule no State allows other States to exercise powers of the Government within it. A person who commits a wrong in State *'A'* and then goes away to State *'B'*, State *'A'* cannot enforce its laws until the person comes back to its territory. If there is an extradition treaty between State *'A'* and State 'B', State *'A'* can apply for extradition; in which case State *'B'* surrenders the person to State *'A'* which can then try him for the offence committed.

A State finds it difficult to punish a person who has committed a crime elsewhere mainly because of lack of jurisdiction. Such persons are therefore sometimes surrendered to the State where the crime has been committed. Such surrender is known as extradition. According to Oppenheim extradition is the delivery of an accused or a convicted individual to the State where he is accused of a crime or convicted of a crime, by the State on whose territory he happens to be for the time being[1].

Grotius was of the view that a State of refuge has a duty either to punish the offender or surrender him to the State seeking his return. The principle of 'prosecution or execution' was recognised by him as a legal duty where the offender is found. This legal duty is based on natural law. But International Law recognizes no right to extradition without a treaty[2].

---

1. International Law, Vol. I, 9th Edn. (1992), p. 949.
2. *Factor* v. *Labubenheimer*, 290 US (1933) p. 287.

A legal duty to surrender arises only when the treaties are concluded by the States. Only in exceptional cases a State may extradite a person on the basis of reciprocity or courtesy but not because of any legal duty[1]. For example, India does not have any extradition treaty with Portugal but when Abu Salem, an accused in 1993 Bombay blast, fled to Portugal along with his wife Monica Bedi, Portugal agreed to extradite Abu Salem to India after India gave an assurance that he would not be given a death sentence.

The Doctrine of Double Criminality governs extradition treaties. That is, the wrongful act must be an offence in both the countries – the requesting and the extraditing country.

India in the recent past has concluded extradition treaties with many countries like Canada (1987), U.K. (1992), Russian Federation (1998), UAE (1999), U.S.A(1999), Spain(2002), France & South Africa (2003). India's proposal to Pakistan for an extradition treaty was rejected by Pakistan saying that time had not yet arrived for such a step.

It is a customary rule of International Law that political offenders are not extradited, that is, they are granted asylum (shelter) by the territorial State. Indian Extradition Act of 1962 has been amended in 1993. It lays down a comprehensive list of offences which shall not be regarded as political offences.

Extradition is not practiced in civil cases. In civil cases, generally every State gives remedy in its own court wherever the wrong may have been committed. Judgments given in foreign countries are recognized in India subject to Section 13 of the Civil Procedure Code, 1908.

Section 13 lays down that a foreign judgement is conclusive as to any matter directly adjudicated upon between the same parties or their privies except when it is not pronounced by a court of competent jurisdiction; not given on the merits of the case; founded on the incorrect view of the International Law; refusal to recognise Indian law in cases where it is applicable; proceedings in which judgment is given are opposed to natural justice; judgment obtained by fraud; or if it sustains a claim founded on a breach of law in force in India.

II. Territorial Nature of Law

Territorial nature of law means that the law is applicable to all persons, things, acts, and events within that territory. It does not apply to things, persons etc. outside the territory. Territory includes all public vessels and aircraft. To say that law is territorial in nature is different from saying that law enforcement is territorial. That law enforcement is territorial is easy to understand because enforcement has to be done by force and force is a physical affair and is manifested in space. But laws consist of rules and rules have no local habitation. The concept of territorial nature of law is, therefore, more abstract in nature and more conceptual. The concept can be broken into three parts:

(a) The rules of law themselves do not purport to apply extra-territorially outside the territory

(b) Law enforcers do not regard them as applying extra-territorially

(c) Other States also do not regard them as having extra-territorial jurisdiction.

---

1. Starke's International Law, 11th Edn., (1994), p. 318.

As far as India is concerned it is a Union of States. The Constitution establishes a Central Government at one level and State Government at the other. There is a division of power between Centre and State Government. Centre can make laws on matters mentioned in Union List of 7 Schedule. The State Governments can make laws on matters mentioned in State list; & on matters mentioned in the Concurrent List – both Central and State Governments can make laws. Article 245 of the Indian Constitution itself lays down that the laws made by the Parliament shall be applicable throughout the territory of India and that made by the State Legislature shall be applicable within the State concerned. For example, laws made by Karnataka Government are applicable only in Karnataka.

- Thus when Karnataka amended the Hindu Succession Act and introduced Section 6 (A) conferring coparcenary rights to daughters, the Act was applicable only in Karnataka. But when the Parliament amended the law to the same effect, coparcenary property rights were extended to daughters throughout India.
- Under the Hindu Marriage Act, the Act is applicable to those married according to the Hindu Law domiciled[1] in India but residing outside India. Thus the territoriality of the law extends to persons *residing* outside the limits of India subject to conditions laid down under the Act, *viz* that they must have an intention to return back to India and stay there permanently.
- Which law is to be applied depends upon the court which is hearing the case. E.g., in U.S.A, there is a dual system of law. Federal law and Federal courts; State law and State courts. Before 1938 the Federal court could take a different view of the Kentucky law from that taken by the Kentucky court itself. Such a situation raises a jurisprudential question 'which is the law of Kentucky?'. Is it as decided by the Federal court or by the Kentucky court? The answer could only be that it depends on the court in which the case is brought. It would also give the future litigants freedom to choose the forum depending on the desired judgement going by the doctrine of precedent.
- What is important to be noted is that territoriality of law is not logically necessary part of law. Hence applicability of a system of law is determined by reference to personal qualifications such as nationality, race, religion and not by reference to territorial considerations. E.g., in India, before the codification of the laws, the law that was applied to Hindus and Muslims were their personal laws. Even to this date, in certain aspects they are governed by their personal laws. E.g., Muslims are governed by their personal laws w.r.t. marriage, divorce and succession. Hindus are governed by their personal laws w.r.t. coparcenary property, subject to certain amendments introduced by the legislature and the Parliament.

---

1. Domicile – is the fact of residence coupled with an intention to stay there permanently. For example, you take up a job in USA as a doctor and meanwhile you are renovating your house in India and also constructing a Hospital. Your intention is to return to India though for the time-being you are residing in USA.

All the statutes in India mention that the law is applicable to the whole of India (except the State of Jammu and Kashmir due to its special constitutional status) or the whole of the State concerned as the case may be. **One exception** to the general rule is that there can be extra territorial operation of the law if there is sufficient nexus between the object and the State. In *Wallace* v. *Income-tax Commissioner, Bombay,*[1] a company registered in England was a partner in a firm in India. The Privy Council applied the doctrine of territorial nexus and held that the entire income made by the company could be taxed in India. Major part of its income coming from British, India gave a sufficient nexus between the object and the State. In *State of Bombay* v. *R.M.D.C.,*[2] Bombay State levied a tax on lotteries and prize competitions. Tax was extended to a newspaper printed and published in Bangalore but had wide circulation in Bombay. Prize competitions were conducted through this paper. Hence there was sufficient territorial nexus.

Likewise our laws pertaining to marriage, divorce, succession and domestic relations apply only to those persons who by residence, domicile, or otherwise are sufficiently connected with the territory of India. Section 4 of the Indian Penal Code is applicable to offences committed by Indians outside India.

So far as the law of procedure is concerned it is that of the forum before which the case is constituted and not that of the country of the litigants or of the place where the cause of action took place. Foreign judgments are enforced based on the rules of conflict of law in its country.

---

1. AIR 1948 PC 118.
2. AIR 1957 SC 628.

CHAPTER 10

CONSTITUTIONAL LAW

SYNOPSIS

INTRODUCTION

Organization of a modern State is complex. It is divided into two parts:

(a) the fundamental elements which are contained in the Constitution.

(b) the secondary elements *i.e.* the details of the State structure. But it is difficult to draw a neat line to demarcate these two parts. It is also difficult to draw a line between Constitution law and the other branches of the legal system. In this Chapter, we will study about matters like legal validity of the Constitution, contents of Constitutional Law etc.

I. Features of Constitutional Law

1. Fundamental Principles and Other Rules

Constitutional law consists of a body of rules which determine the constitution of the State. The more important, fundamental and far-reaching principle is, it is likely to be classified as Constitutional law. The other laws have to be in conformity with these principles. The more detailed, and more specific rules will be covered under the 'other rules'.

2. *Contents of Constitutional Law*

Constitutional law would include:

- the structure of the legislature, its constitution, its powers, functions,
- structure and operations of subordinate legislatures as possessed by colonies (this was applicable when Britain had colonies subject to its jurisdiction),
- whether the country should have a federal structure or a unitary structure,
- structure of the executive, its functions and powers and its area of operation,

- the division of executive and legislative powers between the Union and the States in case of Federal States,
- a Charter of rights called the Fundamental Rights. These are of special importance in every country. So much so that under Article 13 of the Indian Constitution, a law which takes away or abridges the Fundamental right is void to that extent,
- structure of the higher judiciary treated in outline and not in detail, structure of the other courts of inferior jurisdiction like the Magistrate Courts, Civil Courts and the detailed rules of practice of the Supreme court and the High Court would fall under the second part.

3. Written Constitution and Unwritten Constitution

The distinction between Constitutional law and the remaining portion of the legal system is made definite in some countries by incorporating the above contents in a written Constitution as in India. The terms of the written Constitution cannot be amended by the ordinary forms of legislation. Such Constitutions are said to be rigid. They may also be partly rigid and partly flexible as in India. For example, the Constitution of United States of America is contained in a document agreed upon by the founders of the Commonwealth. The provisions cannot be altered without the consent of three fourth of the legislatures of the different States. England does not have a written Constitution. It is, therefore, flexible. It can be altered like any other law under their legal system.

4. Written Constitution in India

In India we have a written Constitution. Article 368 lays down the powers and the procedure for amending the Constitution. The Bill has to be passed in each House (LS and the RS) by a majority of the total membership of that House and by a majority of not less than two thirds of the members of that House present and voting. Ordinary legislations can be amended by a simple majority. If amendment is in respect of the election of the President, manner of his election, extent of executive power of the Union or the State, representation of States in the Parliament or the Lists of subject-matter in respect of which the State and the Union can make laws (Seventh Schedule) or in respect of amending the provisions themselves, it requires ratification by the Legislatures of not less than half the number of States.

5. Legal Validity for the Constitution

An intricate and an interesting jurisprudential question that arises is: if Constitutional law is defined as a body of legal rules which determine the Constitution of the State – from where does the Constitution itself derive its legal validity? The Constitutional law includes the basic rules of recognition of the State's legal system (*i.e.* the rules conferring power on the different organs of the State.) so how can that very legal system give validity to the Constitution. [It would be like saying that "the *thing created by the creator* is giving validity to the *creator itself*"] hence Constitution cannot derive its validity from the legal system. Does it then mean that the State and Constitution are prior to the law and that what we call as Constitutional law is a matter of fact and practice?

After a long freedom struggle, India got independence. The Cabinet Mission plan led by Lord Pethick Lawrence presented a scheme laying down principles and procedures for framing a Constitution for India. It also devised a detailed scheme for election and working of the Constituent Assembly. Elections to the Constituent Assembly took place in July, 1946. An interim Government of 14 members was formed.

The first session of the Constituent Assembly began on December 6th 1946. The Muslim League members did not attend. It demanded 2 separate Constituent Assemblies – one for Pakistan and one for Hindustan and declared that it would never participate in any single Constitution making body.

Indian Independence Act, 1947 enabled the representatives of India and Pakistan to draft their own Constitutions and to provide for the difficult period of transition.

Two independent Dominions were set up in India known as India and Pakistan headed by the Governor General for each Dominion appointed by the King.

Powers of the Legislature of the Dominions were to be exercised by the Constituent Assembly. The Constituent Assembly was to be supreme. British Acts passed after 15th August, 1947 were not to be applicable to them.

The Assembly took 2 years 11 months and seventeen days to finish the task of framing our Constitution *i.e.,* from 9th Dec 1946 to 26th Nov 1949. Until the new Constitution was framed, the Government of India Act 1935 passed by the British was to remain the constitutional law of India. Our Constitution was adopted on 26th November 1949. Thus note two points: one, that the authority to frame the Constitution was given under a law enacted by the British and a scheme framed by them; and secondly, for 2 years, 3 months and 10 days after we got our independence it was the Indian Independence Act 1935 enacted by the British which was in force. Hence, it is critically commented that the irony of the situation is that our Constitution has received its normative legal validity from a legislation passed by the British. It is submitted that, all said and done some arrangement had to be made for the transition period. The Indian Independence Act was by and large agreed to by our leaders who were in the forefront of the Independence movement. And there is a limit beyond which one cannot go on searching for legal validity. Moreover the Preamble and the scheme of the Constitution makes the people supreme who are ultimate in giving legal validity to the Constitution. It is humbly submitted that the criticism is too technical and devoid of practical significance – atleast as of this date.

a. There are 3 ways of answering the question raised:

(i) *Pre-existing law*: In certain cases Constitution is determined by *pre-existing law*. For example, when independence is granted to a colony from the mother country under its own legal system it is the legal system of the mother country which gives legal validity to the newly independent State.

(ii) *Extra-legal origin*: Apart from the above mentioned case, every Constitution has an *extra-legal origin* which depends upon actual facts and usages. For example, the thirteen American colonies revolted against British in defiance of the British laws and succeeded in obtaining *de facto* establishment in the colonies they were recognized as legally valid from the courts of those colonies. Yet they were in fact based on an illegal foundation. So from where does such a Constitution derive its validity?

(iii) *Obligatory nature of Constitutional rules*: We have seen earlier (under law as a system of rules) that existence of a rule depends upon the external observance and an internal respect for the obligatory nature of such usage. This is also applicable to the rules of the Constitution. But the rules of the Constitution themselves being basic rules it cannot derive its validity from some other basic rule. Hence the basic rule of the Constitution is said to be customary in nature. Even in written Constitutions there must be a customary rule that written Constitutions have authority or else a pre-existing rule that the method by which it was framed was valid. The distinguishing feature between this customary rule and other customary rules is that this customary rule cannot be altered or abrogated by Statute or judicial decisions. For if they do so they would be abrogating the authority of that from which they themselves draw their respective powers.

Thus, customary rules also are of two kinds:

(a) those giving validity to the constitutional rules.These rules cannot be amended

(b) other customary rules: these can be altered by legislation – say if they are opposed to public policy or if they are unreasonable, etc.

6. Constitutional Doctrines may not be in Fact True

Another important factor about all Constitution is that all Constitutional doctrines may not be in fact true. They may exist *de jure* but not *de facto* or they may exist *de facto* but not *de jure*. For example, in India, President is the Executive head of the State; all executive actions are in his name; he has to give assent to the Bill; but in fact administration is carried on by the Ministry and his assent to the Bill is only a formality. I submit that in view of the Globalization policies under which the whole economy is thrown open globally, it would not be any exaggeration to say that though the Indian Constitution claims to be socialist, it has in fact grown to be capitalist; though concentration of wealth is to be avoided under the directive principles of State policy. This is exactly what is happening in practice; health of the workers, children, citizens is to be the prime concern of the Indian Government, the policies under which items like gutka, cola and cigarettes are allowed to be manufactured and sold; the policies under which Big Bazaars and Metros are allowed to wash out the small time village side vendors etc. all speak of the factor that Constitutional doctrines may not be in fact true.

However, there is an attempt to bring Constitution in law and Constitution in practice in tune with each other. Note that, in a competition between practice and law, practice was prior to law, but now it may be that practice may continue to run ahead of law. This creates a discordant between Constitution in law and Constitution in fact. Yet Constitution *de jure* and Constitution *de facto* tend towards coincidence. There is an effort to bridge the gap between the two.

In most countries, a statement of the strict legal theory may differ from the statement of the actual facts. A complete account of a Constitution therefore involves a statement of Constitution custom as well as of Constitution law. It involves an account of the organised state as it exists in practice and in fact, as well as of the reflected image of this organisation as it appears in legal theory.

The objective facts tend to mould legal theory to bring it into conformity with itself. This conformity may be brought about through legislation or through creative functions of the courts.[1]

Conversely, the accepted legal theory endeavours to realise itself in the facts The law may thus react upon and influence the Constitution from which it springs, it cannot create a Constitution *ex nihilo,* but it may modify to any extent one which already exists. Constitutional practice may alter, while Constitutional law remains the same and vice versa, but the most familiar and effective way of altering the practice is to alter the law. The will of the body politic as expressed through the legislature and the courts will commonly realise itself in Constitutional fact no less than in Constitutional theory.

---

1. Though in theory courts only interpret the laws – in reality – they do 'make' or 'create' laws in a limited framework of rendering judgment.

CHAPTER 11

THE ADMINISTRATION OF JUSTICE

SYNOPSIS

INTRODUCTION

The whole State system is directed towards administration of justice. In each civilisation the whole set up- be it the civil or the criminal administration of justice would be to suit the understanding of justice in that time frame. The concept of justice has changed during a passage of time and consequently the mode and manner of administration of justice also has undergone a sea-change. In this Chapter we will analyse the concepts involved in the administration of justice and the theories in connection therewith.

I. Necessity of Administration of Justice

1. Government Control Necessary for Orderly Society

Human beings have conflicting interests resulting in clash of interests. In an unorganized society these conflicting interests are resolved by the concept of 'might is right'. "A herd of wolves is quieter and more at one than so many men, unless they all had one reason in them or have one power over them."[1] All men bestowed with one reason is next to impossibility and hence it is one power that would bring order in the society. Without power, civilization is unattainable, injustice is unchecked and triumphant and the life of man is 'solitary poor, nasty, brutish and short'. Howsoever the society may seem orderly and the men may be seen to obey the laws of reason the element of force is present in the society. If force or power is not exercised at all because men are orderly it does not mean that Government control has disappeared but it means the final triumph and supremacy of Government control.

2. System of Law Based on Public Opinion and Coercive Measures

In an organized society legal rules provide for distribution of rights and maintenance of law and order. Maintenance of law and order has an inherent element of force in it. Force is suggested as a temporary measure in the development of a perfect civilization; that in orderly societies it is sufficient to state the rights and the duties of the citizens. It is argued that it is for this reason that there are a large number of suits for declaration of the rights of the parties or for declaration of the law on a particular point.[2] But here again such a Declaration Suit serves its purpose because there is a system of law enforcement which has a significant place in the legal system. The system of law is based partly on the valuable support it derives from public opinion and partly on the coercive measures of enforcement. Public opinion cannot be a substitute for legal sanctions. Public opinion alone without sanctions will lead to group interests and coercion alone without any favourable public acceptance of the coercive measures would place the law on an unstable ground. Hence, social sanction along with institutionalized law enforcement is necessary for an orderly society. Or else people would take law into their hands and criminal justice would be attained by private vengeance and civil justice would be attained by violent self help.

---

1. Jeremy Taylor, Works, XIII, 306, Heber's Ed. quoted in Fitzgerald, P.J., Salmond on Jurisprudence, 12th Edn., p. 88.
2. Declaratory suits are suits filed only for the declaration of one's right. The plaintiff does not claim any relief against the defendant. For example, suit for declaration that he is plaintiff is an adopted son or that he is the owner of a particular property.

As Locke says in his *Treatise on Government* – in the State of nature, law of nature alone is in force, and every man is charged with the execution of it in his own case. But in a Civil State, the law of nature is supplemented by the civil law. Here civil law is maintained by the force of organised community. This makes maintenance of law of nature by the forces of private men unnecessary and also not permissible. Evils of State of nature were quite obvious – 'might' was the yardstick to measure 'right'; and every man was constituted a judge in his own cause. Administration of justice developed slowly over a passage of time. In the earlier stages arbitration & mediation were offered to the parties and the parties had the option of accepting or rejecting the offer. It was only with the growth of Government's power that the State attempted to suppress the ancient barbarous system by force through settlement by courts of law.

II. Civil and Criminal Justice

1. Wrongs of two Kinds: Civil and Criminal

Blackstone classifies wrongs into 2 kinds: Civil and Criminal wrongs. Civil wrongs are private wrongs and Criminal wrongs are public wrongs. Civil wrongs are infringement of private rights and Criminal wrongs are violations of public rights and duties which affect the whole community. A crime is harmful to the whole community though the immeaiate victim is the individual. A civil wrong is therefore deemed to infringe the rights of the individual and not harm the society in general.

2. Differences between Civil and Criminal Wrong

Civil wrong	Criminal wrong
It is a private wrong.	It is a public wrong.
Action is initiated by the individual aggrieved. For example, all rights under Contract Act are *rights in personam* and only the aggrieved can proceed against the person who has committed the breach of contract.	State initiates the action because public is aggrieved and State is the injured party.
Actions are initiated in Civil courts.	Actions are initiated in Criminal Courts like that of Magistrate Courts or Sessions Court.
Appellate courts are the same.	Appellate courts are the same.
Nature of proof: probability of evidence is sufficient.	Guilt to be proved beyond all reasonable doubt.
If successful – it results in a judgment for payment of debt, or for an injunction, possession, restitution, custody of child etc.	Judgment results in acquittal or conviction; successful criminal prosecution results in punishment in the form of imprisonment for the term prescribed or death penalty or fine or release on probation.

3. Differences between Civil and Criminal Wrong are not Rigid

These differences are not rigid. For example:

a. *Wrongs resulting in civil and criminal remedies:* There are offences which result both in penal and civil remedies. *E.g.* trespass and defamation are both criminal wrongs and also a tort. Non-payment of maintenance amount under Section 125, Cr. P.C. entails imprisonment of the husband.

Likewise, under Section 12(3) of the Contempt of Courts Act where a person is found guilty of a civil contempt, the Court if it considers that a fine will not meet the ends of justice and that sentence of imprisonment is necessary- shall instead of sentencing him to simple imprisonment direct that he be detained in a civil prison for a term not exceeding 6 months.

b. *Civil proceedings resulting in exemplary or punitive damages:* Civil proceedings may result in exemplary or punitive damages. For example, under the Indian Contract Act even if no damage/loss has actually resulted due to violation of the contract yet exemplary damages are awarded in recognition of the right that has been infringed.

c. *Portion of fine paid to aggrieved:* A portion of the fine imposed in criminal proceedings if realized may be directed to be paid to the aggrieved party. For example, under Section 5 of the Probation of Offenders Act, 1958[1] the court may direct the offender to pay compensation for loss or injury caused to any person by the commission of his offence.

d. *Some civil wrongs more harmful than criminal wrongs:* Some civil wrongs can cause greater general harm than some criminal offences. For example, Gas leak in Bhopal Gas Tragedy due to negligence in proper maintaining of the pipelines etc proved more harmful than – say – a theft. Likewise negligence of a contractor in using substandard material for constructing a bridge leading to collapse of bridge causes a greater general harm. Of course, in both the cases the situation will give rise to both civil and criminal remedies.

III. The Purpose of Criminal Justice: Punishment

Punishment can be considered in two different aspects:

1. *Institutionalized Imposition for Some Definite End*

Institutionalized imposition of penalty must be distinguished from individualized imposition of penalty. For example, parents punishing a child at home is individualized imposition of punishment. In institutionalized imposition there is a meticulous machinery and a meticulous procedure that is set up to deal with wrongs and crime.

Punishment as a means to an end: Punishment as a means to an end can serve to:

- Deter potential offenders known as the *Deterrent theory*
- To prevent the actual offender from committing further offences- known as the *Preventive theory*
- Reform the offender and turn him into a law abiding citizen-known as the *Reformative theory*

2. *Punishment as an End Itself*

In this sense punishment is only a retribution to the wrong doer. It serves no purpose. This is the *Retribution theory.*

---

1. It is an Act which makes special provisions for dealing with persons committing the offence for the first time.

IV. Four Different Theories of Punishment: Deterrent; Preventive; Reformative; Expiation

1. Deterrent Theory Works in 2 Ways

a. *From the angle of the actual offender*: The theory is based on the principle that "punishment makes every offence an ill bargain"[1] for the offender. Offence results because of the conflict of the personal interests (whether real or supposed) of the wrong doer and the society. He gives precedence to his own interest while committing the crime. When the deeds injurious to the society are made punishable conflict of interest disappears. Here the wrongdoer's interest in committing theft is met by punishment of imprisonment of say 3 years. True, he has interest in committing crime; but he has an equal interest in keeping himself out of the prison where he loses his freedom and has to undergo harsh treatment. With undergoing the punishment the apparent clash between his own interest and the society's interest disappears.

b. *From the angle of the potential offender*: it acts as a deterrent.

2. Preventive Theory

The object of punishment is to prevent repetition of the crime by making the offender incapable of again committing the offence. Death is an extreme form of disablement where repetition of crime is impossible. Imprisonment disables him temporarily and is therefore preventive.

Deterrence acts on the motives of the offender. Disablement consists primarily in physical restraint.

3. Reformative Theory

Reformation brings about a change in the character of the actual offender who is before the court. This theory believes that there is divinity in every human being; that nobody is a born criminal and that with proper approach he can be reformed. The emphasis under this theory is more on the person committing the crime than on the crime. It concentrates on educating and disciplining the criminal. Prison is used as a training ground rather than as a place of punishment. Probation, parole, and suspended sentences, transcendental meditation etc. are reformative measures and serve as examples of this theory. Death penalty has no place under this theory. Even other forms of corporal punishment are rejected as brutal and degrading to those who suffer and also to those who inflict them.

a. *Conflicting approaches*: The purely reformative theory admits only punishments which are educative in nature. It rejects those which are deterrent and disabling. The deterrent theory rejects all those penal measures which are not sufficient to dissuade offenders from committing further offences. They do not believe that prisons must be converted into comfortable dwelling houses or hospitals where education and training is imparted. There are some criminals who are incorrigible *i.e.* beyond correction, yet they cannot be allowed to go without any punishments and punitive treatment. Protection of society demands that the offender be punished in order to restrain him from further committing crime. Reformative measures may lead the offender to take the legal system lightly and instead of deterring the potential offender it may embolden him to commit further crimes under a thinking that if caught he would be given a comfortable treatment of education and training.

A balance has to be struck between the deterrent and the reformative theory. The stress on reformative theory was because in the earlier days punishment was

---

1. Locke.

unreasonably harsh and inhuman[1] and the reformative measures were just not thought of. Reformative theory therefore was the result of a reaction to the deterrent theory. Certain factors were not at all realized and addressed like the fact that criminals are not normal and healthy human beings; that crime is the result of physical and mental abnormality. Too much attention was paid to the crime and too less to the criminal. However it is equally true that the criminal justice system needs a tougher base to handle crime than the reformative measure. The criminal system has to be coercive in nature so that it becomes successful in restraining normal human beings from the dangerous path of crime. If reformative theory is applied to murder and all murderers were subject to the sphere of medicine rather than that of penal jurisprudence on the ground that they are insane the fallacy of the argument is obvious. Law is necessarily a rough and a ready instrument and men must be content in general to be judged and dealt with by it on the basis of their common humanity and not on that of their special idiosyncrasies.

A balance has to be struck when the cases call for diminishing responsibility as in the case of extreme youth, mentally unbalanced nature, partial imbalance of judgment due to external or internal factors etc. Reformative measures can be used with profit to the society and the individual concerned.

4. Retributive Theory

The theory regards punishment as an end in itself and is too primitive. It is based on the idea of settling abstract justice. For example, to compel the wrong doer to pay compensation is a means to alleviate the suffering of the victim. But if it is only to settle or balance the account of abstract justice between the wrongdoer and the person wronged it would not fit into the civilized legal system.

Society's sense of retribution has its own limited purpose because a society which neither feels angry or hurt at the outrageous conduct would hardly result in an effective legal system. But at the same time, decisions pertaining to crime must be taken not on sentimental and emotional basis but on objective analysis of the situation as a whole. Decisions taken at the heat of the moment or only with a sentimental outlook are likely to result in erroneous judgment and that may result in an error on the other side.

5. Expiation Theory

Under this theory guilt is cancelled by suffering the penalty awarded. To suffer punishment is to pay a debt due to the law that has been violated. Once that is done justice is redeemed. 'Guilt plus punishment is equal to innocence.' The criticism against this theory is that if we are to compel the wrong doer to make actual compensation it sounds reasonable. But to compel him to make restitution in the abstract (*i.e.* repaying the debt due to law) to no actual person is morally incorrect.

However the advantage of this theory is that it acts as an important limiting principle in the penal context. The theory can be looked at from a different angled to assert that:

1. Punishment only to counter the offence is not acceptable but the converse is a valuable point. Punishment must not be inflicted unless there is an offence,
2. Punishment must be in proportion to the offence, and
3. Once punishment is undergone the slate must be wiped clean.

---

1. On the racks etc. (Convict made to lie down on the rack with hands & feet tied & the screws tightened up – So as to cause the body to shrink, as a result of which blood starts oozing out from nose, mouth etc.).

6. *Indian View Point on Sentencing Jurisprudence Seen Through Court Observations*

(a) In *Hiralal Malik* v. *State of Bihar,* AIR 1977 SC 2236 (2239) the Supreme Court has reiterated Justice Henry Alfred McCardie's observation that "trying a man is easy, as easy as falling off a log, compared with deciding what to do with him when he has been found guilty. Hence the ultimate goal must be to make an offender a non-offender."

(b) In Md.Giasuddin v. *State of Andhra Pradesh*[1] the Supreme Court speaking through J. Krishna Iyer states that there is divinity in every man which finds recognition in our Constitution for it recognises the dignity of the human being and is aimed at the development of his all-round personality. He believes that the drawback in our criminal process is that they are built on the foundation of impressive opinions and dated values, ignoring empirical studies and deeper researches. We have a new class of crimes arising due to the more stresses and strains in this age than before. This is due to restlessness arising out of frustrated ambitions and expectations. A holistic view of sentencing and a finer perception of the effect of punishment, leads to discarding the traditional concept of sentencing in which punishment was equated with 'physical torture'. Meditational relaxation and psychic medication and like exercises are bound to be more fruitful. Therefore, the emphasis has to be as much on man as on the system, on the inner imbalance as on the outer tensions. He advocates yogic ways of normalising the individual and the group. A balance has to struck. The guilty has to be punished and at the same time mercy as distinguished from an emotional hate be meted out, so as to bring out the divinity in him. The court's approach has to be at once socially informed and personalised. One major deficiency in our criminal trials is that we devote only to finding out whether the man in the dock is guilty. But our approach should be guided by the observation made by the Law Commission of India which has suggested that a proper sentence is a composite of many factors, including the nature of the offence, the circumstances- in which the offender is placed, the age of the offender, the professional and social record of the offender,..." his education, home-life, temper and social adjustment, the emotional and mental condition of the offender, the prospects of his rehabilitation, the possibility of his returning to normal life etc.

(c) In *Ediga Annama* v. *State of Andhra Pradesh,* AIR 1974 SC 799 the Supreme Court has held that modern penology regards crime and criminal as equally material in passing the right sentence, "although in our processual system there is neither comprehensive provision nor adequate machinery for collection and presentation of the social and personal data of the culprit to the extent required in the verdict on sentence. A scientific system of sentencing requires the court to focus not only on the crime but also on the criminal so that the reformative component is as much operative as the deterrent element and so at times facts of a social and personal nature sometimes altogether irrelevant have to be brought to the notice of the court when the actual sentence is determined. Though deterrence through threat of death may still be a promising strategy it cannot be the only strategy and hence what is needed is the composite factors of penal strategy

(d) In *Rajendra Prasad* v. *State of Uttar Pradesh*[2] it was held that under Section 354(3), Cr. P.C. where conviction is for an offence punishable with death, or imprisonment for life, or a term of years, the judgement must state the reasons for the sentence awarded & in the case of the sentence of death 'special reasons' for such sentence. 'Special reasons' under Section 354(3), Cr. P.C. must relate not only to the crime as such but to the criminal & death sentence can be ordered

1. AIR 1977 SC 1926.
2. AIR 1979 SC 916.

only if "public order & social security" demand it. The judge must ask himself- is it reasonably necessary to extinguish the lamp of freedom & consequently the flame of life? & reasonableness depends on a number of variables like "cultural, social, economic & otherwise". Death sentence must be awarded in the rarest of the rare cases.

However note that J. Sen opines in his dissenting opinion in *Rajendra Prasad's case* that the Constitutionality of the death sentence was not before the court in this case. It was upheld as not violating Article 14, 19 and 21 – in *Jagmohan Singh* v. *State of Uttar Pradesh*, AIR 1973 SC 947.

(e) The Supreme Court has expressed serious concern over the increasing number of cases of sexual assault, involving rape and murder of minor girls. Two judges of the apex court, however, differed on the quantum of sentence while upholding the conviction of a person in a rape and murder of a 10-year-old girl, who was a student of class four, in Surat district of Gujarat in 1999. Presiding judge Justice Arijit Pasayat, upheld the death sentence awarded to Ramesh Bhai Chandi Bhai Rathod, a chowkidar, however, the other judge on the bench, Justice Asok Kumar Ganguly said that the case did not fall in the rarest of rare category and therefore commuted the death sentence to life imprisonment. The two judges finally referred the matter to a larger bench on the point of quantum of the sentence. Justice Pasayat, noted, 'If the circumstantial evidence is found to be of unimpeachable character in establishing the guilt of the accused, that forms the foundation of the conviction. It has nothing to do with the question of sentence as has been observed by this court in various cases while awarding death sentence. *The mitigating circumstances and the aggravating circumstances have to be balanced*.' 'In fact in most of the cases where death sentence is awarded for rape and murder and the like there is practically no scope for having an eyewitness as they are not committed in the public view,' he said. 'The case at hand falls in the rarest of rare category as the circumstances highlighted establish the act of the accused and it calls for only one sentence that is death sentence,' he said. Justice Ganguly, however, in his separate judgment while agreeing with Justice Pasayat said that the appellant was guilty of rape and murder of the minor girl, differed on the point of sentence and noted that instead of death sentence, a sentence of rigorous imprisonment will serve the ends of justice. (*Source: http://www.lawyersclubindia.com/news/2009/4/*)

It is thus to be seen that the question of sentencing jurisprudence has remained a mind-boggling area.

V. Civil Justice: Primary and Sanctioning Rights

The right enforced in a civil proceeding is either a primary or a sanctioning right.

1. A sanctioning right is one which arises out of the violation of another right. All others are primary.
    - *E.g.* right to fulfilment of contract is a primary right.
    - Right to damages for non fulfilment – a secondary and a sanctioning right.
    - *E.g.* right to reputation/right not to be defamed is a primary right.
    - Right to damages when defamed is a sanctioning right.

Administration of civil justice is attained at two levels – the first and the primary level is that the courts award the plaintiff that very thing to which he is entitled by contract or otherwise. For example, when *A* agrees to supply 100 tonnes of oil to *B* for a sum of money obviously *B's* primary interest is in getting 100 tonnes of oil and not anything else. This is the primary right. But say *A* does not supply the oil as per the agreement. *B* files a suit. The court may direct *A* to supply the very thing contracted *viz.*, 100 tonnes of oil. This is enforcing the primary right. But if it is just not possible to compel *A* to supply the oil the next alternative is to award compensation. This is enforcement of secondary right called as the sanctional enforcement. But at times it is either not possible or not expedient to enforce the primary right. In such a case the next best alternative is to award damages.

VI. Secondary Functions of the Court of Law

Administration of justice discussed above depicts the narrow sense of the term. It is forcible defense of right and suppression of wrong with the use of physical force by the State. Every case involves two parties – the plaintiff who complains that his right is infringed, a defendant against whom the complaint is made, the advocates arguing for each side, the court listening to the case of each party and then giving its judgment and the State executing the judgment using its power.

In its wider sense administration of justice includes all the functions of the courts of justice whether or not they conform to the above pattern. These are secondary functions of the courts of law. These secondary functions come under the category of 'civil administration of justice'. 'Civil' used in the residuary sense of 'that which is not criminal'. The courts or tribunals primarily established for the purpose of administering justice in its narrow sense are found to be useful for performing other analogous functions which are secondary in nature. They are:

1. Petition of Rights

In England proceedings against the State could be taken only by a petition of right during the earlier days, but now it can be taken by an ordinary action. Though the case is tried in the ordinary manner, the element of coercion is lacking because State being a judge in its own cause cannot exercise constraint against itself. In India, under Section 80 of the Code of Civil Procedure, 1908, 60 days' notice is to be given before a suit can be instituted against the State and a special procedure is provided for the purpose.

2. Declaration of Right

The plaintiff does not complain of the violation of his rights but he seeks assistance of the court for the declaration of his rights because his rights are uncertain. He desires an authoritative decision of his rights. For example, declaration of legitimacy or advice to the trustees regarding their legal power, declaration of nullity of marriage, declaration that plaintiff is the adopted son etc.

3. Administration

Administration of the estate or distribution of property. For example, administration of trust liquidation of the company.

4. Titles to Right

Judicial decrees are used for creating, transferring or extinguishing rights e.g. an adjudication of bankruptcy or letters of administration.

5. Supervision of the Lower Courts

Superior courts are given power to supervise the courts below them. In India Article 227 of the Constitution gives such power to the High Courts.

VII. Indian Position

We have several Tribunals established under various Acts which help in the administration of justice. Following are some of the examples:

1. Right to Information Act, 2005

Access to information in the custody of public authorities is an important gateway to realize one's rights. Even to file a case in the courts one needs authentic information to be placed before the courts. This is now possible under the RTI Act. The Act does not settle disputes but it gives a systematic tool for organizing and preparing for the case to be instituted in the court. If the public information officer gives wrong information or insufficient information or if he wrongly withholds information, Information Commissioners are created under the Act to whom a complaint can be lodged. They have the same powers as of the Civil Courts under the Civil Procedure Code, 1908 [Section 18(3)] and power to impose penalty for not giving information. In this sense they too have been constituted as part of the administration of justice in the wider sense of the term.

2. Consumer Protection Act, 1986

It is designed for better protection of consumer interests; it provides for establishment of Consumer Councils, District Forum and State and National Commission for the settlement of consumer disputes regarding deficiency of services or goods. Strict rules of procedure are not applicable; there are no court fees payable, advocates are not permitted as of right in order to reduce the technical formalities which are involved in ordinary litigations.

3. Industrial Disputes Act

Conciliation and Arbitration is provided under the *Industrial Disputes Act.*

4. Legal Services Authority Act

Provides for settlement of disputes through Lok Adalats.

5. Family courts under Family Courts Act

They are special courts which provide for compulsory conciliation in order the protect the family bonds.

6. Civil Procedure [Alternative Dispute Resolution (Karnataka) Rules], 2005

In order to give effect to the amendments to the Code of Civil Procedure the Karnataka Government has framed the *Civil Procedure [Alternative Dispute Resolution (Karnataka) Rules], 2005.* Alternative dispute resolution mechanism as an alternative method to resolve disputes is becoming popular. Though the concept of reconciliation is not new as such what is new is that the court is bound to formulate terms of settlement after the first hearing if it is of the opinion that there appears to be a possibility of settlement.

It is relevant to note that the amendments to Section 89, Code of Civil Procedure, 1908 making conciliation and mediation compulsory before the trial could commence full fledged, was challenged in *Salem Advocate Bar Association* v. *Union of India,* AIR 2003 SC 89. The Supreme Court held the amendments to be valid and constitutional. C.J. Kirpal observed that Section 89 has been inserted to see that all cases filed in the court need not be necessarily decided by the court itself. Having regards to delays in dispensing justice "it is imperative that resort should be had to alternative dispute resolution mechanism with a view to bring an end to litigation at an early date.

7. Arbitration and Conciliation Act, 1996

The Act has been enacted to cover arbitration, conciliation and mediation at three different levels – international arbitration, domestic arbitration and commercial arbitration. It also provides for a fair arbitral procedure to minimise supervisory roles of the courts in arbitral procedures to permit arbitral Tribunal to use mediation, conciliation or other modes – towards attaining speedy disposal of the dispute in the interest of efficient administration of justice.

Under Section 10 and 10A of the Industrial Disputes Act the appropriate Government may refer an industrial dispute to the Conciliation Board to promote the settlement of the dispute. The employer and the workmen can even voluntarily refer the industrial dispute for arbitration under Section 10A of the Act.

Conciliation officers also can hold conciliation proceedings in the prescribed manner for bringing about a settlement of the industrial dispute between the parties under Section 12 of the Act.

8. Ombudsman

Traditional organs like the Legislature and the Judiciary do not provide an adequate and effective control mechanism over the administration. Hence ombudsman are constituted. Ombudsman is in a very strong position to redress individual grievances arising out of bad administration. Ombudsman has an access to departmental information. Now a common man has access to information under the Right to Information Act. It is an external agency to probe into administrative faults. Citizens' complaints are investigated by experienced staff outside the Department. In India, the Lok Pal Bill introduced in the Parliament lapsed three times. Yet 12 States have enacted Lok Ayukta Laws – Orissa, Maharashtra, Rajasthan, Bihar, UP, MP, AP, HP, Karnataka, Haryana, Chattisgarh, Uttaranchal. There is no uniform pattern. In some States they look into corruption and in some they also look into mal-administration.

Following are some other important Ombudsman in India:

(1) Banking Ombudsman: The Banking Ombudsman Scheme enables an expeditious and inexpensive forum to bank customers for resolution of complaints relating to certain services rendered by banks. The Banking Ombudsman Scheme is introduced under section 35 A of the Banking Regulation Act, 1949 by RBI with effect from 1995.

(2) Insurance Ombudsman: With an objective of providing a forum for resolving disputes and complaints from the aggrieved insured public or their legal heirs against Insurance Companies, the Government of India, in exercise of powers conferred on it u/s 114(1) of Insurance Act, 1938 framed "Redressal of Public Grievances Rules, 1998", which came into force w.e.f. 11th November, 1998. These Rules aim at resolving complaints relating to the settlement of disputes with Insurance Companies on personal lines of insurance, in a cost effective, efficient and impartial manner. These Rules apply to all the Insurance Companies operating in General Insurance business and Life Insurance business, in Public and Private Sector.

To implement the above Rules, the Institution of Insurance Ombudsman has been established and is functioning since 1999.

(3) Tax Ombudsman: It is an independent body initiated by the government and comprises of former Income Tax officials or officials from the Indian Revenue Service. These officers have been empowered to settle grievances and take up matters to the highest authority, with the sole aim of resolving it. They act as an arbitrator and are independent of the jurisdiction of the income-tax department.

(4) Ombudsman For LSGI Kerala:

This is a high powered quasi-judicial body functioning at the State level with its head quarters in the State capital. Possibly no other State in India has such an institution to oversee the functioning of local self government institutions.

Under the present law only a former judge of High Court can be appointed as Ombudsman. He can conduct investigations and enquiries into instances of maladministration, corruption, favouritism, nepotism, lack of integrity, excessive action, inaction, abuse of position, etc. on the part of officials and elected representatives of all Local Bodies (Corporations, Municipalities, and Panchayats of all three levels).He can even register cases *suo moto* if instances of the above kind come to his notice. His sittings can be anywhere in the State and at his discretion.He is not fully bound by the rigid provisions of the Indian Evidence Act and the Procedure Codes. Advocates can appear in the cases before the Ombudsman only if specifically permitted to do so for stated reasons. These provisions make the functioning of the institution very flexible and enables conduct of cases fast and inexpensive.

CHAPTER 12
SOURCES OF LAW: LEGAL AND HISTORICAL SOURCES

SYNOPSIS

Introduction

- **I. Differences between Legal and Historical Sources of Law**
- **II. Dilemmas Involved in the Distinction**
- **III. Legal Sources of English Law**
  1. **Legislation**
  2. **Case Law or Judicial Precedent**
  3. **Custom**
  4. **Conventions**

INTRODUCTION

The term 'source of law' is used in different senses. The general meaning of the word 'source' is origin. The sources of law supply the tools, method and technique available to the institution of law in order to carry out its social goals adequately and effectively.

The term 'source of law' has not acquired a uniform signification in Anglo-American jurisprudence. John Chipman Gray drew a sharp difference between 'law' and 'sources of law'. For him, law consisted of the rules authoritatively laid down by the courts in their decisions and he identified the sources of law in certain legal and non-legal materials relied upon by the judges in shaping rules which make up the laws, namely 1) Acts of legislative organs; 2) Precedents; 3) Customs; 5) Principles of morality.According to Salmond, sources of law can be classified into two categories – legal and historical sources. Hence we will study the sources of law as viewed by Salmond.

I. Differences between Legal and Historical Sources of Law

Legal sources	*Historical sources*
1. They are recognized as such by law.	They lack formal recognition.
2. Court decision may be the immediate source of law.	Courts may have based its decision on the writing of a juristic writer say, Mulla's book on Hindu Law; who in turn may have relied upon Kane's Dharmashastra; who in turn may have relied upon Vedic Scriptures. These successive material sources are not recognized by law. Only the court decision *i.e.* (precedent) is recognized. All others are historical sources.

Legal sources	Historical sources
3. Precedent is the source of law 'in law' and also 'in fact.'	They are source of law 'in fact' but not 'in law'.
4. The principle that the 'principle' contained in the precedent has a binding force of law is itself a law[1].	To say that much of the law of Rome has become incorporated into the law of England is just a statement of fact which has no relevance in law.
5. Legal sources are authoritative sources. The courts are bound to accept them.	Historical sources are unauthoritative *i.e.* the courts are not bound to accept them. For example, all the books on jurisprudence by eminent jurists are only historical sources and the court may or may not accept them. If the courts or the legislature accepts it then it becomes a legal source.
6. Courts allow them as of right.	They are not allowed as of right. They influence the course of legal development but they are not authoritative.
7. Decisions of English courts are authoritative in England. Decisions of the Indian courts are binding in India only. Under Article 143 law declared by the Supreme Court of India is binding on all the subordinate courts in India.	Decisions of English courts are not authoritative in India. They are only of persuasive value and hence historical source.
8. They are the only gates through which new principles find entrance into law.	They operate mediately and indirectly *i.e.* if they are to become legal sources it is only through the medium of the legislature or the judgments.
9. Statutes enacted by the Legislature and the immemorial customs are legal sources. Customs are recognized when they satisfy the tests laid down by the legal system (as in India it has to be antique in origin, reasonable, should not be immoral or against the law of the land; not be opposed to public policy etc.).	Customs are historical sources until they are recognized by the legal system as legal source.

Literary source: In addition to historical and legal sources literary source may also be a source of law. This is specially a continental use of the term. They are the original or authoritative sources of our knowledge as distinguished from later commentaries. For example, Vedas are authoritative sources of our knowledge. They are supposed to be divine pronouncements. But Manusmriti is a commentary.

1. Article 143 of our Constitution.

II. Dilemmas Involved in the Distinction

It is to be noted that the distinction between legal and historical sources is not crystal clear. Following are the *dilemmas involved in the distinction*:

1. The decisions of the Privy Council are not binding on any English Court because they used to sit as Appellate courts for the Colonies only. They are only of high persuasive value. In India too they are only of persuasive value.
2. No decision of the High Court is binding on other High Court judges; or on the Court of Appeal or on the House of Lords. Does this mean that they are binding only on the lower courts and not on the higher courts. Hence the situation can be generalized by observing that—
   - there are some rules which are binding,
   - some which are binding only under certain circumstances,
   - and some which are not binding at all but are only persuasive.
3. *Which is the ultimate source of law*: In every legal system all rules have historical sources. They have their origin somewhere though we may not be able to pin point the same. All rules must obtain recognition from some source of law. But the ultimate source of obtaining recognition will depend upon a *grund* norm which is the ultimate principle beyond which it is not possible to reach. These norms must be accepted as self existent. For example, a municipal bye-law lays down that no one shall ride the bicycle in the garden. From where does this rule derive its recognition? From where does this rule making power get its recognition? From a Statute passed by the Legislature? From where does the Legislature get its power? From the Constitution as in India or an Act of the Parliament as in England? We can go only so far in search of the rule of recognition. Doctrine of Parliamentary supremacy in England or Constitutional Supremacy in India does not receive validity from some other source. It is so because of the acceptance of the view that the Constitution or the Act of Parliament is binding and ought to be observed by the society.

As far as India is concerned we can say that the Constitution derives its authority from the People because it is WE THE PEOPLE who have given the Constitution unto ourselves. But even this search for authority cannot go endless. Hence it is appropriate to conclude that in India it is the written Constitution that we have given to ourselves which is supreme *i.e.* the *grund norm*.

III. Legal Sources of English Law

Different systems of law possess different legal sources. Legal sources may be:

1. *Legislation:* Supreme and Subordinate. The Government of the day – the Body Politic makes new rules and laws by consciously deciding to make laws on a particular subject and debating over the matter and following the prescribed procedure for making laws.
2. *Case Law or Judicial Precedent*: The court makes law by evolving new rules while deciding cases. It does not decide to make the law but out of necessity it has to make law to discharge its duty in the

administration of justice and in order to give its decision on the case on hand.

3. *Custom:* Which fulfils the requirements laid down by law for their recognition become law of the land. Under Article 13 of the Constitution of India law includes customs and usages having the force of law.
4. *Convention*: Agreement may be the source of Conventional law. Treaties between Nations fall under this head.

In India Vedas, Shrutis, Smritis and other commentaries can be said to be the literary source of Hindu law.

In conclusion, classified by reference to their legal sources there are 4 kinds of law:

- Enacted law-having its source in legislation.
- Case law (Judgment) having its source in precedent.
- Customary law having its source in custom.
- Conventional law – having its source in agreement.

CHAPTER 13
SOURCES OF LAW: LEGISLATION

SYNOPSIS

9. *Ejusdem Generis*
10. **Exceptions Where *Litera Legis* (Letter of the Law) is not Applicable**
    a. **Where Law is Logically Defective**
        (i) **Semantic Ambiguity (Open Texture Word)**
        (ii) **Syntactic Ambiguity**
        (iii) **Repugnancy in the Intention Itself**
    b. **Literal Interpretation Leads to Absurdities**
    c. **Mischief Rule**

IX. Indian Judiciary Departs from the Traditional British Practice

INTRODUCTION

We have seen in the previous chapter that there are different legal sources of law, namely- Legislation, Precedent, Custom, Conventional law. In this chapter let us deal with Legislation as an important source of law.

I. Nature of Legislation: Wide and Narrow Sense

Legislation may be used in two senses – in its wide sense and in its strict sense. In its wide sense, it includes all methods of law-making, in its strict sense it means laying down legal rules by the sovereign or subordinate legislator.

While studying Legislation as a source of law we are concerned with Legislation in its strict sense of the term *i.e.* as laying down legal principles by the sovereign.

1. *In the Wide sense of Legislation*

In its wide sense it includes:

a. *Additions or alterations in law:* All acts which have the effect of adding to or altering the law.
b. *New principle through court:* When judges lay down a new principle through their judgment they can be said to exercise legislative and not just judicial power. E.g. *Keshvanand Bharati* v. *State of Kerala,*[1] laid down the doctrine of basic structure of the Constitution for the first time; the whole concept of Public Interest Litigation, the principle of sustainable development in *Vellore Citizen's Forum* v. *Union of India.*[2]
c. *Every expression of will of the legislature*: Legislation includes every expression of will of the legislature whether directed to making of rules or not. As for example, Acts ratifying a treaty, altering the coinage, declaring war etc. They come within the meaning of legislation in the broad sense of the term.

2. *In the Strict Sense of Legislation*

It is understood as a source of law. In this sense the following are the points to be noted:

a. *Legal rules laid down by legislator:* Legislation is laying down of legal rules by a sovereign or subordinate legislator either through enactments or subordinate legislation.

---

1. AIR 1973 SC 1461.
2. AIR 1996 SC 2715. In the International Sphere sustainable development as a concept came to be known for the first time in stockholm Declaration of 1972. The same was applied & recognised in Vellore's case.

b. *Rules for future:* There is a difference between law-making by the legislator and by the courts. Legislators lay down rules for the future and without any reference to disputes. The courts lay down legal rules only while applying the law to the disputes before them. Legislative law making is central to the function of the legislator. Judicial law making is only incidental to the function of the courts. Its main function is to resolve disputes.

c. *Enacted law:* Laws which have their source in legislation may be described as enacted law and the rest as unenacted. Or it may be described as Statute law and the rest as common law. The term Statute is limited to only the Act of the Parliament or the State Legislature. It would not include delegated legislation. Blackstone uses the term written and unwritten law to draw the distinction. These terms are derived from Romans. By *jus non scriptum* they meant customary law. The rest whether enacted or unenacted was *jus scriptum.*

According to Blackstone – English law has its origin either in legislation or in custom. Common law was customary and therefore unwritten. All the rest was enacted and therefore written law.

In India—We have a written Constitution. All laws whether enacted by the Parliament or the State Legislature or the unwritten laws or the customary laws have to be in conformity with the Constitution or else the Courts have the constitutional power to declare them void.

Article 366(10) of the Constitution defines 'existing law' as 'any law' Ordinance, order, bye-law, rule, or regulation passed or made before the commencement of this Constitution by any legislature, authority or person having power to make such a law, ordinance, order, bye-law, rule or regulation. Under Article 372 all laws in force in the territory of India immediately before the commencement of the Constitution continue in force until altered or repealed or amended by a competent legislature or other competent authority. Such existing laws can be adapted and modified to bring them in conformity with the provisions of the Constitution.

II. Legislation may be Either Supreme or Subordinate Supreme Legislation

1. No Control by Other legislative Authority

Legislation is either supreme or subordinate. Supreme Legislation proceeds from supreme or sovereign power of the State. It cannot be annulled or repealed or controlled by any other legislative authority. Subordinate Legislation proceeds from an authority other than the supreme power and depends for its continued validity on some superior authority.

2. Absolute Obedience is not the Test of Sovereignty

According to Austin the sovereign is a body which enjoys general obedience; owes obedience to none; and is an unlimited sovereign. He misses the point that sovereignty is a question of law than of fact. It means that sovereign is a body whose decrees qualify as law within the legal system even if the laws are disobeyed. It is not so much a body which enjoys obedience in fact as it is a body whose decrees qualify as laws within the system. In other words its declarations enjoy the status of law within the legal system, though as facts reveal-laws are disobeyed for whatever reason. Existence of sovereign necessitates existence of the rules of law which define:

- The identity and composition of the sovereign .
- Procedure for legislation.
- The areas on which the sovereign is competent to legislate.

These are not limitations on the States' sovereignty. These provisions occur in written Constitutions as in India. In India the Constitution lays down how the Lok Sabha and the Rajya Sabha are constituted at the Centre; how the Legislative Assembly and the Legislative Council are constituted at the State; the election and nomination formalities; how a Bill for making a law is to be moved; on what areas the Centre and the State can make laws; these are not limitations but it is only natural and logical that a written Constitution should contain all these details.

III. Doctrine of Parliamentary Supremacy: Legally Omnipotent

In England the doctrine of Parliamentary Supremacy implies that the Parliament is not only supreme but also *legally omnipotent*. It means that the Parliament is all-powerful; it has no legal limits upon its power. An Act of the Parliament cannot be held void for unreasonableness as in India. The doctrine of parliamentary supremacy was propounded by Dicey.

The sovereignty of Parliament means that Parliament is legislatively supreme. It can make and unmake laws. There is no body which can declare its legal enactments to be of no effect. The only limit on the legislative power of the Parliament is that it cannot bind its successors in power. However controversial a statute may be the judge is bound to follow it. This statement is now qualified since Briton's entry into E.E.C. The E.E.C rules take precedence in the event of conflict with statute or common law.[1]

This doctrine raises certain questions:

- If the Parliament is all powerful, can it by a law limit the powers of the succeeding Parliaments? If this can be done, then the powers of the later Parliaments would be less than that of the earlier.
- Take the example of the Statute of Westminster 1931. It enacted that no Act of the United Kingdom Parliament should apply to the Dominion without the consent of the Dominion. The question is, is the Statute binding on the present Parliament or is it free to disregard it? What will happen if the present Parliament passes a law contrary to the Statute of Westminster? There would then arise a conflict between theory of Parliamentary supremacy and actual fact.

A good theory is one which fits into the facts. The question that could be asked is: why should it be impossible for the Parliament to bind itself? Arguments to assert that it is impossible for the Parliament to bind itself is based partly on logic and partly on law. The difficulties are similar to those which arise in the idea of the House of Lords being bound by its own decision. In both the situations, it is a vicious circle. In *London Street Tramways Co.* v. *L.C.C.*,[2] the House of Lords held that it is bound by its own decisions. But the proposition is binding in the House only if there is a rule of law that the House of Lords is bound by its own decision. Same is the case with the Parliament. Parliament can bind itself only if there is a rule to that effect.

1. Padfield: Law made simple, p. 60.
2. (1898) AC 375.

The basic rule is that what Parliament enacts is law. The question is whether the Parliament can by law modify or alter this law. Can the Parliament dispense with all the sub rules which lay down the procedures for passing a statute? Hart points out that Parliament can commit a legal suicide by dissolving itself and enacting that it should never be recalled (1st case); it could also transfer all its powers to another body (2nd case). The rule that what Parliament enacts is law still remains. But in the first case, the Parliament will *not need to act* and in the second parliament *is not there to act*. Where power is transferred to another body that body has the authority to make laws but this will not extinguish Parliament's own power to make laws.

In India the Constitution is supreme. Parliament can never be said to be omnipotent. Of course questions have arisen from 1951 onwards as to whether Parliament has unlimited powers to amend the Constitution in several cases[1]. It is now recognized that the powers to amend are subject to the rule that the basic structure of the Constitution cannot be amended.[2] What the basic structure is being decided as and when the cases are coming up before the court.

IV. Subordinate Legislation

Because Parliament is legislatively supreme it can grant powers to make rules or orders to some other person or body. Rules etc made by such other body is known as subordinate legislation. Though in theory Parliament must enact all laws of the land, in practice it neither has the time nor the expertise to do so. Hence the growth of subordinate legislation "for every 400 words of law that the American Congress has enacted, there are 500,000 words of implementing regulations."[3]

Subordinate Legislation means enactments by legislative bodies inferior to the sovereign. Such legislation may be subordinate in the sense that:

- It can be repealed by the sovereign.
- In case of conflict between the sovereign legislation and the subordinate legislation – the former prevails.
- Power to legislate is of the derivative nature. That is the power is derived from some higher body.

Under this power either rules may be framed or directions may be issued. Directions issued by the executive are known as administrative quasi–legislation and rules framed by the Government under the delegated legislative powers are known as administrative legislation. In India, directions derive their authority under Article 73 of the Constitution – at the Central level and Article 162 at the State level. Rules have a statutory authority. Hence rules are on a higher level

1. *Shankari Prasad* v. *Union of India*, AIR 1951 SC 458 and *Sajjan Singh* v. *State of Rajasthan*, AIR 1965 SC 845 held Parliament has unlimited powers to amend the Fundamental Rights; in *Golaknath* v. *State of Punjab*, AIR 1967 SC 1643 held that the Parliament cannot amend the Constitution so as to take away or abridge the Fundamental Rights.
2. This judgment has been criticized. *Keshvanand Bharati* v. *State of Kerala*, who wins? (1974) SCC JS 29 by Prof. Tripathi says it was only one out of the 13 Judges who spoke of basic structure. Constitutional Quicksands of Keshvanand Bharati and the Twenty Fifth Amendment (1974) 1 SCC JS 45 by Prof. Upendra Baxi. He says it is unforgivably naïve for anyone to claim to have discovered the *ratio decidendi* of the case.
3. Reed Dickerson: American Case Book series, 1981.

than the directions, though power to legislate in both the cases is of a derivative nature. Under Article 73 and 162, executive power of the Union/State is co-extensive with powers of the Parliament/State Legislature to make laws.

In England all forms of legislative activity recognized by law other than the power of the Parliament are subordinate and subject to parliamentary control.

Following are the forms of subordinate legislation:

1. *Colonial:* The powers of the self Government entrusted to the colonies are derived from the Imperial Legislature. For example, India and America as colonies derived its powers from the British. But within its own limited field it is supreme.
2. *Executive*: Legislature being very busy; and not having the time and the expertise needed to frame rules in detail, it delegates the task of framing detailed rules to the executive after laying down the broad policies and the guidelines. It supplements statutory provisions by framing detailed rules. For example, under the Right to Information Act it is the rules which lay down what are the fees to be charged per page of information, per floppy, etc.; under Environmental Protection Act; under Legal Services Authorities Act rules are framed by the Executive.
3. *Judicial:* Judiciary possess delegated legislative powers. Higher courts frame rules to regulate their own procedure and the procedure of the subordinate courts. For example, we have the High Court Rules of Practice; the Supreme Court Rules of Practice in India.
4. *Municipal:* Municipal bodies are delegated powers to frame bye laws to carry out various activities entrusted to them. For example, under the Karnataka Municipal Corporation Act detailed rules were framed to demolish buildings which were illegally constructed.
5. *Autonomous*: Law gives to certain groups of private individuals limited legislative authority touching matters which concern themselves. For example, a University may make statutes binding on its members. This kind of subordinate legislation is called autonomic. The other four are instances of legislation by the State itself.

There is a similarity between autonomic law and conventional law. Conventional law is the result of an agreement and hence binding only on the parties to the agreement. Autonomic law is imposed by a superior authority in invitos and is therefore a true form of legislation.

V. Legislation and Other Sources of Law

The growth of legislation as a source of law can be seen in 3 phases of the development of the legal system.

1. During the Primitive Days

Law was regarded as *'jus'* – The principles of justice. In those days the function of law was considered to be not to make laws but to 'enforce' laws *viz.*, those immemorial customs which were sanctioned by religious faith or practice and sometimes claimed to be of divine origin. For example, in India Vedas are considered to be of divine origin; here the part played by human legislation in the development of legal system was necessarily small and may be even non-existent.

2. *Traces of Political and Legal Development*

The next phase was when only those principles sanctioned by *religion or immemorial usage* which were expressly or tacitly accepted by the Prince or retained by him without any alterations were recognized as law. In other words, it was recognised that it was within the powers and functions of the political rulers to change and subvert even the principles sanctioned by religion or immemorial usage. These beliefs mark a considerable progress along the road of political and legal development.

3. *'Lex' i.e. the 'Will of the State'*

In advanced civilizations statute law has gained such superiority that that all other forms of law are more or less considered to be abnormal variations. Today law is considered as *'lex' i.e. the 'Will of the State'*.

VI. Advantages of Legislation Over Precedent

Precedent is supposed to be the most formidable rival of legislation.

1. *Legislation can undo what it has Ill-done*

Legislation not only makes new laws but also has abrogative powers. *It can undo what it has ill-done.* That is – it can alter/amend/abrogate the existing law. It can make corrections if it has gone wrong at some stage and amend the law. In fact, most of the amendments to an enacted law are an example of either correcting the wrong or an attempt to bring the law in tune with the existing realities or with current expectations or demands of the people.

Legislation is an instrument of legal growth and legal reform. Precedent can provide only constitutive efficacy.[1]

In a strict system of binding precedent its operation is irreversible. Precedent can make a good law, even better than the job done by legislation; it can clarify and explain what has been done by the legislature. But it cannot undo the wrong or the ill it has done unless and until the case comes up in appeal or in review or a similar case comes up where it can overrule its own ruling. But it cannot purposively sit upon the judgment and alter it the way the legislature can do with the law that is doing injustice. For example, during internal emergency in India in 1975 the Supreme Court of India gave its ruling in *Habeas Corpus* case that during emergency when the enforcement of fundamental rights are suspended no *Habeas Corpus* petition can be filed before any High Court whether on the grounds of legal or factual *mala fides*. Though this ruling was criticized and did immense injustice to a large number of detenues, yet nothing could be done to set right the wrong that was done by the ruling as the court becomes *functus officio* after rendering the judgment. Here again it was the Parliament through 44th Constitutional Amendment which tried to set right the wrong done by the 42nd Amendment.

---

1. Constitutive efficiency: Efficiency is directly connected with the nature of the Constitution of the body concerned, the court in the present context. Courts are constituted to solve disputes. Hence, its contribution to legal growth depends upon the nature of dispute which come before it and the issues involved. For example, letters were treated as writ petitions (epistolary jurisdiction of the courts) by the courts only because a letter was written by a particular person to the judge complaining of legal wrongs in Fertilizer Corporation Case.

2. *Division of Labour between the Legislature and the Judiciary*

Legislation ensures increase in efficiency by division of labour between the legislature and the judiciary. Legislature makes the law and the judiciary interprets it.

Precedent unites law-making and law enforcing in the same hands.

3. *Formal Declaration of the Law*

Notification in the Official Gazette satisfies the rule of natural justice that law shall be made known.[1]

Precedents operate retrospectively[2] in the sense that they are created and applied to facts which are prior in date to the law itself. That is the facts first occur; dispute arises in relation to the facts; it is referred to the courts; and it is only then that the courts make law to explain and solve the dispute. The meaning of the statute may be vague and doubtful. In such a case its meaning has to be established by the court and the decision of the court will be later than the date of the operation of the statute. Case laws are created and declared in the very act of applying and enforcing it.

But this distinction of the benefit of formal declaration of law must not be overemphasized. *Firstly* because as an exceptional measure statutes also are made retrospective in operation. But there is no retrospective operation of criminal laws creating criminal offences. *Secondly* modern laws are so complicated and numerous that an ordinary man becomes aware of the existence of the law only after he has violated it. In India, of late, legal awareness lectures and camps mandated by the Bar Council of India, by the legal education curriculum, by the High Court directives; free legal aid and advice under the Legal Services Authorities Act, 1986; and the information disseminated through electronic media like TV and Radio and skits are alleviating the difficulty and helping in making the laws of the land known to the general public in simple language. *Thirdly* though statutes are not retrospective in operation as a matter of law they may upset settled expectations. For example, under the Indian Contract Act impossibility of performance due to operation of law makes a contract void, ...say, *A* agrees to sell his land to *B*. on the date the contract is to be performed the Government has passed a law prohibiting the sale of any land in that area or the Government may have acquired the property. The law has upset the settled expectations.

Similarly every case law is not compulsorily retrospective. The court may lay down a new rule but apply the existing rule to the instant case. For example, in *Indira Sawhney* v. *Union of India*, AIR 1993 SC 477,[3] the Supreme Court of India laid down the rule that there shall be no reservation in promotions after a particular date but did not disturb the already existing promotions in reservations. Likewise even where the case law is retrospective it is a gradual

1. Of late debates in the legislature are telecast live and hence laws are made known while they are being made and public opinion is generated while law is being made.
2. Bentham criticizes the concept of judges making laws. He says – judges make laws for men the way men make laws for their dogs. Men wait till the dog does something that you don't want it to do and then you beat it. This is the way judges make laws for men quoted in Fitzgerald, P.J.: Salmond on Jurisprudence (New Delhi, Universal Law Publishing Co. Pvt. Ltd.) 12th Edn., p. 127.
3. However the Parliament amended the Constitution to nullify the effect of the judgment and introduced Article 16(4A) providing for reservations in promotions.

process and limited in its scope. It rarely represents a clean and an abrupt break with the existing law.

4. Legislation can be made in Anticipation of the Circumstances

Legislation can be made in anticipation of the circumstances but courts have to wait for a concrete case before anything vague or ambiguous or obscure in the legislation can be set right. That a concrete case will come up before the courts is only a chance. Case law is always *ex post facto*. The principle of natural justice that law must be known before it is enforced is violated. Legislation can set right the doubt or the vagueness as soon as its attention is drawn to it. Case law is therefore essentially incomplete, uncertain, and unsystematic. If statute law shows the same defect it is due to the lethargy or incapacity of the Legislature.

5. Statute Law is Superior in Form

Statute law is superior in form. Case law is buried in a mass of law reports of bygone days. Salmond observes; 'case law is gold in the mine – a few grains of the precious metal to the ton of useless matter while statute law is coin of the realm ready for immediate use."[1] Here also the modern technology has helped to mitigate this deficiency. Softwares which compile judgments year-wise; subject-wise; judge-wise have made it possible to get the judgments one is looking for at the click of a button. Though of course in form statute law would be more systematic than judge made law, precedent is merged in concrete details of the case. Specially when there are a large number of judges on the Bench and each gives his own verdict it is difficult to find out the exact rationale on which the final decision is based. For example, in *Keshvanand Bharati's* case[2] there were 13 judges and 13 different opinions; the judgment runs into 1000 pages; it was for the first time in the history of Indian case laws that the judges gave the summary of the judgment and there was a comment in the Parliament that at least in such crucial matters can the judges not arrive at some uniform conclusion.

There are some plus points in case law too. It is not bound by authoritative verbal expression and therefore there is no barrier between the courts of justice and the very spirit and the purpose of law they are called upon to administer. While interpreting laws courts are concerned with the true meaning of the words used by the legislature if the words of the statute are not clear. Prof. Clarke points out in his comments on Austin that "Case law is the outcome of the practical needs considered by men of the highest practical experience". "The judge is the interpreter of the social mind" and he can easily adapt the law to the changing wants of those amongst whom the law is administered. Case law is easier to understand than statute law as it is easier to understand a legal principle by noticing how it is applied in an actual case. In addition, as case law is one that is formulated by legal experts it is bound to be more superior in quality to statutes passed by inexperienced legislators.[3]

1. K. Krishna Menon: Outlines of Jurisprudence, 3rd Edn. p. 73.
2. Statutes begin by laying down the object; the title, the definitions; and then the substantive and the procedural provisions, the exceptions, the date of operation etc. This makes it systematic.
3. K. Krishna Menon: Outlines of Jurisprudence, 3rd Edn., p. 71, 72.

6. Legislature or Judiciary – Which is Supreme is Debatable

The question whether Legislature which makes legislation is superior to the Judiciary which lays down precedents is a matter of considerable debate. In one sense, it is the Legislature/Parliament which is supreme. There are a number of instances (refer the 4th, 6th, 9th, 11th, 25th, 26th, 46th, 77th, 81st, 93rd amendments to the Constitution) where law is enacted or amended to nullify the effect of a judgment. It may be for several reasons like- to overcome a difficulty created by the judgment; it may even be in order to please or appease a particular section of the society; it may be because the prominent section of the society is unhappy with the judgment and are lobbying to get it altered through legislation.

For example, the very first amendment to our Constitution was in order to remove the difficulties created by the Supreme Court rulings in three cases concerning Article 19. Under Article 19(2) of the Constitution reasonable restrictions can be imposed on freedom of speech and expression on the ground of security of State. In *Romesh Thapper* v. *State of Madras* (AIR 1950 SC 124) the Supreme Court held that the term "security of State' – a ground on which a reasonable restriction can be imposed on the freedom of Speech and Expression- refers only to serious and aggravated forms of public disorder and not ordinary breaches of public order and public safety. In *Brij Bhushan* v. *State of Delhi*,(AIR 1950 SC 129) under section 7 of East Punjab Safety Act, 1949, order was issued against the Printer, Publisher and Editor of the English Weekly Organisor directing them to submit for scrutiny all news and views regarding Pakistan before being published. Such pre-censorship was struck down by the court as it curtailed freedom of speech and expression under Article 19(1)(a) of the Constitution. To overcome the difficulty created by these two decisions – three more grounds were added on which restrictions could be imposed on the freedom of Speech and Expression – 'public order'; 'friendly relations with foreign State' and 'incitement to offence'.

In *Moti Lal* v. *State of Uttar Pradesh,* AIR 1951 All 257, the Uttar Pradesh Government refused to issue permits to private owners of road transport vehicles in order to enable the State to take over particular services. The Motor Vehicles Act required Private owners to obtain permits from the regional authority. But State owned buses were exempt from the necessity of taking permit. The Allahabad High Court held that the State could not claim any special treatment as it would violate Article 14 of the Constitution which guarantees equality before law and equal protection of the laws. The Parliament by the first Amendment added an Explanation to Article 19(6) making the right of the citizen to carry on trade and business subject to over-riding right of the State to create a monopoly in any trade or business.

Likewise the 93rd Constitutional Amendment provided for reservations in favour of Scheduled Castes and Scheduled Tribes and the educationally backward class of citizens in educational institutions including the private educational institutions except the minority educational institutions referred to in Article 30(1) of the Constitution. This amendment was because of the Supreme Court ruling in *T.M.A. Foundation* v. *State of Karnataka,* AIR 2003 SC 355 and *P.A. Inamdar* v. *State of Maharashtra,* AIR 2005 SC 3226 that the State cannot make reservations of seats for admissions in privately run educational institutions. In

Islamic Academy v. *State of Karnataka*, AIR 2003 SC 3724 the court had held that the State can fix a quota for admissions to these institutions but cannot fix the fees. To overcome the problems created by these judgments – the State amended the Constitution.

It is thus to be seen that though the Courts have the power of judicial review over legislative and executive action under which they can declare a law or an executive action to be void, the legislature can nullify those judgments by bringing an amendment to the laws. Thus in a limited field both can be said to be supreme. However what is needed for efficient administration of justice – is not a tug of war between the two organs but a harmonious interaction.

VII. Codification

Advantages of enacted law are so attractive that in modern days there is a tendency to reduce the whole *corpus jus* into an enacted form.

Codification must not be misunderstood to mean abolition of case law or precedent as a source of law. Case law will continue to grow even when the Code is complete. Substance and body of law shall be enacted law and the case law shall be incidental and supplementary. Even in most carefully drafted legislations some ambiguity, some vagueness or new uncontemplated situations may arise where courts will have to step in. Thus, out of the Code itself a body of case law grows. It is expedient to codify the explanatory case law from time to time.

An interesting compromise between case law and codification is the American Law Institutes 'Restatement of American Law'. The Restatement is in the form of a Code but it is not statutory. It has no official sanction. Yet it has considerable authority in the courts of USA. Its authority rests on the eminence of the jurists who have framed it. Restatement merely declares the existing law without attempting to suggest improvements. But where the decisions are in conflict, the framers of the Restatement have adopted what they consider to be the preferable rule and not necessarily one supported by the greatest mass of authority.

In India, the most ancient case of codification can be said to be the Code of Manu where law and religion were interwoven. Codification in the present sense of the term began in 1834 during the British Regime. The first Law Commission was appointed in 1834 under the Chairmanship of L. Macaulay. Indian Penal Code and the Code of Civil Procedure were drafted. CPC was passed in 1859 and IPC in 1860. Indian Contract Act, Indian Evidence Act and Negotiable Instrument Act were embodied in the Statute soon thereafter.

Today in India, Criminal law is entirely codified and is commonly applicable to all the communities in India including the Muslim community. Hindu law regarding marriage, succession, guardianship, adoption and maintenance is codified. Law relating to co-parcenary property is pàrtly codified (*see* section) 6 and 30 of the Hindu Succession Act and the 2005 Amendment to the Hindu Succession Act) Mohammedan Law is mostly uncodified and there is an opposition to its codification. Some portion of the law is codified like Muslim Women's Protection of Rights on Divorce Act, 1986; (which mostly incorporates the personal law itself without any reformative provisions); the Dissolution of Muslim Marriages Act, 1939 and the Wakf Act. Property laws are still governed by their personal laws itself.

Codification may also be in the form of consolidation. That is law on the subject may be scattered in different statutes; case laws, customary laws etc. The Legislature may consolidate the law by codifying it also with minor improvements. For example, the Code of Civil Procedure is a consolidating statute.

VIII. The Interpretation of Enacted Law

Enacted law is embodied in an authoritative formula. Interpretation means the process by which the courts seek to ascertain the meaning and intention of the Legislature through the medium of the authoritative forms in which it is expressed *i.e.* through the enacted piece of Legislation itself. The legal authority of an enactment is derived from the letter of the law and also its spirit. Other forms of law like custom do not have the letter of law to stand in between the spirit of the law and its judicial application. Hence it is in the case of enacted law that the question of interpretation or construction arises.

Interpretation is of two kinds, literal or grammatical and functional. Literal interpretation regards exclusively the verbal expression of the law. It is *litera legis i.e.* the literal construction of law.

On one hand there is the strict grammatical or literal construction of the statute, where what is seen is the literal or plain meaning of the words used by the Legislature. On the other hand, there is free interpretation. It is a search for the true intention of the legislature. Free interpretation departs from the letter of law and seeks for more satisfactory evidence of the true intention of the legislature.

Following are the principles to be borne in mind while interpreting the Statute:

1. Duty of the Court is to Explain Law

The traditional view is that the duty of the court is to explain, interpret and apply the law and not to make law.

2. Legislature has not made the Rules of Interpretation

In order to ascertain the meaning of a statute the courts make use of various rules of interpretation. These *rules are not legislature made rules.* They are rules that have been evolved by the courts themselves while interpreting the statute. They are not binding upon the future courts. Different rules of interpretation have been evolved to ascertain the meaning of legislation.

3. True Intention of the Legislature to be Applied

The courts have to either apply the principle of *litera legis* (literal construction) or *sententia legis i.e.* the true intention of the legislature.

4. Litera Legis

In all ordinary cases courts must apply the principle of *litera legis.* They must take it for granted that the legislature has said what it has meant and that it has meant what it has said. *Litera legis* is the exclusive and conclusive evidence of *sententia legis.* In other words, the language and the words used are an evidence of what is intended by the legislature. Judges do not have the liberty to add to or take away from the words of the statute or to modify it because they have reason to believe that the true *sententia legis* is not expressed by it.

5. *Dictionary Meaning*

Ordinary meaning of the word is ascertained by referring to the dictionary or its scientific or technical meaning that it has acquired. Words are also interpreted with reference to the interpretation clause or the definition clause that is given in the statute or by the Interpretation Act, 1889 in England or the General Clauses Act, 1897 in India. Courts are also guided by the judicial decisions on the statute itself. Words are also considered in the sense which they bore when the statute was enacted.

6. *Noscitur a Socis*

Meaning of the word is to be judged by the company it keeps. The meaning is to be gathered from referring to the surrounding sections, the whole Act and at times the whole area of Legislation. So gathered, the context may give the word a meaning which is different from the one in the dictionary. As observed by J. Gajendragadkar, the rule means that when two or more words susceptible of similar (analogous) meanings are coupled together they are understood to be used in their cognate sense. They take their colour from each other *i.e.*, the more general is restricted to a sense similar to a less general. For example, Article 194(3) of the Constitution refers to powers, privileges and immunities of a House of Legislature. The Supreme Court held that words "Powers' takes its colour from the words 'Privileges and Immunities of the House, which are necessary for the conduct of its business and not to legislative powers. *State of Karnataka* v. *Union of India*, AIR 1978 SC 68.

7. *Expressio Unius Est Exclusio Alterius*

Mention of one excludes the other. For example, under the Indian Contract Act an agreement in *restraint* of trade is void under section 27. Under section 28 an agreement in *absolute restraint* of legal proceeding is void. The court held that the absence of term 'absolute' in section 27 and its presence in section 28 means that, has been deliberately, with a specific intention, left out in section 27. Hence it was held that under section 27 whether the restraint on trade is partial or absolute it is void; but under section 28 partial restraint on legal proceedings are allowed. That is the reason why we come across agreements with a clause stating that if a dispute arises only the Bangalore court, Madras court etc. will have the jurisdiction. However this maxim is subject to the doctrine of *ex abundanti cautela,* which means 'as a matter of abundant caution'. That is before excluding the jurisdiction of the other courts, the court must ascertain whether the use of one was merely a matter of abundant caution and not with an intention to exclude the other.[1]

8. *Expressum Facit Cessare Tacitum*

Express words put an end to implication.

9. *Ejusdem Generis*

It restricts the meaning of the general words to things of the same kind as the preceding particular words. For example, in interpreting the phrase "suit, proceeding or any other legal proceeding" the Supreme Court held that the words 'other legal proceedings' were restricted to 'proceedings in the court of law.'

---

1. *Asstt. Collector of Central Excise, Guntur* v. *Ramdeo Tobacco Co.*, AIR 1991 SC 506.

10. *Exceptions where Litera Legis (Letter of the Law) is not Applicable*

a. Where the law is logically defective. Logical defect may be of 3 different kinds
   - *Semantic ambiguity*: A word in the statute may be ambiguous due to the 'open texture' of the language or due to its generality. For example, when a person steers a broken down vehicle on tow can it be said to be 'driving'?
   - *Syntactic ambiguity*: Arises with the use of formal words like 'and'; 'or' For example, the Indian Penal Code says 'fine or imprisonment' may be awarded. Does it mean either 'fine or imprisonment' can be awarded or does it mean that both can be awarded. Here the courts have to go beyond the letter of the law and ascertain the true intention of the law makers.
   - *Repugnancy in the intention itself*: Here the courts correct the defect in the *sententia legis* and the *litera legis*. If the text is defective but the intention is obvious and genuine and perfect the court must ascertain the same and give effect to it. But where neither the text is clear nor is the intention they must give effect to that intention which the legislature is presumed to have had if the ambiguity was within their knowledge.

b. *Literal interpretation leads to absurdities*: Where literal interpretation would lead to absurdities and unreasonableness. For example, clerical errors; use of positive instead of negative sentence.

c. *Mischief rule:* Mischief rule has its origin in Heydon's case. It requires the judges to look at the common law, the mischief in the common law which the Statute intends to remedy, the Act is then to be construed so as to suppress mischief and promote the remedy.

In *Garris* v. *Scott,* (1874) LR 9 Exch 125 the statute provided that animals carried on board a ship should be kept in pens (enclosures). The defendant carrier had not kept the plaintiff's sheep in pens because of which they were washed away in a storm. If they were safely penned they could be saved. Plaintiff's suit for breach of statutory duty was rejected by the court because the statute provided for penning of animals to prevent infection spreading from one owner's animals to those of another and it could not be used for providing in a remedy for a totally different mischief.

But in *Smith* v. *Hughes,* (1871) LR 6 QB 597: 40 LJQB 221, Street Offences Act, 1959 was enacted with an intention to clean up streets to enable people to walk along the streets without being solicited by prostitutes. In this case, prostitutes attracted the attention of passers by standing in balconies or windows and not actually on the streets. Held it was within the mischief sought to be prevented. Hence the precise place from where prostitution was solicited was irrelevant. (1966) 1 WLR 830.

In *India* we follow similar rules of interpretation. Yet the judiciary has evolved a large number of rules to suit the requirements and aspirations of Independent India.

IX. Indian Judiciary Departs from the Traditional British Practice

As opined by J. V.R. Krishna Iyer – though legally speaking, British Empire left the Indian soils – it bequeathed to us the Anglo-Saxon system of law which is exotic, elitist and die-hard. Their concepts continued to fascinate the Indian intellectuals. Considering West to be the Best hampers our own creative genius. He believes that while weaving the progressive strands in British Justice into post-independence jurisprudence it is important to re-kindle our indigenous institution, value system, legal practices and blend them with the enduring excellence found in the English speaking law. As and when cases have come up before the courts judges like Justices Krishna Iyer, Bhagwati and others have tried to indianise the rules of interpretation so as to suit the local conditions. Following are some examples which mark a departure from the traditional English practice:

- *Interpretation of Article 32 of our Constitution*: Article 32 makes litigating for a fundamental right itself – a fundamental right. In *Bandhua Mukti Morcha*, AIR 1984 SC 802, Article 32 was interpreted in a new light so as to make the provision 'a friend of the poor and the illiterate'. It simplified the procedure for filing a writ under Article 32 – even letters by public spirited persons could be treated as writs. In *M.C. Mehta* v. *Union of India* (AIR 1987 SC 1086), Supreme Court held that Article 32 confers not only power itself but imposes an obligation on the Supreme Court to protect the fundamental rights of the citizens in the interest of justice. Hence it has powers to fashion new tools and strategies and forge new remedies.
- *Actualising social justice:* In *Azad Rickshaw Pullers Union* v. *State of Punjab*, AIR 1981 SC 14 Punjab Cycle Rickshaw Act, 1976 prohibited non-owners of Rickshaws from plying the Rickshaws in order to free them from exploitation by owners of rickshaws. Though a well intentioned legislation it would have left hundreds of rickshaw pullers high and dry. So Justice Krishna Iyer gave a comprehensive scheme for facilitating rickshaw pullers to become the owners of the Rickshaws. It is a case where judicial justice and legislative power have interacted together to produce pragmatic justice.
- *Writ of Habeas Corpus:* In *Kanu Sanyal* v. *District Magistrate, Darjeeling* – Justice P.N. Bhagwati made a bold departure from the British practice while granting *Habeas Corpus* writ and held that nothing in Article 32 requires the production of the body of a person detained before the application is heard because production of the body of a person was a procedure adopted due to compulsions of the system of justice then prevailing
- In *Rohtas Industries Ltd.* v. *Rohtas Industries Staff Union*, (1976) 2 SCC 82 (93), the Supreme Court refused to award compensation to the employer for the illegal strike causing loss of profit to the employer. Justice Krishna Iyer points out that English decisions awarding damages in such cases were a response to the societal requirements of the industrial civilisation of the 19th century; and the law of torts was shaped to serve the economic interest of the trading and industrial community. But today right to form associations is a fundamental right under the Indian Constitution and the Constitution is sensitive to workers rights. So he says that English torts cannot be incorporated without adaptation under the Indian system.

CHAPTER 14

PRECEDENT AS A SOURCE OF LAW

SYNOPSIS

INTRODUCTION

A precedent is a statement of law enunciated by the superior court in the course of rendering a judgment which has to be followed by that court and by the inferior courts. This brings in certainty in legal matters and the litigant has an idea of how the court will act in similar situations and facts. In the course of rendering decisions on actual disputes the courts explain and expound the law; they clarify and clear the ambiguities in the Legislation; in the process they make statements of law which operate as a source of law. Thus, the theory of precedent plays an important role in the development of jurisprudence of the country. In India, under Article 143 of the Constitution, law laid down by the Supreme Court is binding on all the courts in India.

According to Osborne's Concise Law Dictionary a precedent is "A judgment or decision of a court of law cited as authority for deciding a similar set of facts. It is a case which serves as an authority for the legal principle embodied in its decision. The common law has developed by broadening down from precedent to precedent. A case is an authority for what it actually decides."[1]

I. The Authority of Precedents

1. Judicial Precedent: A Significant Feature

Judicial precedents are a significant and a distinguishing feature of English law. This is because the great body of common or unwritten law in England is almost entirely the product of decided cases. These decided cases are accumulated in a voluminous series of reports from the close of the 13th Century when Edward the First ruled England. In Rome and in the Continent, precedents do not carry the same authority as in England. They are both evidences of law and are of persuasive value but nothing more. In England, precedents are authoritative probably due to the powerful and authoritative position occupied by the English judges. Judges of the King's courts were a small and compact body of legal experts, working together in harmony. They imposed their own views of law and justice upon the whole realm. They succeeded in establishing a single homogeneous system of common law with little interference from local custom or from Legislation. In England, the Bench has always given law to the Bar. In Rome, it was the other way round as there was no permanent body of professional judges capable of doing the work done for centuries in England by the royal courts. In India under Article 143 of the Constitution judgments of the Supreme Court bind the subordinate courts.

2. Doctrine of Precedent: Two Meanings: Loose and the Strict

The doctrine has two meanings: by the loose meaning it means that the precedents are reported, they may be cited and will probably be followed by the courts.

---

1. Roger Bird: Osborn's Concise Law Dictionary, 7th Edn. (Universal Law Publishing Co. Pvt. Ltd.).

In the strict sense, it means that the precedent are not only of great authority but must be followed.

3. *Critical Analysis of the Doctrine of Precedent (Advantages and Disadvantages of the Doctrine)*

Holdsworth supports the doctrine in the loose sense and Dr. A.L.Goodhart attacks it in its strict sense. There is no dissatisfaction with the practice of citing cases and of attaching weight to them. The dissatisfaction is with the practice of treating precedents as absolutely binding. There are arguments and counter-arguments on both the sides. On the plus side the practice of treating precedents as binding brings in certainty of law and predictability of decisions. At times predictability is more important than approximation to an ideal. An extremely unsatisfactory decision can be reversed by a future statute.

- The *counter-argument* is that the pressure on parliamentary time is so great that it would hardly get time to bring in amendments to set right the wrong done or dissatisfaction created by case law. When it has done it, it has done by creating exceptions to the common law. Over ruling by the superior courts is another way to set right the things but that involves substantial expenses to the litigant. The method of restrictive[1] distinguishing leaves the 'distinguished decision'[2] standing and hence creates unnecessary refinements and illogicalities.

Compromise between the two views lies in making the decisions of the superior court binding on the lower courts but the courts would not be bound by the decisions of the courts of co-ordinate jurisdiction because such courts are of equal authority.

II. Theories of Precedent : 1. Declaratory 2. Authoritative and Persuasive

1. *Declaratory Theory of Precedents*

a. *Judges do not make law:* According to this theory, judges do not make law. They only declare the law. Hale says in the history of common law that it is only the King and the Parliament which can make law, though precedents have great weight and authority in expounding and declaring the law.

b. *Judges only declare the law:* According to Blackstone judges are "sworn to determine not according to their own private judgment but according to the known law and custom of the land". Power to make law is not delegated to them. They have to only find the law, explain it and apply it to the given situation. Hence they only declare the law.

c. *Limitations of the theory:*

(i) *Declaratory theory not applicable to the courts of Chancery*: The declaratory theory did *not fit in the courts of Chancery.* Courts of Chancery are courts where decisions are given based on equity, justice and good conscience. It could not be said that principles of equity were founded either on

---

1. *Method of restrictive distinguishing means* – The court refuses to follow a previous decision by drawing a delicate or a subtle difference between the earlier case and the one under consideration.
2. The prior decision is distinguished by the court in a latest case to assert that though it may look similar to the latest case, in fact it is dissimilar. Such prior decision is the "distinguished decision".

custom or Legislation. Hence they could not be said to be declaratory. They were made by the Chancellor based on his concept of just and unjust. He thus made law for himself and for his successors.

(ii) *Not applicable to common law:* Declaratory theory seems to be *not applicable to common law.* Judges do more than just applying the laws in the course of giving judgments. They extend the rule of law; they narrow it down. They evolve a new rule by comparison with an existing rule. At times they create a totally new principle.

d. *Courts do more than Just declaring law:* Social opinion and social necessities are more or less in advance of law. Law is stable whereas the societies are progressive. Henry Maine points out that the gulf between the archaic English common law and the social necessities of the progressive English society was being narrowed down by the English judges by formulating, extending, modifying and improving the principles of equity though they had to go on professing that they were only declaring the law and not making the law. Thus there was 'virtual legislation' though it was unacknowledged. Our Supreme court has pointed out that 'legislative modifications of laws is bound to be confined to major changes' while 'gradual and orderly development of law can only be accomplished by judicial interpretation'.[1] Judges thus bridge the gap between the needs of the society and the existing law. J. Bhattacharjee observes that 'if you cannot reach the goal without the connecting bridges then those who construct the bridges really make the road worth its name; if you cannot understand what is said or written without the gaps therein being filled up by the judges, then the judges who fill up the gaps are really the makers of the statement.'

The entire Administrative law provides a best example of the observation that courts do not just declare the law. As Dr. Upendra Baxi puts it in his introduction to the Book on Jurisprudence[2] – Administrative Law is flourishingly judge made. Administrative law has developed as and when disputes regarding excessive or improper use of power by the Administrators have come up before the courts. The courts have attempted to lay down the checks and balances over the powers of the Administrators; Legislators and Executives. They have tuned the concept of delegated legislation; they have expressed the different dimensions of the principles of natural justice and laid down the circumstances when hearing is allowed or disallowed. The courts have put a check on arbitrary use of power – either by the Legislature or the Executive. For example, it has laid down that when power is exercised for purposes other than for which it has been conferred by the Constitution or Statute. When the Will of the power-wielders becomes the sole justification for the exercise of power – it is arbitrariness. A substantial portion of Administrative law consists in the role played by the Judiciary in checking such arbitrariness and canalising the power by developing the concept of natural justice. To take just one example, before the decision in

---

1. *V.D. Dhanwatey,* AIR 1968 SC 683 (696) quoted in J. Bhattacharjee, A.M.: Judicial Activism & the World Judge's Conference, (1984) 3 SCC JS 1.
2. I.P.Massey: Administrative Law, 5th Edn., p. XII.

Kraipak[1] it was laid down both under our law and also the English law that the principles of natural justice could be claimed only in *quasi*-judicial functions. Kraipak marks an epoch making case because it demolished the artificial and conceptual distinctions between Administrative function and *quasi*-judicial functions and de-linked natural justice from quasi-judicial functions. In simpler words – after the decision in *Kraipak,* the concept of natural justice is applicable not only in *quasi*-judicial and of course judicial functions; but also when the authority is discharging administrative functions. This is because rules of natural justice aim at securing justice or preventing miscarriage of justice and the basic goal to be attained is to arrive at a just decision. Ultimately, it is again the courts which have asserted that – howsoever you label a function – whether as an administrative or executive or *quasi*-judicial – it must be discharged with fairness.

III. Kinds of Precedents

Authoritative (conditional and unconditional)

1. Authoritative Precedent

a. *Judges must follow*: An authoritative precedent is one which the judges *must follow* whether they approve it or not.

   Persuasive precedents are *not binding* on the judges, but they may take them into consideration and attach such weight as they deem fit. Hence, authoritative precedents are legal sources of law; persuasive precedents are merely historical.

b. *Authoritative precedent may be conditional or unconditional*: Sir John Salmond classifies authoritative precedents as conditional and unconditional. It is unconditionally authoritative if under all circumstances it must be followed by the lower courts. A precedent which is conditionally authoritative may be rejected under certain cases as for example, where the decision is so unreasonable or erroneous that it would be a mockery of justice to follow the precedent. It is not a simple case of error or unreasonableness but a gross case of error or unreasonableness.

c. *Examples of Persuasive Precedent*: Following are the persuasive precedents:

   (i) *Foreign Judgments:* In India foreign judgments are given effect provided they satisfy the conditions laid down in Section 13 of Civil Procedure Code.

   (ii) *Commonwealth court decisions*: Decisions of the superior courts in other parts of the Commonwealth

   (iii) *Judgments of the Privy Council*: Privy Council used to hear appeals from Commonwealth countries. Judgments given by the Privy Council while hearing appeal from one Commonwealth country is persuasive with respect to other Commonwealth countries.

   (iv) *Obiter dicta:* Obiter dicta *i.e.,* statements of law made by the court while passing a judgment which are not necessary for the disposal of the case. They are passing observations which the later court

1. *A.K. Kraipak* v. *Union of India,* AIR 1970 SC 150.

regards as unduly wide. J. Krishna Iyer in *Mohinder Singh Gill* v. *Chief Election Commissioner,*[1] has observed that 'an obiter binds none, not even the author...'.Yet, when the obiter comes from the Supreme Court it would be highly persuasive and it sets the tone for speculation of how the future courts may react to a like situation.

(v) *Authoritative text books*: Authoritative text books and commentaries.

(d) *Doctrine of Precedent in India.*

(i) After independence, the decisions of the Privy Council are not authoritative but of high persuasive value.

(ii) Article 143 of the Constitution lays down that the decisions of the Supreme Court are binding on all the courts in India and hence highly authoritative.

(iii) The decisions of one High Court are not binding on the other High Courts. They are only persuasive in nature as the courts are of co-ordinate jurisdiction.

(iv) In the same High Court, the decision of a Single Judge is binding on another single judge, but not on a court of Appeal.

(v) The decision of the larger Bench of the same Court is binding on the smaller Bench of the same Court.

(vi) The lower Courts are bound by the ruling given by the State High Court to which they are subordinate. Even when there are conflicting opinions between different High Courts the subordinate Court is bound by the ruling of the High Court to which it is subordinate. For example, a District Court in Karnataka is bound by the ruling of the Karnataka High Court.

(vii) When on the same point of law, there are different opinions given by different High Courts and then later the Supreme Court gives a ruling on the same point it is the Supreme Court which must be followed in all the High Courts.

(viii) Unreported judgments have as much authority as reported ones.

Difficulty with persuasive and authoritative precedent is that the same decision may be authoritative in one court while persuasive in another. For example, ruling given by the Karnataka High Court is authoritative in Karnataka courts but only persuasive outside Karnataka.

IV. A Precedent may be Disregarded in Two Ways: Overruling and Refusal to Follow

a. The court may overrule it. Overruling is the act of a court of superior jurisdiction. A precedent overruled loses all its authority. It becomes null and void like a repealed statute. A new precedent is substituted for the old.

Overruling and reversal are different. When a decision of the lower court goes in appeal the appellate court may reverse it. Reversal of the ruling occurs in the same case. Overruling occurs when the appellate court decides in another

1. AIR 1978 SC 851 (859).

case that the precedent case is wrongly decided and should not be allowed. Here the court is not making the law but only declaring the correct law. The overruling decision is retrospective in operation. Hence all transactions on the strength of the supposed rule will be governed by the overruling decision. But if by making the overruling decision retrospective it would cause hardship the court may direct that the decision would be prospective in operation. For example, in *Indira Sawhney* v. *Union of India*[1] case it was held that reservations in promotions are not valid. But the decision was made to operate only after 5 years from the date of judgment in order to avoid hardship.[2] Reservation in promotion was held constitutional in *General Manager* v. *Rangachari,*[3] but the Supreme Court overruled it in *Indira Sawhney* v. *Union of India.*

b. *The court may refuse to follow it.* Refusal to follow is the act of the court of co-ordinate jurisdiction. Two courts of equal jurisdiction do not have the authority to overrule each other's decision. Thus both the decisions of the courts of co-ordinate jurisdiction stand side by side until overruled by the superior court. Until then law would be uncertain. For example, under the Transfer of Property Act the Allahabad, Lahore and Jammu and Kashmir High Courts[4] have held that the Pujari's right to receive future offerings which may be given by the devotee is transferable; the Calcutta High Court[5] has held that it is not transferable. The Supreme Court has not yet given its ruling on the point. The issue is still open and the law uncertain.

V. Circumstances Weakening the Binding Force of the Precedents

A precedent is binding because it brings in certainty and predictability in the state of law. Facts and the law would have been urged and considered by the court. Hence it also raises a presumption of correctness of the facts and the law. Hence untill overruled or refused to be followed the precedent is binding.

Following are the Eight Circumstances which Weaken the Binding Force of the Precedents:

1. *Abrogated Decision*

- *Decision ceases to be binding if a statute or statutory rule inconsistent with it is subsequently enacted.* For example, in India, *Mohd. Ahmed Khan* v. *Shah Bano Begum*[6] lost its authority after the Parliament passed the Muslim Women's (Protection of Rights on Divorce) Act, 1986. The Supreme Court held that as long as a Muslim divorced woman is not able to maintain herself and does not remarry her husband has to maintain her. The ruling was nullified by the Muslim Women's (Protection of Rights on Divorce) Act, 1986 which restricted the husband's liability to the iddat period as defined in the Act which in turn incorporates the meaning of iddat prevailing under the Muslim Personal Law. Likewise 24th Amendment to the

1. AIR 1993 SC 477.
2. The Parliament amended the Constitution by introducing Article 16(4A) and provided for reservations in promotion thereby setting the judgment at naught.
3. AIR 1962 SC 36.
4. *Nand Kumar* v. *Ganesh Das,* 58 All 457; *Subh Ram* v. *Ram Kishan,* AIR 1943 Lah 265; *Badri Nath* v. *Punam,* AIR 1973 J&K 7 FB.
5. *Nityagopal* v. *Nanilal,* 47 Cal 470.
6. AIR 1985 SC 945.

Constitution nullified the famous *Golak Nath* case. In *Golak Nath* v. *State of Punjab,*[1] the Supreme Court had held that amendment under Article 368 is 'law' within the meaning of Article 13 of the Constitution. Therefore if it takes away the fundamental right it is void to that extent. 24th Amendment overruled Golaknath by laying down that a Constitutional amendment is not 'law' within the meaning of Article 13. In *Keshvanand Bharati*[2] the Supreme Court has upheld the validity of the Amendment.

- *If it is reversed or overruled by a higher court.* Until 1940's the Court of Appeal in England, considered itself bound by its own previous decision though it was manifestly inconsistent with the later decision of the House of Lords. Only when the House of Lords expressly overruled it, the Court of Appeal did not follow its previous decision. In *Young's* case,[3] the Court of Appeal accepted the new principle that it is not bound by its own decision if it cannot 'stand with' a subsequent decision of the House of Lords.

2. *Affirmation or Reversal on a Different Ground*

For example, the lower court decides the case in favour of the plaintiff on ground A. The appellate court affirms it but on another ground B and says nothing of ground A. In such a case, it is opined that the decision does not lose all authority. It may be followed by the court which thinks the particular point is rightly decided.

3. *Ignorance of Statute*

That is judgment given – *Per incurium.* According to Osborne's Dictionary it means 'through want of care'. Decision of the court which is mistaken. The decision is given without court's attention being drawn to the relevant authority. A precedent is not binding if it is rendered in ignorance of statute or a delegated legislation (*i.e.,* rule having the force of law.) It is not binding even if the earlier court knew the statute but failed to appreciate its relevance to the matter on hand. Such decisions are said to be given *per incurium* (*i.e.,* in ignorance of).

4. *Inconsistency*

Inconsistency with the earlier decision of the higher court: A precedent loses its binding force if it is inconsistent with the decision of the higher court as being *per incurium.*

5. *Inconsistency between Earlier Decisions of the Same Rank*

A court is not bound by its previous decisions that are in conflict with each other.

The rule is applicable to the House of Lords also.

This may arise because having regard to the vast number of precedents, through inadvertence the earlier case may not be cited in the later one. If the new decision is in conflict with the old one which is binding it is given *per incurium* and is not binding on a later court. In such a case the court is free to choose between conflicting decisions whether the earlier ones or the later; a reported or

1. AIR 1967 SC 1643.
2. AIR 1971 SC 1461.
3. [1944] KB 718 (729) (CA).

an unreported decision and can even prefer the decision of the court of co-ordinate jurisdiction rather than its own.

6. *Precedent Sub Silentio or not Fully Argued*

When a particular point of law involved in a decision is not perceived by the court or present to its mind the precedent is said to pass *sub silentio*. For example, a case before the court involves two points – point *A* and point *B*. The case is such that no pronouncement can be made on point *A* unless a pronouncement is made on point *B*. But the point *B* is not argued or considered by the court. But the judgment in favour of the party is based on point *A*. The decision is not an authority on point *B*. Point *B* is said to pass *sub silentio*.

An illustration on the point is *Gerard* v. *Worth of Paris Ltd.*,[1] an employee was discharged from the company and he obtained damages against the company for wrongful dismissal. He applied for a *garnishee* order in respect of a Bank Account standing in the name of Liquidator of the Company. The only point argued was on the question of priority of the employee's claim and the Order was granted. Whether garnishee order can be properly made on an account standing in the name of the liquidator was not considered at all. When this very point was argued in a subsequent case before the court of Appeal the court held itself not bound by its previous decision.

This rule goes back to the year 1661 when the counsel said "a hundred precedents sub silentio are not material. *Rights* v. *Warner*.[2]

One reason why precedents have a binding force is that it is a matter that has been fully argued and decided and hence it should not be allowed to be reopened. Hence an *ex-parte* decision (where the losing party has not represented at all) cannot be regarded as possessing absolute authority as there is no assurance that all the relevant considerations have been brought to the notice of the court, even if it does not fall within the *sub silentio* rule.

A precedent is not destroyed *merely because* it was badly argued, inadequately considered, and based on faulty reasoning. Thus an arbitrary line is drawn between total absence of argument on a particular point (an *ex-parte* decision) which would deprive the precedent of its authority; and inadequate argument which would normally not destroy the binding force of the precedent. But it would be a ground for impugning the precedent only if it is absolutely binding and indistinguishable.

In India, the Supreme Court has observed that the binding effect of the judgment does not depend on whether a particular argument was considered or not, provided the point with reference to which an argument was subsequently advanced was actually decided by the Court.[3]

7. *Decision of Equally Divided Courts*

Where an Appellate court is equally divided (*e.g.*, 2 Judges on the Bench one gives verdict in favour of the appellant and another in favour of the respondent) the usual practice is to dismiss the appeal. In the House of Lords it is the decision appealed from which is the decision of the House. In other courts, the position

1. (1936) 2 All ER 905 (CA).
2. (Ward) 1 Keb 66 1 Lev 8.
3. *K.B. Balkrishna Rao* v. *Haji Abdulla Sait*, (1980) 1 SCC 321.

was less clear. However, this problem does not arise today as the practice is to sit in uneven numbers in the appellate courts.

8. Erroneous Decisions

Decisions contrary to the statute or inconsistent with the rulings of the higher court are not binding. Likewise, decisions may be founded on wrong principles or may conflict with the fundamental principles of common law. Strictly speaking the courts should be free to reject such precedents. In practice, perfection has to be sacrificed in the interest of certainty. Where a decision has stood for some length of time, it would be regarded as having established the law on the point, people may have made contracts on the strength of it, it would be basis for expectations and dealings. Hence it is better to allow the erroneous precedent to stand rather than upset the whole set-up.

Communis error facit jus this is the reason why after holding in *Indira Sawhney* v. *Union of India,* AIR 1993 SC 477 that reservations in promotions are unconstitutional – the judgment was to be given effect to only after 5 years.

Thus an erroneous decision stands until overruled by the higher court. This means that an erroneous decision of the House of Lords can be corrected only by the statute. L. Denning in his dissenting judgment[1] held that the House of Lords could disregard its own decision which conflicted with the fundamental principles of common law. Later in *Scruttons Ltd.* v. *Midland Silicones Ltd.,* the House of Lords[2] by a majority of 4 to 1 disregarded their own previous decision in *Elder Dempster and Co.* v. *Paterson Zochonis and Co.*[3]. Two of the judges distinguished the prior case in order not to follow the decision. The other two considered themselves free to question the previous decisions of their own House when not consistent with established principles. This marks a relaxation in the strict rule that the House of Lords is bound by its own decision.

In India, the Supreme Court is not bound by its own decision.

VI. *Ratio Decidendi*

A judicial decision consists of following parts:

Ratio decidendi: This is what the court decides generally, it is the rule of law for which the judgment is an authority. It is the only part which is conclusive as against the persons who are not parties to the case.

Res Judicata: That part of the decision which is binding only on the parties and their privies.

Obiter Dictum: These are passing observations made by the judge or reference to hypothetical situations while giving the judgment. They are not binding.

Res Judicata: Once the case is heard by a court of competent jurisdiction, all appeals are disposed of or time for filing appeal is over, all parties to the dispute and their successors are bound by the court's finding on the issues raised between them and on questions of fact and law necessary to the decision of such issues. This is in order to give finality to the decision and to put an end to the litigation. This is known as *res judicata*. It is dealt with under Section 11 of the Code of Civil Procedure, 1908. At times the judgment may be conclusive against

---

1. *London Transport Executive* v. *Betts,* (1959) AC 213 (157).
2. [1962] AC 446.
3. [1924] AC 522.

the third parties also. It is known as a judgment *in rem i.e.,* against the world at large. For example, in a petition for declaration of nullity of a marriage the court's decision is conclusive not only against the parties but also against the third parties.

VII. *Precedent, Stare Decisis* and *Res Judicata*[1]

A precedent broadly signifies the use of past decisions as a guide in giving other decisions. In this sense it is not peculiar to the common law system. The special characteristic of common law is that precedents are treated as having *law quality* in themselves and that they are *binding*. This means they must either be followed or else distinguished. *Law quality* is the principle on which the case is decided which is known as the *ratio decidendi*. Bindingness depends on the hierarchy of the courts. That is the higher courts' decisions bind the lower court and not *vice versa*.

Stare decisis is the convenient nomenclature which distinguishes the common law doctrine of precedent from that of the broad doctrine of precedent common to all developed systems.

As opined by Rupert Cross[2] a precedent may be binding and not merely persuasive in England because *stare decisis* is , generally speaking, a hard-and-fast rule in England. It is a great deal more than a mere maxim of judicial conduct to be followed if other things are more or less equal.

The main differences between *res judicata* and *stare decisis* are as follows:

1. *Res judicata* applies to the decision in dispute, while *stare decisis* operates as to the ruling of law involved.
2. *Res judicata* binds only the parties and their privies. As *Stare decisis* relates to the ruling of law and hence is binding on everyone including those who come before the court in other cases.
3. *Res judicata* is applicable to all courts. *Stare decisis* is applicable only as regards the decisions of the higher courts.
4. *Res judicata* takes effect after the time for appealing against the judgment is over. *Stare decisis* operates at once.

The doctrine of precedent in English law is of considerable antiquity. *Stare decisis* is relatively modern. There was never a suggestion that the judges were bound by them. *Stare decisis* is one of the foundations on which English law rests. The factors leading to the emergence of the doctrine of *stare decisis* are peculiar to the history of England and they are as under:

1. If people are to decide their disputes through peaceful methods rather than self-help, like cases should be treated alike. This minimizes arbitrariness and caprice. This is attained by using the previous decisions as paradigms (examples). In the process, lines of similar decisions evolve in course of time. Out of these, common principles can be extracted.
2. England did not have a written Code. The Normans[3] who had half conquered the realm did not want to impose their code in England.

---

1. Dias: Jurisprudence, 4th Edn., (162-163).
2. Cross, Rupert: Precedents in English Law, p. 4.
3. The Northern French People who conquered England in the 11th Century.

Instead they tried to win confidence of the people by relying on local customs while solving disputes. This led to the distillation of the common general principles known as the common law. These principles were respected because they were believed to be the expressions of natural law and hence just and reasonable. Common law had become the people's champion against governmental oppression. Hence no one dared to suggest that it should be replaced with a code.

3. The caliber of the judges and their resistance to the Royal endeavour to override individual rights added to the prestige of the judges.
4. For the doctrine of *stare decisis* to be applicable there had to be (i) reliable law reporting, and (ii) settled judicial hierarchy and clear cut rules of binding authority (*i.e.,* decisions of which of the courts are binding.)

VIII. Law Reports[1]

History of *stare decisis* is the history of law reporting. Habit of relying on precedent gradually improved law reporting. Law reporting has gone through the following passage:

1. In the earliest period, it was memory which was relied upon. Judges referred to the Registrar's books where facts, the steps in the suit, and the principles were set out. Until the end of 15th Century the writers hardly quoted any decisions. The noted exception was Bracton who compiled a Notebook of 2000 cases as material for his treatise. He stated his view of what a rule should be and added an illustrative case.
2. Then came the Year Books. They were anecdotal in character laying down the points of pleading rather than the principle. They were useful but not reliable. Citation was only out of memory. Original record was the only official source of information. Access to the records was available only to the lawyers acting for the Crown.
3. Then came the private compilations. Noted amongst them were Reports of Dyer, Plowden, Coke. None of the above were similar to citations as we understand today.
4. In the 17th century an idea emerged that the decisions of the Court of Exchequer were of binding authority because they were given by judges in groups. Strangely enough the decisions of the King's Bench, Common Pleas, or the House of Lords were not considered binding. One reason was that lay peers took part in the deliberations which embarrassed the lawyers. Another reason was that this assembly did not distinguish between its legislative and judicial functions. Both were covered under parliamentary privilege. Publication of judicial proceedings would be a breach of privilege.
5. In 1813 Dow began a series of House of Lords reports.
6. Publication of Burrow's reports from 1757 to 1771 marks the beginning of the modern practice of reporting with their head notes, facts, argument, and decision with a proper report of the judgment. The doctrine of *stare decisis* cast its first shadow.

---

1. Dias: Jurisprudence, 4th Edn., pp. 166-168.

7. In 1865, *i.e.*, 80 years later, a series of reports known as "Law Reports was inaugurated by the Incorporated Council of Law Reporting. They were revised by the judges before publishing.
8. In 1936 came the All England Law Reports. It was a weekly service.
9. Today the cyber revolution has made law reporting possible on line. There are a number of sites and addresses where the judgments are thrown open to the knowledge of the people more or less simultaneously with the passing of it.
10. In India we have the All India Reporter, the Supreme Court Cases, the Indian Law Institute publication etc. In addition Reports classify the judgments State High Court-wise; Supreme Court-wise. Reporters are very meticulous. They give the list of the cases that are overruled, followed, reversed. Classification is made subject-wise, topic-wise making it easy to search the decision.
11. Softwares like that of Manupatra etc., give the judgments topic-wise; judge-wise, period-wise at the click of the mouse. In addition the Government of India has also made the decisions available online free of cost.

IX. The Hierarchy of Authority

The general rule is that a court is bound by the decisions of all courts superior to it. A High Court judge is not bound by a previous High Court decision, though he would normally follow it on the grounds of judicial comity. If he refuses to follow it he cannot overrule it. Both the decisions stand side by side until a higher court settles the point.

To this general rule following are the qualifications:

1. Courts of inferior jurisdiction do not create binding decisions even for courts lower in rank. Courts of inferior jurisdiction are bound only by decisions of courts of superior jurisdictions *i.e.*, High Court, the Court of Appeal and the House of Lords in England; in India the High Courts and the Supreme Court.
2. *Is the house of lords bound by its own decision?* As of date it is not bound by its decision.

Before 1898, no court was absolutely bound by its own decision. In *London Tramways* v. *London County Council*, the House held that it was bound by its own decision. The rule is subject to certain exceptions: the House is not bound by the decision made in ignorance of statute; it is not bound when there are 2 conflicting decisions. It is not binding when the *ratio decidendi* of the previous decision is so obscure as to be undiscoverable. The ruling was criticized. Pullock commented that no other court of the last resort has fettered its own discretion in this way.

X. Hierarchy of Courts[1]: English and Indian Courts

A brief sketch of the hierarchy of the courts in England and in India is essential to appreciate the Doctrine of Precedent. It is as follows:

1. Cross, Rupert: Precedents in English Law, p. 5

Hierarchy of the Civil Courts in England:

Beginning from the lowest level, there are

- County and Magistrate Courts with a limited jurisdiction over cases of first instance
- High Court whose judges exercise an unlimited jurisdiction over such cases
- Divisional Courts - which are part of the High court , and enjoy a limited appellate jurisdiction in addition to hearing certain special application in the first instance.
- Court of Appeal which hears appeals from the County Courts and the High Court.
- House of Lords which hears appeals from the English Court of Appeal, the Court of Sessions in Scotland and the Court of Appeal in Northern Ireland.

Hierarchy of the Criminal Courts in England:

Beginning from the lowest level:

- Magistrate Courts exercise an important summary jurisdiction over cases of the first instance
- Convicted person has right of appeal to the Quarter Sessions in a summary case
- Most important appellate and supervisory work in relation to summary jurisdiction is by Divisional Courts of the Queen's Bench Division of the High Court. Trials on indictment take place at the Quarter Sessions or Assizes.
- Person convicted on indictment may appeal to the Court of Criminal Appeal
- Appeal to the House of Lords provided the requisite leave is obtained.

Hierarchy of Civil Courts in India

Starting from the lowest rung of the ladder, we have

- The Civil Court (Junior Division)
- The Civil Court (Senior Division)
- The District Court (to handle both Civil and Criminal Matters)
- The High Courts of each State. High Court Benches are established in several States like that of State of Karnataka,
- The Supreme Court.

Classes of Criminal Courts in every State in India (Section 6 of the Code of Criminal Procedure, 1973.)

- Courts of Session at the District level
- Judicial Magistrate of the First Class and in any Metropolitan area, Metropolitan Magistrate. Where the population exceeds one million - it is a Metropolitan area. Bombay, Madras, Calcutta and Ahmedabad are deemed to be Metropolitan area.
- Judicial Magistrate of the Second Class, and
- Executive Magistrate.
- High Courts
- Supreme Court.

XI. *Ratio Decidendi* and *Obiter Dicta*[1]

1. One essential feature of the doctrine of precedent in common law is that rules of law are developed while being applied to live issues raised between actual parties and argued on both sides. It means that they are created by judges while acting in their capacity as judge and not as say teachers or in their extra judicial capacity while giving lectures etc. If statements of law are made in any other capacity, they are not binding.
2. As against persons who are not parties to the suit the only part of the case which is conclusive is the general rule of law for which the case is an authority, known as *ratio decidendi*. It is a rule applied by and acted on by the court.
3. In the course of delivering a judgment a judge may make various observations not relevant for the disposal of the case. He may illustrate his reasoning by referring to hypothetical situations and the law which he considers to apply to them. As it is not a live issue before the court, the counsel would not adduce full argument. Under the circumstances it would be unwise to attach the same importance to such observations as would be attached to the actual decision of the case on which the case is disposed of. These observations are *obiter dicta* and without any binding force. For example, in *Unnikrishnan* v. *State of Andhra Pradesh,*[2] case the question of right to primary education was not in issue at all. It was right to higher education which was in issue. Yet a pronouncement was made declaring right to primary education as a fundamental right under the Constitution of India. This was only an *obiter* observation.[3]
4. Though *obiter dicta* are not binding they are important. They tend to rationalize law and suggest solutions for problems that may arise in future. Obiter observations from House of Lords or the judges of the Supreme Court who are masters in their areas may carry more weight than that of the lesser judges.
5. *Ratio decidendi* is the rule acted upon and applied by the court in the given case. The difficulty lies in finding out this rule. The rule may have been too widely stated; it may have come up for the first time, hence all possible situations may not be within its contemplation. Yet the original court is not obliged to ponder over situations that may arise in future or lay down exceptions to it. No two cases would be exactly the same. Later courts therefore are not totally fettered by the earlier decision. They may narrow down the rule or restrict its application. For example, in *Keshvanand Bharati's*[4] case the Supreme Court laid down the general rule that basic structure of the Constitution shall not be amended. It was the later judges, as and when the cases came up, started laying down what the basic structure is[5].

---

1. Note: plural of dictum is dicta.
2. [1993] 1 SCC 645.
3. This obiter may have set the tone for 86th Constitutional Amendment in 2002 making education of Chidren between 6 year & 14 year – a fundamental right.
4. AIR 1973 SC 1461.
5. *E.g.*, that judicial review is the basic structure or that secularism is the basic structure.

But the question is: should we wait for the later decisions to tell us what the *ratio decidendi* of the present case is. In *Bridges* v. *Hawkesworth*,[1] it was held that when a customer found money lying on the floor of the shop he should have the possession of it. In 1896, an exception was carved to this rule in *South Staffordshire Water Co.* v. *Sharman*.[2] In this case the defendants found 2 gold rings in a mud pool. But the pool was wholly and solely occupied by the plaintiffs. Outsiders did not have access to it. Hence the plaintiffs were allowed to take them as the pool was not open to the public.

Secondly, difficulty arises when judgment is unsupported by reasonings or supported by different reasonings or there may be a large number of judgments delivered in the same case each supporting the decision but on different grounds. Classic example is *Keshwanand Bharati* case where the 13 judges gave 13 different rulings making it so difficult to find out the ratio of the case that the judges probably sensing the difficulty for the first time gave the summary of their judgment.

XII. Methods of Determining the *Ratio Decidendi*

1. *The Reversal Method of Prof. Wambaugh*:

Take the proposition of law laid down by the judge; reverse it or negate it. If the reversal alters the actual situation then the proposition is the ratio or a part of the ratio. If the reversal makes no difference then it is not a ratio. That it is ratio is a general rule without which the case would have been decided otherwise. This test is of no use where no proposition is laid down or where several reasons are given for the decision. Each proposition may be reversed and yet the decision remains because it is based on many propositions.

2. *Dr. Goodhart's method or the Material test method*

The ratio is to be determined by ascertaining *the facts treated as material by the judge* together with the decisions on those facts. Here the emphasis is on what the judges *do* rather than on what *they say*.

Advantages of the test:

- It is the only way of finding out the ratio when no judgment is given.
- It stresses the point that a proposition of law is authoritative only to the extent it is relevant to the facts in issue in the case.
- It is valuable in pointing out that we cannot always rely on the judge's reasoning in a case since this may be patently faulty. This is likely to happen where the judge supports his decision with arguments of policy and justice.

  "when there is a link between the material facts and the reasoning given by the judge, it becomes more objective in nature. Thus, judges cannot be said to be only declaring law but also applying their judicial reasoning in solving the disputes."

The only drawback of the test is that the test is not in actual use by the judges. In practice the courts seem to be paying more attention to the judge's own formulation of the law than that permitted under the test.

> "that is-the fact in issue may not be linked to actual proposition of law. Fact in issue is a fact alleged by one party and denied by the other. For example, in *Unnikrishnan's* case the point in issue was whether right to higher education in Medical and Engineering colleges is a fundamental right under the Constitution but the Supreme Court introduced its own

1. (1851) 21 LJ QB 75.
2. (1896) 2 QB 44.

proposition that – right to primary education is a fundamental right. Note that the fact in issue is not related to the proposition laid down."

Difficulty arises when the court deals with the law without first finding the facts. They depart from the normal situation where rule of law is enunciated and applied to the facts as found. In these cases facts are assumed and in some the actual facts do not fit into the law as enunciated.

The observations of the Supreme Court in *State of Orissa* v. *Misra,*[1] are relevant. "A decision is only an authority for what it actually decided. What is of the essence in decision is its ratio, and not every observation found therein nor what logically follows from the various observations made in it." In *Rajput Ruda Meha* v. *State of Gujarat,*[2] the Supreme Corut has held that a *mere discussion* by a court after pondering over the issue in depth would not be a precedent binding on the court.

XIII. Judicial Reasoning

If the role of the judge is to only apply the law and not to create it as under the Declaratory theory of law, all he has to do is to ascertain the law and apply it to the given situation. This view can be put in the following syllogistic form:

All fact situations of type A entail legal consequences B (known as the major premise)

This is a fact situation of type *A*

Hence the legal consequence is *B*.

But real life situations are not so simple. Following may be the difficulties:

1. *The law may not be that clear*. In such a case the court will first have to arrive at a proposition. For example, after the rule in *Rylands* v. *Fletcher*, is laid down it becomes easy to apply it to the fact situation where anything likely to do harm is kept by the person and it escapes and causes harm. But for the judges in *Rylands* v. *Fletcher*, there was no such rule. For them the major premise was not established. Likewise in India we have any number of cases where propositions have been laid down for the first time by the courts because the major premise was not clear. For example, after *Maneka Gandhi's* case, the courts freely started reading the *fundamental rights under Article 19 and the other liberties which may not be fundamental rights specially mentioned in Part III of the Constitution, but which go to constitute personal liberty of a man* within the meaning of 'personal liberty' under Article 21. But this was unique proposition that the court in *Maneka Gandhi's* case had to lay down for the first time and it required quite a lot of judicial heroics to arrive at the point. Just and fair procedure was read as a part of Article 21; Legal aid to the poor was read as a part of Article 21 long before the Parliament enacted the Legal Services Authority Act, 1986.
2. *It may not be easy to apply the second premise.* The rule may be authoritatively laid down but the question may be whether it is applicable to the facts of the case?

To decide a case not already covered by an existing rule of law the judge has to seek guidance from the existing law. There may be persuasive authorities like foreign judgment; decisions of the domestic law on closely related topics; analogous cases on other branches of law; practical social result of his decision.

1. AIR 1968 SC 647.
2. (1980) 1 SCC 677.

CHAPTER 15

CUSTOM AS A SOURCE OF LAW

SYNOPSIS

I. Early Importance of Custom

Customs are the practices of a particular community or group which regulated the conduct of the society in their relationship with each other.

During the early stages of the development of a legal system, customs were an important source of law. As the legal system grows its importance diminishes. Customs were an important instrument in the development of the English legal system. In England the theory was that whatever was not the product of legislation had its source in custom. Law was either written statute law or unwritten common law or customary law. Judicial precedents were regarded not as source of law but only as evidence of the customs which prevailed in the society. But as of date the true sources of the bulk of English law are statute and precedents and not statute and customs and the common law is essentially judge made law and not customary law.

Blackstone said that Municipal law of England may be divided into two kinds:

- *Lex non scripta* – the unwritten law. It includes the general customs and also the particular customs of certain parts of the community.
- *Lex scripta* – the written or statute law.

This is true of the earlier period. But even today custom has not lost its law creating efficacy.

According to Paton custom is useful in two ways: It provides the material out of which the law can be fashioned because it usually takes a great deal of intellectual effort to create law *de novo*. Secondly, psychologically it is easier to secure respect for law, when it is based on a custom which is immemorial.

In India, customs are recognized as law by the Constitution itself provided the conditions of reasonableness, certainty etc. are satisfied. Just as the courts may recognize the customs and apply them in their judgment the Legislature too has recognized the customs. For example, the customary forms of divorce under Hindu Marriage Act, 1955; the whole of the Muslim law on marriage, divorce, property law, are custom based; Muslim Women's Right to Property Act, 1986 incorporates the traditional meaning of *'iddat'* which is the focal point of the Act.

Under Section 48 of the Evidence Act opinion evidence of a witness on the existence of a family or community custom is admissible. Custom may be proved by the persons likely to know of its existence. For example, it is not necessary that the parties to the customary dissolution of marriage be examined personally.

II. Essence of Custom

1. Custom embodies those principles of justice and equity and good conscience which have appealed to the conscience of the Nation. It is a strange mixture of religion, practice and taboo. State could enforce customs which commanded respect and obedience.
2. As Dias points out[1] the 'ought' proposition stems from a value judgment, which is sometimes concealed. Thus in the statement "X is your father; so you ought to help him", the 'ought' is derived not from the fact that he is the father, but from the unstated moral attitude attaching to the parent-child relation. Customs is to society what law is to the State. Each expresses man's ability to decide on the principles of 'what is right and just' and incorporate it as a code of conduct. It is not the development of a practice as such but the growth of the conviction that it ought to be followed that makes it a model for behaviour. Many such models spring up in the society. But all of them do not qualify as law. The question is when does the custom or the practice gain acceptance as law.[1]
3. Existence of established usage is the basis of rational expectation of its continuance for future, hence even if the custom is not ideally reasonable it is given effect to so as not to upset settled expectations.

III. Kinds of Customs: Legal and Conventional

Customs having the force of law are of two kinds: Legal customs and Conventional customs. Legal customs may be either local or general.

1. *Legal custom*: It is one whose legal authority is absolute. It *proprio vigore* (in itself) possesses the force of law. It is general legal custom when it is observed by all the members of the society. It prevails throughout the country and is the law of the land. It is local legal custom when it is observed only by the residents of a particular locality. It prevails in some defined locality and is a source of law only in that place.
2. *Conventional custom or usage*: It derives its authority because it has been incorporated in the contract between two or more parties either expressly or impliedly. It does not have a *proprio vigore* force as in the case of legal custom.

---

1. Dias: Jurisprudence, 4th Edn., p. 247.

IV. Conventional Customs

It is also referred to as a usage. It is an established practice incorporated in a contract which gets legal recognition. Generally the larger part of a contract is implied rather than express. Express terms lay down only a skeleton which is filled up by implied terms. Law supplies these implied terms. If the parties do not intend to follow the implied terms, they must expressly provide to the contrary. For example, the Sale of Goods Act, 1930 and the Partnership Act, 1932 has several sections which lay down that *'unless a different intention appears'* certain provisions are applicable. For example, the Partnership Act lays down that unless a different intention appears death of a partner will dissolve the firm. Hence if the parties intend that the Firm must continue even if one of the partners die they must expressly include a clause to that effect in their agreement. The Sale of Goods Act provides a lot of terms pertaining to the character of goods, price to be paid in future etc. which are presumed. This is because law presumes that when persons enter into a contract in a matter on which there is established usage they intend to contract with reference to that usage and make it a part of the agreement. Hence if they have a contrary intention it must be made clear in the contract. These terms called presumed intention are gathered from law from a) what is reasonable and b) what is customary. What is reasonable depends on the facts and circumstances of the case; what is customary depends on established usage and other factors.

Conventional customs got incorporated into law in three stages:

(a) *Factual question:* It is a question of fact whether a particular convention or usage is in practice. Evidence adduced in a particular case determines this question.

(b) *Judicial notice by courts:* Courts take judicial notice of the question. Facts of which courts take judicial notice need not be proved is the rule of evidence.

(c) *Incorporation by statute:* Statute incorporates the established practice in the law of the land.

V. The Extent of Conventional Custom

(a) Like a legal custom, conventional custom also can be either a local usage as in the case of agriculture or tenancy or a general custom like that prevailing throughout the realm. It does not require immemorial antiquity as in the case of legal custom. Sufficient if it is well established for a considerably long time.

(b) Conventional custom operates like express agreement within the limits of the maxim *modus et conventio vincunt legem.* Certain parts of law are absolute and usages cannot over ride them. Some parts of the custom operate only to the extent they are not modified by law.

(c) Another restriction is that when general usage has received judicial recognition and become a part of precedent it cannot be altered by the growth of later usage in conflict with it.

VI. Legal Custom

It is a custom in the stricter sense as opposed to usage. It is *per se* a source of law. Legal custom is of two kinds – local and general.

A valid custom must satisfy the following requirements:

1. *Reasonableness*: There must be a certain measure of conformity with justice and public utility. It does not mean that the courts can disregard a custom because in their opinion a better rule could be formulated. One reason for recognizing customs is that law does not favour upsetting the arrangements based on its presumed legal validity. But if the custom is obviously and seriously repugnant to reason and justice the courts discard it on the ground that it is unreasonable. For example, in *Anandi Devi* v. *Raja Ram,*[1] it was held that the custom amongst Sadh Vaishnav under which the husband could divorce his wife by merely tearing a piece of cloth from his turban was held to be unreasonable. Likewise customary divorce amongst Komma Reddies where the wife throws away the 'thali' and the husband picks it up was held to be unreasonable.[2] But in Barai Chaurasiya community under the custom *'chuttam chutta'* a marriage could be dissolved by agreement of the spouses. It was held to be a reasonable custom.[3]
2. *Conformity with statute law:* Custom must not contradict with the statute law. Whatever be its antiquity or length of usage if it is opposed to the statute law it is the statute law that prevails and not the custom. But the enactment may provide that it is subject to any custom to the contrary. For example, the Indian Contract Act, 1882 provides that nothing contained in the Act shall affect any custom or usage of trade.
3. *Observance as of right:* That is the custom must have been followed openly and without force and without requiring the permission of those adversely affected.
4. *Immemorial antiquity:* It must have existed for such a long time as to be beyond the memory of man. It is said to be time immemorial if no living man can remember it or give evidence of it.

The three main sources of Dharma or law under the Hindu law are Sruti, Smriti and Sadachar. Sadachar means customs. They could be local, class and family customs. The Privy Council held in *Hurpurshad* v. *Sheo Dyal,*[4] that a custom is a rule which has obtained the force of a law in a particular class or community or in a particular district. It must be ancient, certain and reasonable and must not be in derogation of the general rule of law, must not be opposed to public policy or morality and must not be expressly forbidden by the legislature. The custom must be ancient but unlike in England it need not be time immemorial. But if it is of comparatively recent origin the court may hold that the custom is proved only in respect of the parties to the suit and not other parties.

VII. Custom and Prescription

Custom is a long practice operating as a *source of law*. Prescription is a long practice operating as a *source of right*. Historically, prescription is a personal

1. AIR 1973 Raj 94.
2. *Timmaku* v. *B. Rangappa,* AIR 1977 Kant 115.
3. *Madho Prasad* v. *Shakuntala,* AIR 1972 All 119.
4. (1876) 3 IA 259 (285).

custom one restricted to a particular person whereas local custom is limited to an individual place.

In India, Section 26 of the Indian Limitation Act lays down the law of acquiring easement right by prescription. For example, where access and use of air or light to any building has been enjoyed peaceably, as an easement, as of right without interruption for 20 years or 60 years in case of Government property; any way of water course or the use of any water or any other easement is enjoyed peaceably, openly by a person claiming title thereto without interruption for 20 years such right shall be absolute and indefeasible.

VIII. Theories of Customary Law

There are two theories:

(a) *German jurisprudence:* Which regards custom as a formal source of law and not a material source of law. Salmond rejects this theory. He says custom is material and not formal source of law. The State may draw the material contents of the rules from the custom to which it gives the form and nature of law.

(b) *Austinian theory*: True legal source of customary law is to be found in the precedents in which custom receives judicial recognition and enforcement for the first time. It is thus a variety of case law. Hence it does not acquire the force of law until it has actually come to the notice of the courts and received judicial approval.

CHAPTER 16
CONCEPTS: LEGAL RIGHTS

SYNOPSIS

4. **Proprietary and Personal Rights**
5. **Rights *in re propria* and Rights *in re aliena***
6. **Principal and Accessory Rights**
7. **Primary and Secondary Rights**
8. **Legal and Equitable Rights**
9. **Vested and Contingent Rights**

INTRODUCTION

'Right' is one of the concepts studied in Jurisprudence. Rules are expressed in terms of concepts and concepts are the tools of judicial reasoning.

A wrong is an act contrary to the rule of right and justice. Law consists of rules to regulate human conduct. These rules prescribe rights and duties for the smooth administration of justice. When there is a breach of duty and a violation of right, law steps in with its remedial measure. The concept of right and duty are closely connected with the concept of wrong. The concept of wrong arises because duty has not been performed and because a right has been infringed.

I. Wrong

1. *To be understood in two senses – Injuria and Harm:* A synonym of wrong is injury. The term injury must be understood in two senses:
   - In its primary sense - it means *injuria i.e.,* contrary to *jus i.e.,* violation of a legal right.
   - Secondary perverted sense, it means harm/damage *(damnum)* whether rightful or wrongful and whether inflicted by human agency or not. A mere loss without the violation of a legal right does not give rise to a cause of action though there are cases where *injuria(legal wrong)* without *damnum (actual loss)* is sufficient to constitute a tort.
2. *Moral or a legal wrong:* A wrong may be either a moral wrong or a legal wrong. A moral or a natural wrong is an act which is morally wrong. It is opposed to natural justice. A legal wrong is an act which is contrary to the rule of law. It is authoritatively determined to be wrong by the yardstick of law. It is therefore treated as wrong for the purpose of administration of law. It may or may not be a moral wrong. Likewise a moral wrong need not be legal wrong.
3. *Punishment is not essential element of legal wrong:* In ordinary cases, legal recognition of an act as wrong involves the punishment or suppression of it by the physical force of the State. But such force is not the essential characteristic of legal wrong. There are other forms of effective legal recognition.

II. Duties

1. *Positive acts of duty:* Behaviour is regulated chiefly through duties. A duty is an act which one ought to do. To say that a man is under a duty means that he ought to perform a certain act. Yet not all acts which a man has to do constitute his duty. Duty consists in positive acts and not in just restraining from doing something. A duty not to reveal something is a negative way to describe a positive duty to keep silent.

2. *'Ought' has 3 senses:* the idea of 'ought' in law must be understood in 3 senses[1]:
   - It may connote conduct which is due (obligation or duty) *e.g.* you ought to pay your debt
   - It may connote propriety (correct or accepted usage)
   - It may connote the effective means to an end *e.g.* if you want to talk to X by telephone, you ought to ring him up.
3. *Duty and obligation distinguished:* A duty must be distinguished from an obligation. A typical example of an obligation is one that results from making a promise. The person making the promise of his own accord has incurred an obligation unlike in the case of a duty where a person has the duty prescribed by law whether he wants it or not.
4. *Anything that 'ought to be done' is duty:* Dictates of common morality like that one should not kill or steal – neither fit in the meaning of duty nor obligation in the strict sense of the term. Yet lawyers speak of anything which ought to be done or ought not to be done as a duty in the loose sense of the term. In Jurisprudence, the term duty is used and discussed in this loose sense.
5. *Moral & Legal Duties*: Duties are either moral or legal. They are partly coincidental and partly distinct. Adulterated milk may not be sold whether knowingly or otherwise is a legal duty. But it is not a moral duty if selling takes place without the owner's knowledge that it is adulterated.

III. Rights

1. *Asserts belongingness:* The concept of right is a very important and a significant one in any civilized society. Right is a concept of which a very liberal use is made by a person in order to assert that something belongs to him; in order to assert that the other person is not entitled to take it away from him; and to assert that if taken away he has the right to get it back; and to equally assert that he is entitled to get the State assistance/ court assistance in getting it back.
2. *Right has a corresponding duty*: Right and duty are closely linked. For example, when X says that he has a right to a piece of land what he means is that the rest of the world is under a duty not to deprive him of it; when X says that under a particular contract he has a right to take possession of a certain land from *Y*, it means that *Y* is under a duty to give him the possession. Thus ascribing a right on one person is to imply that someone else is under a corresponding duty.
3. *Interests protected by moral and legal rules:* Rights are defined as interests protected by moral or legal rules. Yet rights and interests are not identical. Interests are things which are to a man's advantage. To say that a person has an interest in his reputation means that it is to his advantage to enjoy a good name. To say that he has a right to reputation means that others ought not to take it away from him *i.e.* that others ought not to defame him.

---

1. R.W.M. Dias: Jurisprudence, 4th Edn., p. 301.

4. *Protected and recognized interests:* Every wrong involves some interest attacked by it and every duty involves some interest to which it relates and for whose protection it exists. In other words, if any act is wrong or unjust it means that human interests are pre-judicially affected by it. If these human interests which are prejudicially affected are legally recognised – they will be protected. *Hence those interests which are recognized and protected by the State are called right.* Hence a right is an interest the violation of which is a wrong.
5. *De facto interests has no protection:* Every attack on the interest is not a wrong either in fact or in law; respect for every interest is not a duty, either legal or natural. Many interests exist *de facto* but not *de jure*. Their violation is no wrong and hence is not entitled for protection.
6. *Moral and legal right:* Rights like wrongs and duties are either moral (natural) or legal. A moral right is an interest recognized and protected by a rule of morality. *A legal right is an interest recognized and protected by a rule of law.* It involves an interest the violation of which is a legal wrong and the respect for which is a legal duty.
7. *Legally protected and recognized interest is legal right:* An interest becomes a subject of legal right only when it is legally protected and legally recognized . Cruelty to animals is a criminal offence. But this does not invest the beasts with legal rights. There is *no duty towards* the beasts. There is only a *duty in respect of beasts*. Therefore it can be said that the interests of the beasts are only to some extent protected by law. He who ill-treats a child violates the duty owed to the child. But when a person ill-treats his dog no *vinculum juris* between the man and the dog is broken because there is no bond of legal obligation between him and the dog. Likewise there is no duty which restrains a person from being drunk, but there is a duty not to be drunk while driving. Here duties contemplate a prescribed pattern of behaviour in specified circumstances.[1]
8. *Rights of inanimate objects:* Rights in objects other than men may also vest in temple, idol, corporations, companies etc.
9. *Non-enforceable rights:* Generally legal rights confer power to initiate proceedings to enforce the rights. But there are exceptions like no suit lies to recover time-barred debts. For example: The Limitation Act allows 3 years to recover the debts. Beyond three years though the right is still there the remedy is barred.
10. *Two theories on whether rights and duties are correlatives:* There are two schools of thought. *Rights and duties are correlatives:* Salmond opines that they are correlatives. That is, there can be no right without a duty or a duty without a corresponding right, just as there cannot be husband without a wife and a wife without a husband. For example, if *A* has the right to get some information under the Right to Information Act there must be some authority, a public authority which is under a duty to give the information. Conversely if *A* is under a duty not to disturb the peaceful possession of the property by *B*, *B* must have a right to such

1. R.W.M. Dias: Jurisprudence, 4th Edn., p. 301.

property. Thus, *every right must be a right against some person who owes a duty to such a person; and every duty must be a duty owed to some person in whom the corresponding right vests.* Every right involves a *vinculum juris or a bond of legal obligation, by which two or more persons are bound together.*

Rights and duties are not correlatives: Relative and absolute duties: The opposite school advocated by Austin distinguishes between *relative and absolute duties.* Relative duties are those which have corresponding rights to them. Absolute duties have no rights corresponding to them. This school believes that duty must be owed to some determinate person and not an indeterminate person. On this view, duties towards the public at large or towards indeterminate persons have no corresponding rights *e.g.*, the duty to refrain from committing a public nuisance say noise pollution. The question is: to whom is the duty owed? To *A*, B, C, D...? or the public at large? or to the government? It makes no difference to whom the duty is owed. The law is clear that there is a duty not to create a public nuisance.[1]

IV. Characteristics of a Legal Right

Every legal right has the following characteristics:

1. *Owner of the right:* The right is vested in the person who is the owner of the right. The owner of the right need not be a determinate person. He is the subject of it; the person entitled to it. In case of a bequest in favour of the unborn person the owner of the right is the unborn child. *En ventra sa mere* child in the womb subsequently born alive can also be the subject of the right. When a duty is owed to the society, the society is the subject of inherence.
2. *Subject of duty:* The legal right is available against another person who is under a correlative duty to respect that right. Such a person under a duty is called a person of *incidence* or the *subject of the duty* or a person *bound.*
3. *Content of the right:* It obliges the subject of duty to do an *act or omission* in favour of the owner of the right. This is the content of right.
4. *Subject-matter of right:* The act or omission relates to some thing termed as the object or *subject-matter* of the right.
5. *Legal right has a title*: Every legal right has a title *i.e.*, the facts by reason of which the right has vested in the owner. This may be by purchase, gift, exchange, Will, by inheritance or any other mode of conveyance recognized by law.

---

1. I submit that even in such a case of public nuisance say by noise pollution – the fact remains that a duty is owed to the public at large *i.e.* an indeterminate class of persons. Now if there is a breach of duty by playing songs on loudspeaker so as to create noise pollution, because of which a particular person (or a class of persons) is prejudicially affected and injured that specific person's right is affected and he can maintain an action. Here the duty owed can be said to be diffused until it becomes concrete when a specific person is injured. The situation can be compared to *Carlill* v. *Carbolic Smoke Ball Company* case – where the Company made a general offer to the public at large; it was accepted by Carlill; the contract was deemed to be concluded when the conditions were complied. Thus arose the necessary *vinculum juris* between the Company and Carlill. Hence when she suffered from influenza in spite of taking the pills in the prescribed manner she was allowed to claim damages from the Company; (1893) 1 QB 256.

Thus for example, *A* purchases a house from *B* for Rs. 2 lakhs. here

- *A* is the owner of the right.
- *B* is the subject of duty.
- All other persons also are the subject of duty because the right available to *A* is available against the world at large.
- Content of the right is the non-interference with the purchaser's exclusive use of the house.
- Subject-matter of the right is the house.
- Title of the right is the conveyance deed like the sale deed.

In the same example *B* would be the owner of the right to receive Rs. 2 lakhs from *A* being the consideration amount for the sale of the house. But here the subject of duty is *A* alone as *B* can demand payment from *A* alone. This is because the content of the right is to receive payment from the buyer alone and is therefore available only against the buyer.

Thus every right involves a three-fold relation in which the owner of it stands:

- It is right *against* some person.
- It is a right *to* some act or omission of such person.
- It is a right to *some thing* to which that act or omission relates.

For example, in *State of Rajasthan* v. *Union of India*,[1] the court did not agree with the contention that right to remain as Member of the Assembly and to draw salary for 5 yrs is right to property.

An ownerless right is not recognized by law though it is not a legal impossibility. Yet ownership of the right may be contingent or uncertain. For example, a bequest for the benefit of the unborn person is a contingent right in the unborn person until it is born.

A right must have an owner and also an object in respect of which the right exists. Object of the right is the thing in which the owner of the right is interested. It may be a material thing like a house or land or it may be immaterial thing like reputation, copyright, commercial goodwill, etc.

V. Legal Rights in the Wide Sense of the Term: 3 Senses

Legal rights in the wide sense of the term: 3 senses– Liberties, powers & disabilities

Legal rights in the strict sense has duty as its correlative. In its wide generic sense, a legal right is defined as any benefit conferred upon a person by a rule of law. In this sense, there are 4 kinds of rights: 1. rights (in the strict sense) 2. liberties 3. powers 4. disabilities. Each of these has its own correlatives *viz.*, duties, no rights liabilities, disabilities. The four pairs of correlatives are:

I. Rights and duties (already dealt with)
II. Liberties and no rights
III. Power and liabilities
IV. Immunity and disability

1. AIR 1977 SC 1361 (1401).

The analysis of rights into 4 pairs of correlatives was a matter of slow evolution and reached its culmination with the work of Hohfield. Hohfield built upon the work of Salmond.

1. *Liberty and no Rights*

- A person has liberty when there is an absence of legal duty imposed on him. Liberty implies 'no duties' on the person enjoying the liberty. The sphere of his legal liberty is an area of activity where law leaves him alone without interfering with his liberty. They may take various forms which represent his interests in doing as he pleases. They are things which he can do without being prevented by law. The term right is often used in this wide sense of liberty. He can do as he pleases with his right but he has no right to interfere with what is another's right. I have a right to express my opinion on public affairs, but I have no liberty to publish defamatory material or seditious matter, or obscene material. In this sense, under the Indian Constitution the fundamental freedoms under Article 19 are liberties and the restrictions under Article 19(1) to (6) indicate that the person enjoying the liberties cannot take liberties with the rights of the others. Thus, fundamental freedom of Speech and Expression; of Assembly; of Association; of Residence; of Movement throughout the territory of India; of Profession are all liberties which gives the citizens the right to do as they please but subject to the restriction that they shall not so exercise their liberties as to interfere with the rights of the others as well as with the interest of the Nation.
- Thus Rights in the strict sense (with duty as correlative) concern with those things which others should do for me; rights in the wide sense of liberty concern with those things which I may do for myself. Both are advantages derived from law but they form two distinct species of the same genus.
- It is often said that all rights whatsoever correspond with duties. They believe that a legal liberty is in fact a legal right not to be interfered with by other persons while exercising those activities. They contend that 'no right' means absence of a right in another (say *A*) to obstruct (say *B*) in exercising that activity in respect of which the latter (*B*) has the liberty. For example, an owner of the land has a liberty to eject a trespasser. This means that correspondingly a trespasser has 'no-right' to prevent the owner from ejecting him. But then generally, when law allows an area for lawful activities it also takes care to see that there is no interference in the exercise of this right by others.
- There are instances where liberties are not accompanied by protecting rights. I may have legal liberty which does not have a corresponding duty of non-interference. E.g. though *A* has given me a licence to go on his land, so I have the right to go on his land, but he too can prevent me from going on the land. In this sense, licence has no other effect than to make that lawful which would otherwise be unlawful.

2. *Powers and Liabilities*

- Power is defined as ability conferred by law upon a person to alter his own rights, duties, liabilities or other legal relations or those of others by his own free Will directed towards that end. For example, power to make a Will. *A* will is made by the free consent of the testator without any compulsion either by law or by any one else. The testator makes the Will with the specific intention of making an arrangement for disposing of his property after his death. Thus his action in making the Will is directed towards altering his right, etc. in relation to his property. It alters the legal relations between the testator and the legatee; it would make the legatee the owner of the property bequeathed after the Will comes into operation. Making a Will is a legal right, it is a legally recognized interest; it is an advantage conferred by law. Yet it is different from the classes of rights which has either duty or no-right as the correlative. My right to make a Will does not correspond to a duty in someone else as in the case of *'right-duty'* concept; neither does it correspond to 'no right' as in the case of *liberty 'no right'* concept.

- Other examples of powers are power of sale vested in a mortgagee; power to alienate property; a landlord's right of re-entry on breach of a covenant; the power to sue and to prosecute; the right to rescind a contract when it is voidable; the various powers conferred on the judges and other authorities for the due discharge of their functions.
- The correlative of power is liability. This means the presence of power vested in someone else as against the person with the liability. It is the position of one whose legal rights (in the wide sense) may be altered by the exercise of power. For example, mortgagee has a power to have the mortgagor's property sold for realizing the mortgage debt *means* that the mortgagor has the liability to have the property sold by the mortgagee. It means that the mortgagor has no right to stop the mortgagee from proceeding to get the property sold. In this sense liability may be co-incident with no-right.
- A liability may be an advantageous position. For example, when I exercise my power to make a gift of a property in your favour *Y* who has the property is under a liability to give you the property. The liability is thus beneficial and not detrimental.
- Powers are either public or private. Public powers are those which are vested in a person as an agent of the State. This power is sometimes called authority. Private powers are powers exercised by a person for his own purpose. Private powers are known as capacity.

3. *Immunities and Disabilities*

In the wide sense, right means immunity from the legal power of some other person. The correlative of immunity is disability (inability or no power). It means absence of power. For example, diplomatic immunities; a diplomat has immunity from civil and criminal proceedings. It means the authorities concerned have no power to institute legal proceedings against him. Likewise immunities enjoyed by the members of the Parliament under Article 105 of the Indian Constitution for anything said and any vote given in the Parliament means disability to initiate proceedings in any court in respect of such speech or vote. Likewise *nemo dat quod non habet* means disability to transfer property which a person himself does not own.

To summarise the 4 classes of rights conferred by law are:

Right in the strict sense – when law limits liberty of others on my behalf. It is that which other persons ought to do on my behalf.

Liberty – when law allows me an area of unrestrained activity. It is that which I may do innocently.

Power – when law actively assists me in making my wish effective. It is that which I can do effectively.

Immunity – when law denies to others a particular power over me. It is that which other persons cannot do effectively in respect of me.

Of the 4 classes 'right' in the strict sense *i.e.* having its correlative as duty is the most important.

The following diagram helps in understanding the inter-relation between the 4 classes of rights:

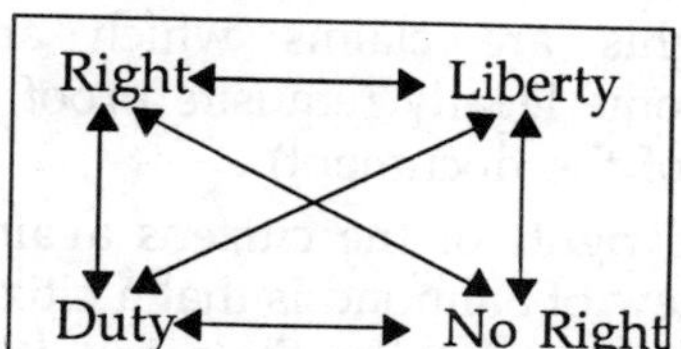

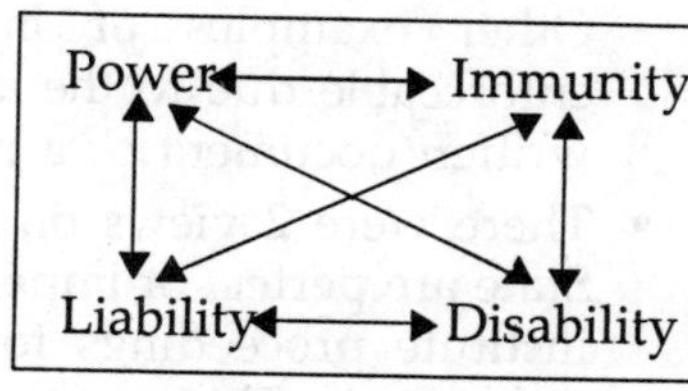

- Vertical arrows connect jural correlatives. It is to be read as "——— — is the presence of ——— *in another*". *E.g.* right is the presence of duty *in another.*
- Horizontal arrows connect the contradictories of correlatives. It may be read as "——— is the absence of —— *in another*". *E.g.* liberty is the absence of right *in another.*
- Diagonal arrows connect jural contradictories. It is to be read as "—— — is the absence of ——— *in oneself*" E.g. no-right is the absence of right *in oneself.*

VI. Kinds of Legal Rights

1. Perfect and Imperfect Rights:

- A perfect right is one which corresponds to a perfect duty. A perfect duty is one which is *recognized and enforced* by law. A duty is enforceable when a civil or a criminal action lies for the breach of it; and if necessary the judgment is executed against the defendant through physical force.
- In all ordinary cases, if the law recognizes the right it enforces it. The rule is *ubi jus ibi remedium,* no right without a remedy. Imperfect legal rights are an exception to the rule. It is a case – where the right is there but the remedy is lost. For example, rights which are lost by lapse of time. The Indian Limitation Act provides a time-limit to execute proceedings. For instituting a suit to recover the debt law provides 3 years from the date on which the debt became due. After 3 years the debt does not get wiped out but the remedy in the courts of law is barred. *That is to say lapse of time does not destroy the right but reduces it from a perfect right to an imperfect right.* The right remains valid for all purposes but not for the purpose of enforcement.

For example, *A* takes a loan of Rs. 10000 from *B* returnable on 1st December, 1990. *A* also pledges his gold ring to secure the repayment. *B* must institute a suit for recovery within 1st December, 1993. if he does not do so, he loses his right to institute legal proceedings to recover the amount. We say that his perfect right has now become an imperfect right. But for other purposes his right remains intact. Thus

- The pledge remains valid. Hence *B* can sell (or cause it to be sold) the gold ring and realize the amount;
- *A* may pay the money in satisfaction of the debt after 1st December, 1993. *A* cannot later recover it on the ground that it was a time-barred debt;
- If *A* acknowledges the debt in writing, the right of action revives and time begins to runs afresh.
- Other examples of imperfect rights are claims which are not enforceable due to the absence of some legally requisite proof (like a written document or a registration of the document).
- There were 2 views on whether the rights of the citizens against the State are perfect or imperfect. The view of Salmond is that a citizen can institute proceedings for a judgment against the State but it is not enforceable. This makes it an imperfect right. The other view of Austin is that a citizen cannot have any rights against the State; that the Sovereign claims obedience from all and owes it to none. And the citizens therefore have no rights against the State. *In the modern days* there is no doubt that the citizens have rights against the State which are perfect rights which have to be exercised subject to certain procedures laid down by the laws. For example in India under Section 80 of the Code of Civil Procedure, 1908 no suit can be instituted unless a two months notice is given to the Government. In England there was a demand for individual rights against the State after the landmark case of Sir Walter Raleigh in the Sixteenth Century.

2. *Positive and Negative Rights*

Positive right corresponds to a positive duty. When *A* has a positive right against *B*, *A* is entitled to something being done by *B*. When *A* has a negative right against *B*, *A* has a right to see that *B* will refrain himself from doing an act which would prejudice *A*. the distinction is of practical importance as it is easier to prevent the harm being done than remedy the harm that is already done. For example, a prohibitory injunction to restrain *B* from encroaching on my land is my negative right and B's negative duty; but a mandatory injunction directing *B* to demolish an illegal structure built on my land is my positive right and *B's* positive duty.

3. *Rights* in rem *and Rights* in personam *(Real Rights and Personal Right)*

- Right *in rem* is a right available generally against the whole world. A corresponding duty is imposed upon the persons generally. It does not mean that the duty is absolutely universal. The duty binds persons in general. If anyone is not bound- then it is an exception.
- A right *in personam* is one which is available against a particular individual only. It need not be against a single individual only. What

is meant is that it is a corresponding duty it imposed upon determinate individuals. My right to recover a debt from the Partnership Firm is a right *in personam*. But the debt may be due from any number of partners.

- The distinction is important in law. For example, my right to the peaceful occupation of my land is a right *in rem*. Hence the world at large is under a duty not to disturb my right. But if I rent out my land, my right to receive rent is available only against the tenant. It is a right *in personam*.
- All rights that arise under the Contract Act by virtue of a contract between the parties are rights *in personam*. They are interests available against the contracting parties. All rights under Torts like a right not to be assaulted, not to be defamed, etc. are rights *in rem*. They are interests protected against the whole world. For example, I contract with *A* to sell all the mangoes grown in my farm. Right to recover the sale amount is available only against *A* as it is a right *in personam*. But my right not to be assaulted is available against the whole world. Now if *A* assaults me, my right to recover damages is available against *A* alone.
- Other examples are: The right of a patentee who has monopoly against the whole world is a right *in rem*; right of the person who has purchased the goodwill of a business is protected only against the purchaser of the goodwill.
- Right *in rem* is generally negative in nature. It is a right to be left alone by the world at large. It is a right to their passive non-interference. Right to reputation is negative right. Rights *in personam* are positive in nature. For example, right to a debt; right to delivery of possession etc.
- *Jus in rem* means a right against or in respect of a thing. Jus *in personam* is a right against or in respect of a person. In truth, every right is at the same time in respect of a thing and also against a person bound.
- The commonest and important kind of *jus in personam* is *jus ad rem*. *Jus ad rem* is a right to a right. Such a right to a right must in all cases be *in personam*. The right which is to be transferred may be a right *in rem* or a right *in personam*, though it is more commonly *in rem*.

4. Proprietary and Personal Rights

Differences between proprietary rights and personal rights

- Proprietary rights are rights concerning property. Man's proprietary rights are also referred to as his 'estate'; his 'property'; his 'assets'. His rights over his house, land, furniture etc. are his proprietary rights.
- Personal rights are his rights regarding his status or person. His rights as a husband, father, mother, are regarding his status.
- Both the kinds of rights have corresponding duties. Example of obligation to pay a debt or deliver the goods is a proprietary obligation. Obligation to drive carefully is a personal obligation. Obligation not to infringe another's copyright is a proprietary obligation. Obligation not to harm another's reputation is a personal obligation.
- Proprietary and personal rights have their corresponding duties, liabilities, no-rights and disabilities.

- Proprietary rights are valuable. They can be calculated in terms of money. Personal rights are not valuable in that sense. They are elements of his well-being.
- Proprietary rights are inheritable. Personal rights are not.
- Proprietary rights may be either rights *in rem* or *in personam. E.g.*, my right to the money in my pocket is a proprietary right *in rem*. My right to the money in the Bank; money which *A* owes me is a proprietary right *in personam*. *A* person's rights of personal liberty; freedom from bodily harm; of reputation are personal and not proprietary. Rights of a husband, father, wife, citizenship, honours, dignities, and official position pertain to personal rights relating to status and not property. A minor's contractual disability is part of his status, but a man's debts are not part of his estate.

5. *Rights* in re propria *and Rights* in re aliena

- The owner of the property has full powers in respect of that property. He has full dominion over the property. This right is known as *jus in re propria*. It is the general right which a person has over his property. Certain rights may be carved out of it and transferred to another person. Such carved out rights are known as rights *in re aliena*. Both rights can be created in respect of the same property. For example, *X* mortgages his house to *Y* to secure the repayment of a loan of Rs. 1 lakh. Jurisprudentially speaking *X* has transferred some of his rights(interests) in the house to *Y* while still remaining the owner of the property. Rights of the mortgagor (owner of the house) *X* is known as jus *in re propria* and the rights of the mortgagee are rights *in re aliena*. Pledge also creates a right *in re aliena* in favour of the pledgee and rights *in re propria* remains with the pledgor who is the owner of the property.
- When rights are carved out of the property as in the above example – the owner of the property no longer enjoys full dominion over the property as he would otherwise have enjoyed. A *right in re aliena* creates an encumbrance over the property.
- Another example is where land is given on rent. The land owner's general right is limited or encumbered by the tenant's right to the temporary use of the property. One encumbrance may be subject to another encumbrance. For example, *A* gives his land on lease to *B*. *B* may sublet it to *C*. Rent in favour of *B* is an encumbrance. Sublease in favour of *C* is a case of one encumbrance itself being subject to another encumbrance. The right subject to encumbrance is termed servient and the encumbrance as dominant. In this sense, in this example, the right of the tenant *B* is dominant with respect to the owner *A* and servient in respect of the sub tenant *C*.
- A right must not be regarded as encumbered merely because of the natural restrictions on them. No rights are absolute. They are always subject to the rights and the interests of others. *Sic utere tuo ut alienum non laedas*- every man must so restrain himself in the use of his property as not to infringe upon the property and rights of the others. While speaking of

rights in *re aliena* we are dealing with the exceptional restrictions due to the existence of *jura in re aliena* and not the normal restrictions represented by the said maxim.

- An encumbrance must run with the right encumbered. Thus if *A* gives his land on lease for Rs. 5000 to *B*; and later sells the land to *D*, *D* acquires the right to recover the rent from *B* because the encumbrance follows the encumbered right into the hands of the new owners. Thus the dominant (that of *B* the lessee) and the servient (that of *A* the owner) rights are concurrent. Other examples of encumbrances running with their servient rights are mortgages and easements.
- Concurrence of the dominant and the servient rights exists in different degrees. It may be concurrent either at law or at equity. When it is concurrent at equity it is imperfect because it is not available against the purchaser for value and without notice of the dominant right. For example, agreement for a lease, equitable mortgage.
- Chief classes of encumbrances are 4:
- Lease – right to possession and use of land vests in another person.
- Servitude – right to limited use of land but not accompanied by possession or ownership.
- Security – is an encumbrance vested in the creditor over the property of his debtor for the realization of his debt.
- Trust – is an encumbrance where there is an obligation annexed to the ownership – *viz.* to deal with the property for the benefit of someone else.

6. Principal and Accessory Rights

A principal right is the main right vested in a person under the law. An accessory right is a secondary right which arises out of the principal right. A right can be affected by the existence of another right. It may be affected in a beneficial manner or in an adverse manner. When it adds or supplements the right vested in the *same owner* it is beneficial. When it limits or qualifies another right vested in a *different owner* it is adverse. For example, *A* pledges his gold ring to *B* to secure the repayment of a loan of Rs. 10,000. *B's* primary right is his right to recover the loan. His right to sell the ring to realize the amount is his accessory right which is beneficial in nature.

7. Primary and Secondary Rights

- Sanctioning right originates from some wrong. It is a right to initiate an action against the wrongdoer.
- Primary rights have a source other than a wrong. Primary right can be either a right *in rem* (my right not to be assaulted) or a right *in personam* (my right that you perform your contract with me). But sanctioning right is always a right *in personam*. When my primary right not to be assaulted is violated by *X* my sanctioning right is available against *X* only. Likewise, if *X* who has committed a breach of contract with me, my sanctioning right is available only against *X*.

- Rights *in rem* are negative in character (right to be left alone without disturbing personal freedoms). They are available against an indefinite class of persons. Violations of such rights consist of positive acts which can be performed by specific persons only. Hence sanctioning rights are rights in personam.

8. Legal and Equitable Rights

- In England, legal rights were those which were recognized by the courts of Common Law. Equitable rights (Equities) are those which were recognized solely by the courts of Chancery. The Judicature Act of 1873 did not abolish either law or equity, but brought a fusion of law and equity. Yet the distinction is important. In India, we do not have separate courts of law and equity. When laws are silent, the courts act in accordance with justice, equity and good conscience. Under Section 151 of the Civil procedure Code – the court has plenary powers to pass such orders as it deems fit in the interest of justice. Under Article 142 the Supreme Court has powers to pass such orders as it deems fit in the interest of doing complete justice.
- Legal and equitable rights differ in the following 2 aspects:
- *Methods of creation*: a legal mortgage of land must be made by a deed. An equitable mortgage can be created by a written agreement or by a deposit of title deeds. *In India,* under Section 58 of the Transfer of Property Act, 1882, equitable mortgage can be created by the deposit of original title deeds with an intention that the property comprised by the deeds shall operate as security for the loan advanced.
- *Efficacy:* Legal rights are more efficacious. When there are 2 inconsistent legal rights or 2 inconsistent equitable rights claimed adversely by two different persons over the same thing- the one prior in point of time prevails. But when there is a competition between a legal and an equitable right, legal right prevails over equitable right even if the equitable right is prior in point of time than the legal right provided the owner of the legal right has acquired it for value and without notice of the prior equity. *In India,* under the proviso to Section 48 of the Registration Act a registered mortgage and an equitable mortgage stand on the same footing - a subsequently registered mortgage will not take priority over the prior equitable mortgage.
- In England, mortgagor's right to redeem is an equitable right.
- In India it is a statutory right.
- In England, a contract to sell property creates an interest in favour of the purchaser and so the seller holds the property in trust for the purchaser. In India, contract to sell property creates no interest whether legal or equitable in favour of the purchaser. There is only an obligation annexed to the ownership of the property.

9. Vested and Contingent Rights

A vested right is a right which is sure to take place, a contingent right is a right which takes place on the happening or non-happening of an uncertain event. A grant of land to *A* gives him a vested right in the property. By 'a grant of land to *A* for life and then to *B* if he survives *A*' gives *B* a contingent right.

CHAPTER 17
CONCEPTS: OWNERSHIP

SYNOPSIS

I. The Idea/Concept of Ownership

Even by ordinary parlance, ownership is a right to do anything you choose with what belongs to you. Salmond defines Ownership as the relation between a person and an object which forms the subject-matter of his ownership. It is a complex of rights which are all rights *in rem*. They are good against the whole world. Thus when we say that *A* is the owner of a house – we are speaking of the relation that *A* has with the house in terms of various rights.

According to Austin, ownership is a right over a determinate thing, indefinite in point of user, unrestricted in point of disposition, and unlimited in point of duration. In other words, ownership is a right over a specific, identifiable thing; with no restriction over the manner of disposing of the property. The owner can sell it or gift it or exchange or bequeath it; and with no time limit for ownership. Once an owner you continue to remain an owner until you decide to part with the rights.

a. The five incidents/characteristics of ownership are as follows:

As Ownership implies a plenary control over the object of ownership. Following are the 5 incidents of ownership:

1. *Right of possession:* The owner has the right to possess the thing he owns. He may not have the actual possession of it. What is important

is that he has *the right to possess it.* If *A's* watch is stolen by *B, B* has the actual possession of it which is wrongfully obtained, but *A* remains the rightful owner of it with an immediate right to possession. If *A* gives his car on hire to *C, A* now has neither the possession nor the immediate right to possession. He is still the owner of it because he has the right to repossess it on the termination of the period of hire. Such a right to repossess is known as the right of reversion. He can even institute an action in the court to protect his reversionary right.

2. *Right to use and enjoyment:* The owner has the right to use and enjoy; to manage it as he likes. This is in fact a right in the wide sense of the term *viz.*, a liberty. The owner has the liberty to use the thing *i.e.* others have no right to interfere with the use of his 'right of use and enjoyment.' He himself also is under no duty not to use it.
3. *Right of consumption, alienation and destruction:* The owner can consume the thing over which he has ownership and exhaust the thing. He may alienate/transfer it in accordance with the existing laws. He may transfer it during his life-time. He may leave a Will under which his property will be disposed of according to his intentions after his death in accordance with the provisions of the law. A non-owner cannot transfer property even if he is in possession of it. This is based on the maxim *nemo dat quod non habet*- no person can transfer better than what he himself has. Under exceptional cases mentioned in the Indian Contract Act and the Sale of Goods Act even a non owner can transfer the property. *E.g.* a pledgee can sell the goods in his possession under certain circumstances[1]. Under the Sale of Goods Act a carrier can sell the goods in his possession when the goods are stopped in transit. In the following cases, pledge by a non-owner is valid:—Pledge by a mercantile agent[2]; pledge by a seller in possession after sales, pledge by a buyer in possession before sale[3]; pledge by a co-owner in possession, pledge by a person in possession under a voidable contract.[4]
4. *Indeterminate duration:* There is no time limit for ownership. Non-owners who are in possession of the thing are entitled to use or possess the thing for a specified time. It has to be returned back after the time. For example, if the lease is for 5 years the lessee must give back the possession after 5 years. Likewise, interest of the bailee comes to an end after the purpose of bailment is over. But the owner's interest is perpetual. Even after his death his heirs or his legatees get the property.
5. *Residuary character:* For example, the owner has leased his land to *A* and an easement right say a right of way to *B*. His ownership now consists of the residuary rights after these lesser rights have been given away. When these lesser rights are extinguished by say passage of time or because the purpose is over all the original rights revive in favour of the owner of the property.

---

1. Section 176 of Indian Contract Act, 1872.
2. Section 178 of Indian Contract Act, 1872.
3. Section 30 of Sale of Goods Act, 1930.
4. Section 178A of Indian Contract Act, 1872.

It is sometimes argued that the term ownership is not applicable to English law because in a case to establish title to property the plaintiff has to only prove that he has a better title than the defendant and not that he has the best title. For example, *A* finds a golden ring. *B* dispossesses it from him. *A* has to prove that he has a better title than *B*. His ownership is good against the whole world except the true owner.

To say that the owner's property is unencumbered does not mean that he has completely unlimited rights. When *A* is described as an absolute owner of the property it means two things:

- That *A* has a clear and an indisputable and a marketable title to the property.
- That he has all the ownership rights allowed by the legal system in question. Ownership rights may be limited by adverse dominant interests of an encumbrancer *e.g.* an easement right. Easement right is a right which *A* has over *B's* property say a right of way or a right to draw water from the well on *B's* land. Here, *A* is the encumbrancer. Encumbrancer himself is the owner of the encumbrance. Encumbrance limits the right of ownership, though by itself it is also a right. The encumbrance is a right in *re aliena.* Likewise adverse dominant interest may be in the form of possession by a tenant whose right of use and occupation limits the right of the owner. Ownership rights may be limited by Town Planning Laws. It is also restricted by ordinary laws of the land. Thus though the title may be indisputable the mode of use and the manner of disposition may be restricted and regulated by the laws of the land.

II. The Subject-matter of Ownership

A man's primary properties are his land and his chattels (goods). But it may include things like interests in other's lands; debts due to him; shares in a company; patents; copyrights; and his interests in trust funds, right to catch fish in another's pond.

1. *Salmond: Subject-matter of ownership was in all cases 'a right'.*

Salmond took the view that the true subject-matter of ownership was in all cases 'a right'. Yet in lay and legal usage, it is natural to speak in terms of owning a land or chattels. Further a man is said, usually *to have a right.* We don't speak in terms of owning a right. For example, we speak in terms of *having a right to free speech or reputation and not in terms of owning the right to reputation. Further one cannot sell or lease his right to reputation. Society regards only certain rights as marketable and therefore only such things can be the subject-matter of ownership. Hence it is preferable to speak both in terms of owning material objects and also the rights. What things form the subject-matter of ownership depends upon the rules of the particular legal system.* At one time, even slaves could be owned; women could be the subject-matter of ownership. But this is history. *Res communes i.e.* air, water in the sea cannot be owned due to their very nature. Possession of stars and moon and sun are altogether not practicable.

When a thing can be owned it may be acquired by the operation of law for example, (intestate succession vests the property of the deceased in his heirs;) or by some act or event (by original acquisition).

2. *Shift of emphasis from absolute ownership to restrictions on ownership to privatization of property:* Ownership no longer has the same pre-eminence that it had centuries ago. From absolute rights we have reached a stage where the owners are made to have regard to the needs of the society. Legislations are passed to prevent exploitation of the tenants; legislations are passed to stop the property developers from building without regard to the general environment; rules prescribe for space to be left for gardens and parks; rules are there prescribing the FSI (floor space index) and the set backs while constructing the buildings. Much that was in private hands has been passed over to the public sectors and to the society in general. But with Globalisation and with countries including India signing GATT emphasis is once again gaining on privatization.

III. Sole Ownership and Co-ownership

Ordinarily a thing is owned by one person only at a time but duplicate ownership is also possible. Examples of duplicate ownership are co-ownership and Trust.

- When two or more persons own the same thing at the same time they are said to be co-owners. There is undivided unity which is vested at the same time in all of them. For example, co-ownership by the partners of the firm. They are co-owners of the goods which constitute their stock-in-trade, of the lease or ownership of the premises; and of the debts owed by their customers to the firm. For example, if 2 partners have Rs. 10,000 in the Bank Account of their partnership. It means that there is a single debt of 10,000 that is owed to them and not two debts of Rs. 5,000 to each of them. Each partner is entitled to the whole debt. Likewise if the firm owes Rs. 10,000 to the Bank each would owe the whole amount of Rs. 10,000. Partition dissolves co-ownership and what emerges is the sole ownership. All the co-owners have reciprocal obligations of restricted use and enjoyment.

1. Co-ownership: Ownership in Common and Joint Ownership

Co-ownership may assume different forms by reason of different incidents attached to it. The two main forms in English law are: Ownership in common and joint ownership. The most important difference is in connection with the effect of death of one of the co-owners. Suppose *A* and *B* are the co-owners

- *In case of ownership in common:* On *A's* death, his rights devolve upon his heirs and successors like any other inheritable right. The co-owners possess the property *per mie* but not *per tout i.e.* per parcel but not per the whole.
- *In case of joint ownership:* It devolves upon the surviving co-owner *B*. *B* then becomes the sole surviving owner. *A's* heirs get nothing. This right of the surviving co-owner to take away the interests of the deceased joint owner is called *jus accrescendi i.e.* the right of survivorship. The co-owners possess the property *per mie* and *per tout i.e. per parcel per the whole.* Therefore the joint owners take the entire property.

2. *Fragmentation of Ownership in Respect of Time*

The rights of ownership can be split between several persons on a temporal plane. A landowner wishing to provide for his sons *A* and *B*:

- May constitute them co-owners or
- He may divide the land into 2 parts and give one to each as a sole owner.
- he may convey land to *A* for life and thereafter to *B*. Here neither son becomes the sole owner of the land nor co-owners. *A* has a life estate vested in possession. *B* has a fee simple remainder in interest not in possession.

The third method enabled the owner to make provision for his sons and also keep the property intact.

IV. Trust and Beneficial Ownership

(a) Trust is an instance of duplicate ownership. It provides for separation of the powers of management and the rights of enjoyment. Trust is an obligation annexed to the ownership of the property. Trust property is that which is owned by two persons at the same time. Thus if *A* gives property to *B* on trust to be used for the benefit of *C*, *B* is the trustee having trust ownership (bare ownership as called by Prof. Campbell); *C* is the beneficiary (*cestui que trust*) having beneficial ownership and *A* is the direct owner of the property. As between the trustee and the third parties the trustee is regarded as the owner of the property. As between the trustee and the beneficiary the beneficiary is the owner. The trustee has no rights of beneficial ownership. He has to utilize and manage the property for the benefit of the beneficiary. His ownership is therefore a matter of form than substance; it is nominal rather than real. Under the Indian Trust Act the trustee is described *as the owner of the property*. The trustee's ownership is in law; the beneficiary's ownership is in equity.

(b) Trust ownership and beneficial ownership are independent of each other in their destination and disposition. In the above example, *B* may assign his trust ownership to *X*, without affecting the beneficial ownership. Likewise *C* the beneficial owner may assign his ownership to *Y* without affecting the Trust ownership.

(c) The purpose of trusteeship is to protect those who are unable to protect themselves. Following are the 4 classes for whose protection generally a trust is created:

- To protect and administer the property for the benefit of unborn persons.
- To protect and administer the property for the benefit of lunatics, infants or of those who are absent.
- Where a large number of persons are interested in common to manage the complexities that arise when the number of co-owners is very large.
- Where persons have conflicting interests in the same property - as in the case of an owner and an encumbrancer or different kinds of encumbrancers in order to safeguard their interests.

(d) A trust involves separation of trust ownership (which is in the trustee) from beneficial ownership (which is in the beneficiary) and vests them in different persons. Hence, the direct owner of the property can declare himself to be the trustee for another person who becomes the beneficial owner and the direct owner gets the trust ownership.

(e) At times a constructive trust is created. Here a person holds the property under such circumstances that it becomes inequitable for him to disregard the claims of others.

(f) Trust and contract:—

- Contracts were enforced in the courts of law whereas trusts were enforced in the courts of equity.
- Though a trust is normally created by an agreement, Trust may also be created unilaterally as where a person creates a trust by his own declaration or conduct while the beneficiary knows nothing.
- Even when a trust is created by a bilateral act no formal offer and acceptance is needed as in contract.
- The rule that a stranger to the contract neither acquires rights nor incurs liabilities has no application to the trusts. It is the beneficiary who benefits from the trust to which he is not a party.
- Contract creates a right *in personam* available against the promisor. The beneficiary's right resembles a right *in rem* as it is enforceable against all third parties, except a bona fide purchaser for value.[1]

(g) Trust and agency:—

Trust and agency are similar to the extent that both the trustee and the agent manage the property on behalf of others. Following are the differences:

- At law trustee is the owner of the property. In agency, property vests in the Principal *i.e.*, the person on whose behalf the agent acts.
- A trustee can give good title to the bona fide purchaser for value without notice of the trust, an agent cannot do so except under some exceptions.
- A trust always involves property that is the subject-matter of the trust. Agency need not necessarily do so.
- A trustee being the legal owner is personally liable on all contracts entered by him in respect of the trust. But when an agent enters into contract with a third party in his capacity as an agent the contract is with the Principal and the agent is generally not personally liable.

V. Legal and Equitable Ownership

Legal ownership had its origin in the rule of common law in England. Equitable ownership proceeds from rules of equity.

The distinction between legal and equitable ownership is not the same as between legal and equitable rights discussed before. These two forms of

---

1. Dias P. 404 (However there are some who assert that the beneficiary's interest is *in personam*. What the beneficiary owns is the totality of his interests which mainly consists of the due discharge of duties and exercise of powers by the trustee. His ownership lies in the totality of claims *in personam* against the trustee.

ownership would still exist even if all rights were legal. Equitable ownership of a legal right is a different thing from the ownership of an equitable right. When a debt is orally assigned by *A* to *B*, *A* remains the legal owner of it but *B* becomes the equitable owner of it. But for this reason there are no two debts. There is only one debt with two owners. The thing which *B* equitably owns is a legal right which is at the same time legally owned by *A*.

The distinction between legal and equitable estates has little importance in Indian law. Such distinction is not recognized under the Indian Trust Act. The trustee is the legal owner of the trust property and the beneficiary has no direct interest in the trust property itself. He has the right against the trustee as the owner of the property. In India a contract of sale does not create any interest in the property in favour of the buyer. Even if the purchaser pays the price and takes possession of the property he does not become its owner until the sale is completed in the manner prescribed. These circumstances may raise certain equities in his favour like a charge on the property for the money paid and can sue for specific performance of the contract.

VI. Vested and Contingent Ownership

Ownership is either vested or contingent. It is vested when the owner's title is already perfect and so he owns it absolutely. It is contingent when the title is imperfect but is capable of being perfect on the fulfilment of some condition and so he owns it conditionally. A vested interest is one which is sure to take effect. It does not depend on any condition. A contingent interest may or may not take effect depending on the happening or non-happening of the event.

An interest created in favour of a person is said to be vested under the following 4 circumstances in India under the Transfer of Property Act:

a. Where no time is specified for it to take effect. For example, *A* gifts a plot of land to his daughter *B*. *B* takes a vested interest in the land as there is no time limit prescribed for it to take effect.
b. It is expressed to take effect forthwith.
c. If it is expressed to take effect on the happening of an event which must happen. For example, if *A* transfers property to *B* for life and on his death to *C*, *C* takes the interest after *B's* death. Death of *B* is sure to happen. Hence *C's* interest is vested interest even during the lifetime of B. He has a present fixed right of future enjoyment on the death of B.

Contingent Ownership

Where on transfer of property an interest is created in favour of a person to take effect only on the happening or not happening of a specified uncertain event the interest is said to be contingent interest.

When the interest depends on *the happening of the event* the interest does not take effect until the event happens. For example, *A* creates an interest in favour of *B* to be paid to him if he attains the age of 18 years. Until *B* attains 18 years the interest is contingent (for it may so happen that *B* dies before completing 18 years). Thereafter it is vested.

When the interest depends on the non-happening of the uncertain event the interest does not take effect until the happening of the event becomes an impossibility. For example, *A* transfers an interest in the property to *B* if a particular ship which is on a voyage does not reach a particular destination within 15 days. The ship drowns. It now becomes impossible for the ship to touch the destination. The contingent interest becomes vested. Contingent ownership depends upon the present existence of an incomplete title. It is more than a mere *spes successionis. Spes successionis* is a chance that a person will inherit or acquire an interest in the property. It cannot be transferred.

If the transferee dies before obtaining the possession the contingent interest fails and the property reverts to the transferor. Contingent interest is not heritable and not transferable whereas vested interest is transferable, divisible and heritable.

Condition precedent and condition subsequent:

A condition precedent is one which has to be first fulfilled before the interest can take effect. Hence the condition precedent involves an investitive fact.

Condition subsequent is one where the interest has taken effect subject to be divested on the happening of the condition subsequent. Hence the condition subsequent involves a divestitive fact. In other words, the transferee becomes the owner but if the condition subsequent happens his ownership ceases. Hence it is to be noted that ownership subject to a condition subsequent is not contingent but vested.

CHAPTER 18

POSSESSION

SYNPOSIS

Introduction

I. Nature of Possession

1. Basic Relationship between Men and Things

2. Possession: Neither a Purely Legal or a Purely Factual Question

3. Unlawful Possession also Protected

II. Possession and Ownership

1. Different Forms: Custody-holder; Detention; Possession; Ownership

III. Possession in Fact

1. *Corpus possessionis* and *Animus possidendi*

(a) *Corpus possessionis*:

(i) Power to Use and to Hold

(ii) Continuous Control – Not Necessary

(iii) Extent of Power

(iv) Power of Excluding others

(b) *Animus possidendi*

(i) *Intention to possess*

(ii) *Animus* – Manifested in three Degrees

IV. Possession in Law

1. Protection of Possession

(a) Sanctioning Rights in Personam

(b) Criminal Penalties

(c) Legal Criteria to Determine Possession

(i) Common Sense Criteria

(ii) Complicated Situation

(iii) Constructive Possession

(iv) Illustrations

(v) Possession in Law without Knowledge

(vi) Possession – A Temporary Title

V. Kinds of Possession

1. Immediate and Mediate

2. Corporeal and Incorporeal

3. Concurrent Possession

4. Juridical Possession

VI. Acquisition of Possession

1. Taking

2. Delivery

a. Actual Delivery

b. Constructive Delivery

INTRODUCTION

We have examined the concept of ownership in the previous chapter. Ownership and possession are closely linked as jurisprudential concepts. In this chapter we will study and analyze the concept of possession.

I. Nature of Possession

1. Basic Relationship between Men and the Things

Possession in ordinary parlance means the capacity to deal with a thing physically. To make living meaningful and to have a peaceful enjoyment of the material things possession is needed. If possession is wrongfully taken away law provides ways and means of restoration of possession. Possession is the most basic relationship between men and the things, says Salmond.

2. Possession: Neither a Purely Legal or a Purely Factual Question

Possession is difficult to define as it is an abstract concept with different meanings in different contexts. For example, I may owe a car; *B* may have the right to possess as it is given on hire to him; I may have taken loan from the Bank to purchase it and hence the Bank may have a right to take the possession if there is a default in payment of the instalments; *C* may steal it from *B's* possession giving a right to *B* to complain and take back the possession. Meanwhile, *D* may steal it from *C* and *C* will have a better claim to possession as compared with *D*. Thus, possession is neither purely a legal concept nor purely a factual question.

3. Unlawful Possession also Protected

Possession must be understood in its various dimensions. Question that arises is why should law protect even *unlawful possession*? This is a favourite question for jurists and philosophers. Three main reasons for the protection of possession advanced were[1]

- It *aids criminal law* by preserving peace because interference with possession has always invited violence. Order is best secured when possession is protected and the true owner is left to seek his remedy in the courts of law.
- Possession is protected as part of law of tort.
- Possession is protected as part of the law of property.

The concept of possession is surrounded with complexity because there is an inevitable conflict between the logic(reasoning, theory) of law and the demands of convenience. The fact that possession was there long before laws governing possession came into existence had its own typical consequences[2]. Legal theory attempts to discover the underlying common thread and judges may not be able

1. Paton: Text book on Jurisprudence, p. 501.
2. Paton: Text book on Jurisprudence, pp. 501, 503-04.

to use that thread in all the cases, hence they attempt to do justice in individual cases before them. Hence Paton observes that English law has never worked out a completely logical and exhaustive definition of possession. This would be true of any legal system including our Indian system.

II. Possession and Ownership

1. Different Forms: Custody-holder; Detention; Possession; Ownership

1. Ownership denotes the relation between a person and the object forming the subject-matter of ownership. Possession is the most basic relationship between men and things. *It may be in the form* of[1]
   - *Custody-holder* Where he lacks full control of the thing or has no intention (*animus*) to exclude others e.g. customer examining a ring in the presence of the jeweller.
   - *Detention* – Full physical control in fact which for some reason is not regarded as possession in law.
   - *Possession* – Legal possession. In most cases the legal concept of possession centres around the idea of physical control. Yet each legal system has 'anamolous' cases where a person in full control in fact is denied possession in law; or where one with no physical control in fact at all is accorded the right of possession.
   - *Ownership*
2. Ownership is more permanent than possession unless possession is accompanied with ownership.
3. Ownership is strictly a legal concept. Possession is both a legal and a non-legal concept.
4. Possession is primarily a matter of fact. Ownership consists of certain legal rights. It is a matter not of fact but of law. The two concepts are therefore used to distinguish between *de facto* possessor of an object and its *de jure* owner between the man who actually has it and the man who ought to have it.
5. Ownership and possession have the same subject-matter. Whatever may be owned may be possessed and whatever may be possessed may be owned. There was a time when trade marks, copyrights, could be possessed without ownership. The legal scenario has changed with the majority of the countries signing GATT. Today we have patent and copyright laws, wherein intellectual property is protected at law also. For example, in India we have the Patents Act, (As amended in 2005 it has recognized both process and product patent.); Geographical Indications Act, 1999. There are rights which can be owned but not possessed because it is transitory. For example, *B* owes Rs. 10,000 to *C*. *C* the creditor owns a right to recover the debt, but it cannot be possessed because as soon as B pays back Rs. 10,000 the right of ownership goes away and there is no question of possession at all.

---

1. Paton: Text book on Jurisprudence, pp. 501, 504-505.

Generally, rights *in personam* do not admit of possession. Exception is where there is a repeated use as in the case of an easement right of way over another's property.

III. Possession in Fact

Mental and Physical Element

Characteristics of possession: Power to use; continuous control; physical control not necessary; extent of power; Power of excluding other people Animus possidendi.

1. ***Corpus possessionis and Animus possidendi:*** According to Salmond, possession consists of *corpus possessionis* and *animus possidendi*:

(a) *Corpus possessionis*: It is the physical element. It has the following characteristics—

(i) *Power to use and to hold*: It is the power to use the thing possessed and existence of the grounds for expectation that the possessor's use will not be interfered with.

Possession in fact is the relation between the thing and the person. Hence ordinarily, it implies physical control over the thing. Actual holding of the pen or a purse or any other object in one's hand; wearing of the clothes, a ring on the finger, a cup of tea in your hand etc. are simple routine examples which are obvious examples of actual possession.

Things which are humanly not possible of possession like sun, moon, stars cannot be the subject-matter of possession.

(ii) *Continuous control – not necessary*: To possess a thing it is not necessary that one must be able to exercise a continuous control over the thing. What is important is that one must be able to resume control whenever he wants. In a primitive society, where there were no laws for protection of possession it could be said that exercising actual control is the only evidence of possession. But in today's society, law protects possession and provides legal remedies when the possession is illegally taken away. Hence there can be more varieties of possession like possessing intellectual property rights.

(iii) *Extent of power*: Whether the physical control is sufficient enough to be regarded as possession depends on various factors, extent of power is a deciding factor. Complete absence of power means absolutely no possession. But this does not mean that to have possession one must have absolute power over the subject- matter. The extent of power required to constitute possession depends upon the nature of the object. Higher the degree of control, stronger is the proof of its possession. Possession of small objects would be in holding it. Even immovable property like a house can be possessed while miles away from the house.

(iv) *Power of excluding others:* When there is absence of actual control - it is relevant to find out whether there is the intention and the ability and power to exclude others and whether law penalizes others for any such interference.

and

(b) *Animus possidendi*: It is the mental element in possession. It has the following characteristics:

(i) *Intention to possess*: It is the intention to possess and appropriate the thing to oneself. There must be an intention to exclude others from possessing it; exclusion need not be absolute; it need not be specific it may be general. *A* may intend to possess all the utensils in the cupboard though he may have forgotten the existence of some of them. He may intend to possess all the coins and the money in his pocket though he may not know the exact cash he is carrying. It is neither necessary nor feasible for him to continuously keep thinking of possessing the objects concerned. General intention to possess them is sufficient. In other words, if his attention is drawn to the question of possession he would assert his intention to possess.

(ii) *Animus* manifested in 3 degrees:

- highest degree of intention: is manifested by totally excluding all others and denying the right of all others to the thing.
- a lesser degree of intention is manifested by persons like bailee, lessee, usufructee mortgagee who possess the property for various purposes and intend to possess the property until the purpose is served and at the same time recognize the superior and the outstanding right of others *i.e.* the owners. Their possession is derivative.
- lowest degree of intention is of persons like servants and agents who merely protect the possession without any intention of asserting any rights in the property on one's own behalf. Such persons are known as representatives.

IV. Possession in Law

1. Protection of Possession

Law protects possession in two ways:

(a) *Sanctioning rights* in personam: The possessor has a right *in rem*, right available against the world at large that he would enjoy his possession without any interference. It is protected by sanctioning rights *in personam*. These sanctioning rights give the possessor civil and criminal remedies against those who violate his primary right.

(b) *Criminal penalties*: Law protects possession by prescribing criminal penalties for wrongful interference and for wrongful dispossession.

(c) *Legal criteria to determine possession*: Before the remedy can be granted it has to be necessarily ascertained whether the plaintiff who complains of interference was actually in possession of the object mentioned. This requires legal criteria to determine whether a person is in possession of an object. *These criteria may be*:

(i) *Common sense criteria*: If the legal system applies only the criteria of common sense then law would consider man to possess only those things of which he is in actual possession. In such a case possession in law would coincide with possession in fact.

(ii) *Complicated situation*: The first criteria is a simple and a straightforward approach to finding out who has the possession of the article. But then possession in fact is a complicated concept as seen above. The nature of the article involved, the attitude and activities of the others would give rise to borderline cases where law has to refine the concept of possession. Thus if I lose a 1000 rupee note when I go to *B's* house and it is found by *C*; or say C sees it but has not yet picked it up, who can be said to be in rightful possession of it. This situation cannot fit into a *straight jacket* solution as above.

(iii) *Constructive possession*: Legal protection is not restricted to actual possession. If *A* wrongfully takes possession of *B's* watch law gives possessory remedies to *B* on the ground that *B* originally had the possession and he ought to have it. This is done by regarding the dispossessed person *as being in possession at law for legal purposes.* This is known as constructive possession. This is a case without even being in actual possession he is deemed to be in possession by a legal fiction. Conversely the actual possession of another person is brought on a lower footing than legal possession.

(iv) *Illustrations*: The crime of larceny theft provides several illustrations. Theft is taking another's goods without his consent with an intention to deprive him permanently of the object stolen. But when *A* gets into an innocent possession of a jewel with consent of the shop owner, law regards the owner as being in possession and *A* as having only the custody of the object and now if *A* runs away with it he has the actual possession of the jewel but it is without the rightful possessor's consent and therefore *A* is guilty of wrongful taking of the possession.

- a bailee who fraudulently misappropriates the goods bailed is guilty of stealing under the Indian Contract Act. Thus his initial possession is lawful but later he commits larceny or theft of the goods.
- if I buy a cupboard in which some valuables are hidden in a secret drawer and the seller never intended to give the possession of the valuables, if I appropriate the valuables it will amount to larceny in English law, though factually possession of the cupboard would include possession of its contents. Here again physical possession is less than legal possession.
- Under the Transfer of Property Act *A* lets out his house to *B* on rent for 5 years. *B* continues to occupy beyond 5 years without the consent of *A*. In legal fiction it is tenancy at sufferance and not trespass. This is because possession is lawful in its inception and wrongful in its continuance.[1] *A* can proceed to recover possession by any legal means straight away without giving him a notice to

1. *Mozam Sheikh* v. *Anand Prasad,* AIR 1942 Cal 341.

quit – but he cannot use force to throw him out. Now suppose *B* the tenant at sufferance is dispossessed by a trespasser *C*. *B* has two remedies against *C* to recover possession. He can sue *C* under Section 6 of the Specific Relief Act, 1963 within 6 months of the dispossession based on the strength of his initial lawful possession. The other remedy is to file a suit within 12 years on his possessory title under Article 64 of the Limitation Act and not proprietary title (title deeds need not be produced). But if C proves his title to the property *B* will have to prove better title or fail.[1]

(v) *Possession in law without knowledge*: At times possession in law is possible without knowledge. If you take a ring lying in my pool you commit a trespass to goods. Though I had no knowledge of the existence of the ring, I possess it in law.

- If I lose my wallet I still retain the possession of it in law. This is because lost articles are deemed to be in the possession of the loser. To lose the legal possession of a thing law requires that I must terminate my intention to retain my rights over it.
- Thus it is to be noted that sometimes possession is possible without knowledge of the subject-matter and sometimes such knowledge is necessary. Common law is not concerned with who has the best title. It is concerned with who has a better right to possess.

(vi) *Possession – a temporary title*: In several legal systems including our legal system possession is a provisional or a temporary title even against the true owner himself. A wrongful possessor who is deprived of his possession can recover it from any person whosoever simply on the ground of his possession. Section 6 of the Specific Relief Act, 1963.

- Of all the divergences between legal and actual possession the most notable is that outside the law, possession is used in the absolute sense whereas within law it is used in a relative sense. Outside law we say that a person has or does not have possession. In law we speak in terms of having possession against another.

V. Kinds of Possession

Possession can be classified into the following heads:

1. Immediate and mediate
2. Corporeal and incorporeal
3. Concurrent possession
4. Possession in fact and in law (already dealt with above).

1. Immediate and Mediate Possession

Possession acquired or retained directly or personally is immediate possession. Possession held by one man through another is termed as mediate. If I purchase a book myself I am in immediate possession of it. If I ask my friend to buy it for me I acquire mediate possession through him. Once he hands it over to me my possession becomes immediate.

---

1. *Nair Service Society Ltd* v. *Alexander*, AIR 1968 SC 1165.

There are 3 types of mediate possession:

a. When I acquire possession through an agent or a servant who *holds it on my account* and claims no interest in the property. The Supreme Court has held[1] that if the agent is not obedient or amenable to directions from the principal or the master, possession by the former cannot be regarded as possession by the latter.
b. Direct possession is in one who *holds both on my account and on his own* but recognizes my superior right to obtain it from him *whenever I choose to demand e.g.* a borrower or a tenant at Will.[2]
c. Immediate and direct possession is in a person who claims it for himself until some time has elapsed or some condition has been fulfilled. He is prepared to deliver it when his temporary claim has come to an end. For example, I pledge my gold ring to *B* as a security for a loan of Rs 10000 Even here as against the third persons I still retain possession. In other words, as against the entire world except *B* the ring is still in my possession. Another example is delivery by attornment. *A* bought a horse from *B* and without any change in immediate possession he lent the horse to seller himself to use as a bailee for one month. It was held that the horse was effectually delivered by *B* to *A*.

Thus in all cases of mediate possession two persons are in possession of the same thing at the same time as in the case of landlord and tenant; bailor and bailee etc. Another example of mediate possession is in the law of prescription. Long, continuous and uninterrupted use of another's land for 12 years or more makes you the owner of the land. Suppose *A* takes wrongful possession of *B's* land; holds it for 6 years and then leases it to *C* for a term of years. After 6 more years – *A* gets a good title as against *B* because as against *B A* has been in continuous possession for 12 years (including 6 years for which he has rented out the premises to *C*).

2. *Corporeal and Incorporeal Possession*

a. Possession of a *material object* is corporeal possession. Incorporeal possession is the possession of anything *other than the material object*. For example, possession of land is corporeal possession. Possession of a right of way or right to light is incorporeal possession.
b. Corporeal possession involves the continuing *exercise of exclusive control* over the material object. Incorporeal possession is the continuing *exercise of a claim* to anything other than the material object. It may be an interest unconnected with the use of material object like a trade mark, a patent or an office of profit.

---

1. *Chiranjitlal* v. *Union of India*, AIR 1951 SC 41.
2. For creating a lease fixing the duration is a must. If duration is not fixed and the lessor puts the lessee into possession of the property the lease is not invalid because the tenant has entered into possession with the permission of the lessor. Lessee is not a trespasser just because the lease does not fulfil the essential condition of fixing the duration of lease. The lessee is a tenant at Will. His tenancy is determinable (can come to an end) at the Will of either the lessor or the lessee. A demand by the landlord for possession determines the tenancy at Will. *Jhalku Singh* v. *Chandrika Singh*, AIR 1961 Pat 350.

c. What is more important for corporeal possession is the existence of the *legal right to exercise exclusive control* and not the actual exercise of such exclusive control. When I lose my mobile phone I still retain the legal right to exclusive control though I have lost the actual control over it. In the case of incorporeal possession it may be thought that I must actually enjoy and exercise the right in order to possess it. Yet, if I have an easement of way over another man's land, mere non-use will not extinguish it. It may constitute evidence of abandonment. Likewise, I continue to possess various rights in *rem* like right to my reputation, my liberties under Article 19 of our Constitution like my liberty to leave the country, my liberty of speech, of movement within the country, of residence, of Assembly, of profession or trade, etc. though I may never actually exercise them or seek to enforce them.

d. Corporeal possession is called the possession of a thing. Incorporeal possession is called as the possession of a right.

e. Under the Transfer of Property Act, 1882, exception to Section 11 provides an example of incorporeal possession. Suppose *A* is the owner of two properties a land X and a house *Y* which are adjoining each other. He sells the land X to *B* and retains the house with himself. For the more beneficial enjoyment of his house *Y* he can impose a condition on *B* to keep a portion of the land open and free and not to construct on it so as to affect light and air to his house *Y*. This condition (covenant) is an incorporeal right available to A and he can enforce it against *B*.

3. *Concurrent Possession*

It was the maxim of civil law that two persons cannot possess the same thing at the same time (*Plures eandem rem in solidum possidere non possunt.*) But claims that are not destructive of each other; which are not adverse to each other can be held by two persons at the same time. Following are the cases of concurrent possession:

a. Mediate and immediate possession co-exist in two persons at the same time as seen above.

b. Two or more persons may possess the same thing in common just as they may own in common.

c. Corporeal and incorporeal possession may co-exist. For example, B has a right of way over *A's* land. *A's* right is corporeal and *B's* right is incorporeal.

4. *Juridical Possession*

The expression juridical possession is the same thing as legal possession in a more impressive form.[1] For example, a possession cannot be said to be juridical where it is taken behind the back of the defendant who seeks to evict him as soon as he learns about his dispossession.

VI. Acquisition of Possession

Modes of acquisition are two:

---

1. *Rahimbux Ashan Karim* v. *Central Bank of India,* AIR 1929 Cal 497.

1. *Taking*

It is the acquisition of possession without the consent and co-operation of the previous possessor. It may be actual or constructive.

2. *Delivery*

Delivery is the acquisition of possession with the consent and co-operation of the previous possessor. It is of two kinds - actual and constructive:

a. *Actual delivery* – It is transfer of immediate possession. It is such physical dealing with the thing as transfers it from the hands of one person to those of another. Delivery by sale is an example of delivery without any mediate possession. Delivery of keys of the house is delivery of the house itself because it gives access to the house.

b. *Constructive delivery*: It is that which is not actual. It is of 3 kinds.

(i) *Traditional brevi manu* – Surrender of the mediate possession of the thing to the person who already has the immediate possession of it. For example, I lend a jurisprudence book to a student to read. While he still has the possession of it I gift it to him. As he already is in possession of the book what is required is the intention to gift it which can be expressed by just telling him to keep it for himself.

(ii) *Constitutum possessorium* – *I.e.* an agreement touching possession. It is the transfer of mediate possession while the immediate possession remains with the transferor. I buy 100 bags of cement from a warehouseman. He agrees to hold them on my account. The goods are delivered to me as soon as this agreement is entered into. It is as though I have taken the delivery of the cement and then brought them back to him and deposited for safe custody.

(iii) *Attornment* – It is the transfer of mediate possession while the immediate possession remains outstanding in some 3rd party. *E.g.* I have 100 bags of cement in the godown of *A* and I sell them to *B*. I have effectively delivered the 100 bags as soon as *A* agrees with B to hold them on account of him and not on my account. In all cases of constructive delivery goods are not physically transferred. It is the intention the *animus* of the persons concerned which suffices.

3. *Continuous of Possession*

We have seen that acquisition of possession involves control over the subject-matter and some intention to exercise control over it. But the continuance of legal possession does not necessitate the continuance of either of these factors. For example, I retain the legal possession of all the furniture and the utensils in the house even if I am out of the house and hence I have no control over it. Likewise continuance of legal possession does not depend on continuance of intention. Thus even if I forget that I possess my wallet, in law I am not prevented from still being in possession. Possession is lost in law if one loses his control of the subject-matter and also gives up the intention of resuming the control.

VII. Possessory Remedies

The legal remedies which exist for the protection of possession are known as possessory remedies. Those which exist for protection of the ownership are known proprietary remedies.

In several legal systems possession is regarded as nine points in law. Possession operates as a temporary title even against the true owner. Even a true owner cannot throw out the wrongful possessor by using force. He has to take recourse to legal measures for recovery. If the true owner has forcibly taken possession it has to be first restored back to the wrong doer and then taken steps to establish ownership. The reasons why possession must be protected have already been discussed above.

Under the Specific Relief Act, 1963 Sections 5, 6, 7, 8 deal with possessory remedies.

1. A person entitled to possession of specific immovable property may recover it in the manner provided by Section 5 of CPC, 1908.
2. If a person in possession of immovable property whatever be his title, is ousted illegally from his possession without his consent is entitled to recover back his possession. But the condition is that he must institute the suit within 6 months of his dispossession. All that the plaintiff has to prove is that he was in possession and that he has been ousted illegally and without his consent. However any other person can establish his title to such property and recover the possession. Section 6. But no such suit can be instituted against the Government.
3. A person entitled to the possession of specific movable property can recover the property in the manner provided under the Civil procedure Code. *E.g.* a warehouse keeper is charged with the delivery of certain goods to *Z*. *B* dispossesses the *Z* of the goods. *Z* can sue *B* to recover the same.
4. If a person has possession of a movable article and he is not the owner of it he can be compelled to *specifically deliver* it to the person who is entitled to the immediate possession of it. Section 8

VIII. Other Remedies

1. Other method of recovering property is by instituting a suit based on title by ownership.
2. Part performance: A person who has taken possession of an immovable property in part performance of a contract to sell the property to him cannot be ousted as being a trespasser because the other legal formalities like registration etc., have not been completed. Possession offers him the protection from being treated as a trespasser. Section 53A of the Transfer of Property Act)

Three rules regarding possessory remedies and the English law:

1. Prior possession is *prima facie* proof of title.
2. The defendant can always prove better title and defeat the plaintiff.
3. If *A* has violated the possession of *B*, he (A) cannot take up the defence that some third person *C* has better title than *B*. *e.g.* *A* is in possession of a car stolen by *B*, in a suit filed by *A* against *B* – *B* cannot tell the court that neither *A* nor he himself has good title because *C* has the title to the car. This doctrine is known as *jus tertii* which is also recognized under our law.

CHAPTER 19

CONCEPTS: LEGAL PERSON

SYNOPSIS

INTRODUCTION

Hitherto we have analysed about rights, duties, powers, immunities, possession, ownership etc. The obvious reference is to the rights etc. of men as human beings. But can animals, idols, temples, mosques, companies and Corporations also possess rights and liabilities is an interesting study under this Chapter on the Law of Personality.

I. Clarification Regarding the Use of the Term 'Person' an Artificial Creation of Law

One is accustomed to using the term 'person' in its ordinary parlance to mean a human being with flesh and blood. This is not the sense in which it is used in legal parlance. It has acquired a special meaning. For a clearer understanding of the term as law students it is desirable to clear some of the confusion at the outset.

As observed by Paton[1] the Latin word *persona* was the equivalent of the Greek *prosopon.* It originally referred to the mask worn by actors in a play to personify God and to represent God. It was later extended to refer to the part played by a human being in legal proceedings and to all sorts of publicly recognized offices or capacities. That human beings and legal persons were not one and the same; that they were not synonyms was quite evident in the classical times when the system of slavery existed wherein slaves were human beings but not legal persons. By the sixth century Boethius defined *personality* as the individuality of a rational being. However the concept of human personality became the centre of intellectual controversy. Legal person and legal personality are an artificial creation of law with its own peculiar features. It is not to be confused with the term person as is understood by a non-legal person. It should be noted that the term has acquired a special meaning.

II. Nature of Personality

A person is any being whom law regards as having rights and obligations and liabilities. Human beings can of course have rights etc., and so they are persons. Human being is the focal point of 'person' and personality is identified by the presence or possession of characteristics peculiar to mankind *i.e.* power of thought, speech, and choice. But *in law* there are men who possess these characteristics but still are not 'persons' recognized as such by law. For example, in the olden days slaves did not enjoy legal personality. Slaves themselves were regarded as property possessed by their masters. The masters owned the slaves; they could be traded like cattle and treated like animals. *Slaves could thus be the object of rights and not the subject of rights.* A monk who enters a monastery is regarded in some systems as being 'civilly dead' and his property is distributed just as if death had in fact taken place.[2] Under the Hindu Marriage Act, 1955 if

1. Paton: A text book of Jurisprudence, 3rd Edn., p. 350.
2. Paton: A text book of Jurisprudence, 3rd Edn., p. 353.

the whereabouts of a person are not known by persons who would have normally known, for a period of more than 7 years it is termed as 'civil death' and divorce proceedings can be filed. Conversely, at law there are persons who are not human beings but still are regarded as legal persons like a joint stock Company, a Corporation.

Under the Indian Penal Code a 'person' includes any Company, Association or a body of persons whether incorporated or not.

III. Attributes of a Legal Person According to Salmond

(a) A person or an entity whom law regards as capable of having rights and duties. This is the distinguishing feature.
(b) Such a person need not be a human being.
(c) Any being who is not capable of having rights is not a legal person even if he is a human being.
(d) Persons are the substances of which rights and duties are the attributes.
(e) Only if the above characteristics are present persons possess juridical significance.
(f) Personality receives legal recognition only from this exclusive point of view. In other words whether the thing is capable of rights and duties is the yardstick with which to find out whether it is a legal person.

IV. Persons are of 2 Kinds: Natural and Legal

(a) Natural person is a human being as understood in its ordinary parlance.
(b) Legal persons are beings – real or imaginary, who are treated as human beings in greater or lesser degrees. Legal persons are also termed as juristic, artificial, fictitious or moral persons. This is personification of the beings which are not in fact human beings. E.g. Corporation is a legal person. It is not a human being but it is treated like human being and is imputed with rights, duties, capacity to purchase property, it can sue or be sued etc. The thing so personified *i.e.,* the corporation in this example is known as the *corpus* and law infuses *animus* (intention) into it.

Personification has the advantage of simplicity of thought and speech. It is an artifice/pretence/trick of speech devised for compendious expression. Device of personification is widely used. We say that the estate of the deceased person owes debts, or has debts owed to it or that it has become insolvent. But then the estate of the deceased person is not a legal person. The rights and liabilities vest in the executors, administrators and the heirs and not upon an artificial person known as estate. For example, under the Indian Succession Act, 1923 the estate of the deceased person immediately vests in the legal representatives, the executor and the administrator of the deceased until it is distributed to its rightful heirs or legatees.[1] It does not remain in abeyance.

Likewise groups of persons are personified. For example, we speak in terms of *'the jury giving its verdict'*; it is in fact the jurors who have given the verdict here we are personifying the jury, but jury is not a corporation; likewise when we say the *'public meeting passed a resolution'* we are personifying the meeting of a group of persons. It is the convenience of language and the easy way to

1. Section 211.

communicate the message or the thought; when we say the *'court passed the judgment'* we are personifying the court. In fact it is the judges who have passed the judgment. But court is not a juristic person; it cannot be sued; it cannot hold property or assign it.[1] What is to be noted is that *mere personification does not make the thing a juristic person.* Legal personality is reached only when law recognizes the associated individual as a single entity which represents them but is not identical with them.

V. Three Main Kinds of Legal Persons

Legal persons being the creation of law to attain some purpose it can be of as many kinds as the law pleases. Following are the three main types: Corporations; Institutions; and funds or estates for special uses

1. *Corporations:* It is a group or series of persons which is treated as a person by a legal fiction. Corporations are of two kinds – corporation aggregate and corporation sole.
2. *Institutions*: A temple, a church, a hospital, a university a library may be regarded as a legal person. Law attributes legal personality to the institution itself.
3. *Funds or estates for special uses*: A charitable fund, a trust may be endowed with legal personality.

Whether law regards any of the three above as a legal person depends upon the rules of the particular legal system. For example, under the Karnataka Universities Act, University is a legal person with a seal and a perpetual succession of its own; a Company incorporated under the Companies Act, 1956 is a legal person.

VI. Agent, Beneficiary and Members of a Corporation

Another important point to be noted is that

- Every legal person has corresponding to it agents or representatives in the world of natural persons through whom it acts.
- It also has beneficiaries for whose benefit it exists and fulfils its functions.
- The beneficiaries and the representatives may be the same persons or they may be different persons. For example, take the case of a Company X with 1000 shareholders. *A* director may be one of the shareholder. The director is the beneficiary and also shareholder.
- In the case of a corporation established for a charitable purpose the beneficiary may have no share/role in the management of its affairs.
- The representatives and beneficiaries must not be confounded with its members. The members are the individuals who form the group or series personified by law and who constitute the corpus of the legal person thus created.
- Shares of the company may be held by other companies. In this sense members of a corporation are themselves a corporation. In case of Mutual Fund Companies the Company itself is a shareholder of different Companies. Here the idea of incorporation is duplicated. Law

1. *Sadhu Madho Das* v. *Pandit Mukund Ram,* (1955) 2 SCR 22.

creates a legal person by the personification of a group of persons who are themselves only legal persons.

Corporation aggregate	Corporation sole
It is an incorporated *group of co-existing persons.*	It is an incorporated series of successive persons.
It has several members at a time.	It has only one member at a time. It is the successive holders of some public office who constitutes the legal person.
They are far more numerous and more important	They are fewer in number and not as important as corporation aggregate
Examples are: A registered company with shareholders as its members; the property of the company is not the property of the shareholders; shareholders are not bound by the debts and liabilities of the company; shareholder can enter into a contract with the company; under the Companies (Amendment) Act company can buy its own shares. In short the Corporation aggregate and its members are distinct from each other.	Examples are: The Sovereign in England; the Prime Minister in India. On the Prime minister's death – his personal property passes to his heirs; when he vacates his office, the property held by him as corporation sole passes to his successor in office; the Comptroller General in India.
The incorporated group is treated as a person by legal fiction.	The legal fiction is that law assumes that there is a natural person who carries out his duties in the office and there is a mythical person in law, – who in law, is the real occupant of the office – who never dies or retires. The natural living person is the agent through whom the legal person performs his duties

VII. Corporations and Unincorporated Partnerships

A firm is not a person in the eyes of law unlike a company. It is not a legal entity as in the case of a company. The debts and the property of the firm are the same as the debts and the property of the partners. Hence his liability for debts of the firm is unlimited. Decree against the firm can be executed against the partners. A decree against the Company cannot be executed against the shareholder. A partner cannot contract with his firm the way in which the shareholder can contract with the company. This is because the firm does not have a distinct identity separate from that of the partners. Death of a partner in a firm dissolves the firm unless otherwise provided in the agreement. A company continues in existence irrespective of the death or retirement of the shareholder. There can be no firm with just one partner, whereas a company can exist with just one shareholder also.

VIII. Limited Liability Partnership in India

Limited Liability Partnership (LLP) Act has been passed in India in the year 2008. LLP is a body corporate and it has a legal entity separate from that of its partners, has a perpetual succession- as in a Company and unlike a

Partnership under the Indian Partnership Act. Like a Company it also has a perpetual succession of its own. Members may come and members may go but the LLP remains subject to the provisions under the Act. It has a minimum of two members. However no maximum number is prescribed unlike under the Indian Partnership Act. If the number is reduced to less than two and the business carried on beyond 6 months with only one partner, with the knowledge that business is being carried on with him alone, such person shall be personally liable for the obligations of LLP incurred during that period. Indian Partnership Act is not applicable to the LLP.

Thus, unlike under the Indian Partnership Act, where the partners are personally liable- under LLP Act – as under the Companies Act- LLP and its partners are different legal persons and hence partners under LLP are not personally liable for the liabilities of LLP. An obligation of the LLP arising in contract or otherwise shall be solely the obligation of the LLP and the partner shall not be liable solely on the ground that he is a partner of the LLP. Section 27(3) & 28(1). But this does not affect his personal liability for his own wrongful act or omission but a partner shall not be personally liable for the wrongful act or omission of any other partner of the LLP.

Schedule I determines mutual rights and duties of the partners *inter se* and also that between the LLP and its partners in the absence of any agreement to the contrary between the partners.

Under Section 26 every partner is an agent of LLP but not of other partners as under the Companies Act and unlike the Indian Partnership Act. Liabilities of LLP shall be met out of the property of LLP.

The LLP is liable if its partner is liable to any person as a result of a wrongful act of omission on his part in the course of business of the limited liability partnership or with its authority. In other words – the partner would not incur any personal liability if the wrong is in the course of the LLP business, for which the LLP would be liable and not the partners. (Section 27).

Under Section 28 of LLP Act a partner incurs no personal liability solely by being a partner of LLP. He shall be personally liable for his own wrongful act or omission but not for wrongful act or omission of any other partner of LLP.

Under Section 30 the partners and the LLP incur unlimited liability for an act of the LLP or its partners done with an intention to defraud creditors of the LLP or any other person or for any fraudulent purpose.

It is opined that having regard to the way in which the public is being duped by the large Finance entities- it is desired to make the liability of the persons or Companies or Firms dealing with people's money – a strict liability where 'intention to defraud' would have no say; and the liability would be determined on the basis of the resulting consequences and the partners/Directors are held personally liable by even attaching their personal property.

IX. Advantages of Incorporation

1. *Efficient management:* When a large number of individuals have a common interest and have to act in common in the management and protection of their interest, incorporation makes things manageable and the working becomes efficient. Imputing a legal personality helps in saving time, energy, cost and facilitates quick and prompt decisions and action. For

example, with thousands of persons having an interest in a commercial activity who should enter into contracts; who should call for meetings; who should file a case and a plethora of such questions arise. Here the concept of incorporation makes things manageable.

2. *Perpetual succession*: Perpetual succession has its own advantages. Members may come and members may go but the corporation continues to function.
3. *Continuity of management and protection of interest*: In a corporation sole a series of persons who come into existence one after the other having a common interest and the action taken by one in the capacity of corporation sole will be binding on the successor and ultimately it procures *continuity of management and protection of interest.*
4. *Limited liability:* Incorporation as a Company enables traders to trade with limited liability, unlike in a partnership firm where there is unlimited liability.
5. *Personal property – distinguishable*: Incorporation helps to distinguish personal property of the shareholders from that of the Company.
6. *Freely transferable shares:* Freely transferable nature of the shares is another advantage. The shareholder can sell his share in the open market without going to the company to withdraw his investments.
7. *Suits*: A body corporate can sue and be sued in its own name.

X. Acts and Liabilities of a Corporation

1. *No Will of its own*: A Corporation cannot have a Will of its own and so it is incapable of acting on its own *i.e.* in *propria persona*. It can confer authority upon an agent to act on its behalf either by the (a) Will of some human beings identified by law for this purpose [for example, the Articles of Association of a Company may appoint the First Directors. The Will or the volition of these persons is the Will of the company] or by (b) the law itself.

2. *Can sue and be sued*: The Corporation can sue and be sued. But it cannot be sued unless the act done was within the scope of the agent's authority and within the purpose of the incorporation. The Memorandum of Association lays down the purpose of the Company and the limits within which its representatives must act. An act done by the representative within the limits so laid down and for the purposes and those incidental thereto are binding on the corporation on the principle of vicarious liability. The principle of vicarious liability is similar to one under the Torts where the master or the Principal is held liable for the acts of his servant or the agent respectively. An act done beyond the legally permissible limits and beyond purposes mentioned in the Memorandum of Association are not binding on the corporation even though done on its behalf as they are said to be *ultra vires* and therefore *null* and *void*. Even the unanimous consent of the whole body of shareholders cannot authorize the company to act beyond the limits so laid down.

In England, the law is settled that a corporation can be held responsible for wrongful acts; acts in which malice, fraud or other wrongful motive or intention is necessary. A company may be sued for libel, malicious prosecution or deceit. They can incur both civil and criminal liabilities.

3. *No action for personal wrongs*: A Corporation cannot maintain an action for personal wrongs because by their very nature such injuries cannot be inflicted on a Corporation.

An idol of a Hindu temple or a mosque is a juristic person and hence can be sued in respect of tort committed by its manager.

4. *Jurisprudential thoughts about liability of the Corporation:* Salmond opines that the concept of *ultra vires* is necessary because the corporation has no Will. But then the counter argument is that law can always regard the Will of the human beings who are the representatives of the corporation as the Will of the corporation itself.

The question that would arise is how fair is it that the shareholders should be punished for the acts of the agents of the corporation? But then though in form they are the agents of the corporation, in substance they are the agents of the beneficiaries *i.e.* the shareholders.

The other question that may arise is : How can the corporation be held liable if the agent has exceeded his authority? For then it would not be the act of the corporation. The answer could be that the legal person cannot in person do what it ought not to do (liability in commission); yet it can in person fail to do what in law it ought to do (liability in omission). Apart from this, liability may arise by the application of the law of employer's liability. The responsibility of a master does not depend upon any authority given to his servant to commit a wrongful act. For example, I authorize my servant to drive a car. I don't authorize him to drive negligently. In fact I also give instructions to drive carefully in the ordinary course of general instructions. Yet if he is negligent I become liable.

Thirdly, the question arises: If the agents do *ultra vires* act the corporation or the beneficiaries may be prohibited from taking advantage of it but why should they be held liable for such *ultra vires* act. The answer is that the corporation like any other employer is liable for the injurious acts of its agents or servants.

XI. Double Capacity and Double Personality

The idea that a man can hold more than one capacity and act in different capacities has helped in making the concepts of legal personalities effectual and workable. Take the example of a company which acts through its director. The director is a human being, as such he has his personal capacity under which he enters into personal contracts; he may inherit his father's property. In his capacity as a director of the company he represents the Company and so he enters into business contracts; he purchases property for the Company etc. He may be a trustee of a Charitable trust, as such he manages the trust property etc. Thus the same individual may fill in different capacities. This is a legal imagination with lot of advantages in performing several activities without mixing up the roles. Often he has power to do certain acts in representative capacity which he would have no power to do in his individual capacity.

The important point to be noted here is that:

1. *No legal transaction with himself*: The mere fact that a man has two or more capacities does not give him the power to enter into a *legal transaction with himself*.

2. *Double capacity does not mean double personality*: Thus a man cannot sue himself or contract with himself though he has different capacities on each side. This rule worked practical hardships. Yet with some exceptions the rule still remains unimpaired even today. For example, under the Transfer of Property Act, 1882 one living person can transfer property[1] to another living person *or to himself* as where he creates a trust and he himself becomes the sole trustee.
3. *Indian examples:* In India too, the same position prevails. For example, under Section 35 of the Transfer of Property Act, 1882, dealing with the doctrine of election when the person who has to elect, holds two capacities, he may elect in one capacity and dissent in the another. For example, *A* has only a life interest in a particular immovable property. And after his death it is to go to *B*. Now *A* gives the estate to *D* and to B Rs. 2000 and Rs. 1000 to *C* who is *B's* son. *B* dies intestate without making the election. *C* becomes the administrator to *B's* (his father) estate. As administrator *C* elects to keep the estate and relinquises Rs. 2000. He can do so and still claim Rs. 1000. What is to be noted is that C has acted in two capacities: As a representative of his deceased father and another in his own personal capacity

XII. The State as a Corporation

A modern state today is engaged in multifaceted activities involving every facet of a person's life and comfort. The question is: Whether the State is a corporation with a legal personality and having all its citizens as members owing allegiance to it and being entitled to protection by it. This is a difficult question to answer. In England there is fiction that Crown *i.e.* the King, not as a natural person but as a body politic, a corporation sole. King includes the Queen has a legal personality; public liabilities are those of the King; whatever is done by the State is in law done by the King; it is royal justice administered by the King through his servants *i.e.* the judges; laws are King's laws which he enacts with the advice and consent of his Parliament; the executive Government is the King's Government which he carries on through his ministers; likewise it is the King's army; the King's Navy etc. Offences against the State are offences against the King. Citizens of the state are not fellow members of one body politic and corporate but fellow subjects of one sovereign lord. Hence State is an organized society but not body corporate.

In India, the Constitution is supreme; all legislative, executive and judicial acts, actions and policies must be in tune with the Constitution; Constitution is given to us by ourselves *i.e.* the people. So the people acting through the representatives whether (elected or nominated) are supreme. These representatives constitute the body politic by name State. The State can be considered to be the corporate body consisting of 3 distinct departments: the legislature, the executive and the judiciary. In case of Companies registered under the Company's Act there is a corporation aggregate governed by the Memorandum of Association and the Articles of Association. Here we have a corporate body wherein the constitution serves the purpose served by the Memorandum of Association and the Articles of Association for it lays down the

1. Section 5 of the Transfer of Property Act, 1882.

purpose, the functions, the powers, the limitations and practically every aspect necessary for the functioning of the State. It is like the people are the creators and also the beneficiaries of a trust or the corporation; the elected or nominated representatives and the holders of constitutional and other public offices are the trustees who are under the mandate of the Constitution to discharge their duties and functions in accordance with the provisions of the Constitution. The President and the Governor are similar to the Directors of the Corporation in whose name action is taken, with a difference that the President and the Governor have to act in accordance with the aid and advice of the Council of Ministers. Laws are passed and contracts are entered into by the State in the name of the President or the Governor who can be compared to the Corporation sole. Hence in India the legal opinion is in favour of considering State as a corporate body.

XIII. Creation and Extinction of Corporation

Law determines the birth and death of legal person *and not nature* as in the case of natural persons. They come into existence at the will of the law and they can be dissolved in the manner provided by law. Corporations may be established by Royal Charter, by statute, by customs and in recent years even through agreements. By their very nature they can be of indefinite duration. The corporation continues to live even if the last of its member is dead. The corporation sole is merely dormant during the interval between two successive occupants of the office, it is not extinct. The extinction of the body corporate is known as dissolution. It severs the legal bond which has held its members together.

In India, we have corporations like the Life Insurance Corporation of India and Indian Oil Corporations which are created by statute. In addition there are any number of Companies registered under the Companies Act.

XIV. Theories about Corporations

There are three theories:

1. *Fiction theory*: According to this theory corporations do not possess any real existence or real personality at all. The misleading feature here is that the lawyer indulges in make-belief. In case of works of fiction the characters indeed lack existence but in case of corporation it is not so. The attributes of a real person are assigned to the corporation for easier management of the affairs.
2. *Realist theory*: It speaks of corporation as possessing a real personality. It is also unsatisfactory. To say that: when I contract with a corporation I have really contracted with a mysterious entity explains nothing at all but creates confusion.
3. *Bracket theory of Ihering or abbreviation theory*: It postulates that in truth a corporation is nothing other than its members and that statements about corporations are disguised abbreviations for statements about all its members is also not satisfactory. For example, if X and Co. owe a debt of Rs. 100 to me it does not mean that each of the members owe me a debt of Rs. 100.

The personality of the corporation thus is neither wholly real nor wholly fictitious. It is *quasi*-real and *quasi*-fictitious.

XV. Unincorporated Associations

There is no such legal person as 'unincorporated association'. In law they are nothing more than group of members. They vary in size and importance. In India freedom to form associations is a fundamental right. It may be a small association to promote cultural activities at a college level, at a residential locality level; it may be an association to cater to the needs of the locality; to tackle the day to day problems regarding roads, water, electricity, cleanliness etc. or it may be trade unions and other professional bodies. The rights and duties of such an association are nothing more than that of its members. The legal position is that the members are all contractually related with each other. The moment a member joins the association he automatically enters into a contract with all others and are bound by the rules of the society or the club etc. The law pertaining to unincorporated associations has still not developed. It can work hardship to both the non-members and the members themselves. For example if a non member supplies goods to a club he can proceed only against those members who have personally made the contract and those who have authorized the contract as principals. For in law there is no such entity as a club. A member may be expelled from his office resulting in social and economic loss or ruin to him, the courts will interfere only to see whether the bodies have acted according to their rules and the rules of natural justice. They will not consider appeals against facts.

Midway between corporations and unincorporated associations stand entities like partnership firms and trade unions. Under the Indian Partnership Act a registered firm has several advantages but registration is not compulsory. A trade union can be a registered or unregistered or a recognized one under the Indian Trade Unions Act, 1926. It is only a registered Union which enjoys immunity from civil and criminal proceedings. However it has been held by J. Krishna Iyer in *Mumbai Kamgar Sabha* v. *Abdulbhai,*[1] that even an unregistered union can espouse the cause of the union. Likewise for filing a public interest litigation it is not necessary that an association must be an incorporated one.

XVI. Legal Status of Animals

1. *Lower Animals:* Human beings are the only natural persons. Beasts or lower animals are neither natural persons nor legal persons. According to Salmond they are only things- they are the objects of legal rights and not the subject of legal rights.
2. *Interests are not recognized:* People who own the animals may possess rights in respect of them. For example, if my horses suffer injuries because of your negligence I will be entitled to claim damages from you. But it is no legal wrong to the beast. It hurts the animal physically, but the legal wrong is done to me; or to the society of mankind. Animals have interests like men but their *interests are not recognized* and protected by law the way in which the interests of the men are protected. The acts of the animals are neither lawful nor unlawful. This is because they cannot distinguish right from wrong; just from unjust; they can neither be imputed with *mens rea* nor strict liability.

---

1. AIR 1976 SC 1455.

3. *No duties to be discharged*: They have *no duties to be discharged*. They are only designed for carrying out some functions which are assigned to them by nature or at times as may be expected of them when they are trained. *Hominum causa jus constitutum* the law is made for men and allows no fellowship or bonds of obligation between them and the lower animals.
4. *Two cases where the beasts possess legal rights:* There are *two cases where the beasts may be thought to possess legal rights.* Firstly, cruelty to animals is a criminal offence and secondly a trust created for the benefit of a particular *class of animals* as opposed to one for individual animals is valid and enforceable as a public and charitable trust. Duties towards animals are conceived as duties towards society.
5. *Trust for individual animals*: If a private trust is created for the maintenance of the pet animals of the testator it does not create a trust enforceable by or on behalf of the non-human beneficiaries. The only legal effect is that the trustees would be authorized to spend the money in the manner indicated and the amount not so spent will go to the testator's representatives as undisposed of.

XVII. Legal Status of the Dead Men

1. Dead men are no longer persons in the eyes of law. They are regarded as things. They have no rights and no interests.
2. Law recognizes 3 things in which he would have been interested when alive: *his body, his reputation and his estate.*
   - *The Body:* The corpse is the property of no one. It cannot be disposed of by Will or other instrument. A permanent trust for the maintenance of a man's tomb is illegal and void. A dead body is supposed to belong to nobody and cannot be the object of theft. However showing indignity to a human corpse is an offence.
   - However under the Human Organs Transplantation Act in India detailed procedures are laid down for human organ transplantation; the whole body also can be dedicated to a hospital for the purpose of research after his death for the benefit of humanity. Hence in these modern days in order to keep in tune with the progress in medical science even a Will to such an effect can be given effect to by the representatives of the deceased or else a person can donate his organs or body as the case may be during his lifetime itself and his wish has to be obviously given effect to after his death
   - *Reputation: De mortuis nul nisi bonum* one must not speak anything but good about a dead person. Hence a libel upon a dead man is punishable under the law only when its publication is in truth an attack on the interests of the living persons and is intended to be hurtful to the feelings of his family and relatives (Section 499 IPC). The right so attacked and defended is in truth, that of the living heirs and relatives of the deceased.
   - *Estate:* This is the most important matter where even after the death of a person his wishes are respected and given effect to. Each legal system has its laws pertaining to testamentary succession.

XVIII. Unborn Persons

1. A man can own property even before he is born. His ownership is necessarily contingent upon his being born. Yet his ownership is present and real. Law permits property to be settled on the unborn child under the Transfer of Property Act, 1882. A benefit can be created in favour of unborn person by a Will subject to rule against perpetuity under which law lays down rules to ensure that property does not remain without vesting in a living person for too long.
2. A child in the womb later born alive is by a legal fiction considered to be a child in being for the purpose of acquisition of property by the child itself or being a life chosen to form part of the period in the rule against perpetuities. Under the Hindu law a person can even reopen the partition effected by the other coparcenors and challenge the alienations made while he was in the womb of his mother.
3. A pregnant woman sentenced to death cannot be executed until she has delivered the child.
4. Abortion is a criminal offence except when it is under the provisions of the Medical Termination of Pregnancy.

CHAPTER 20

TITLES

SYNOPSIS

INTRODUCTION

'Titles' are an important legal concept which determine the right or 'no right' to the property. In the previous chapters, we have dealt with rights, ownership and possession. In this chapter, we will study about the concept of title which has a close link to rights and ownership.

I. Vestitive Facts

1. No Right without a Title

Title is the *de facto* antecedent; right is its *de jure* consequent.: Every right involves a title or a source from which it is derived. Right is used here in its wide sense so as to include privileges, powers and immunities. The title is the *de facto* antecedent of which the right is the *de jure* consequent. For example, I purchase a plot of land from *B* for Rs. 2,00,000 and the sale is registered at the sub-registrar's office. I obtain the sale deed which is my title deed. Now I have a legal right of ownership to the property. Obviously my title is based on the fact that

I have purchased the property from *B* and completed all the legal formalities like registration etc. It is only then that I derive a right in the property. Hence *my title depends on the fact of purchase and my right is its legal consequence.* This is what is meant by: *title is* de facto *antecedent of which right is the* de jure *consequent.* Whether a right is inborn or acquired, a title is required. For example, title to a debt may be a promissory note or a contract; title to life, liberty and reputation is the fact of being born as a human being.

2. *Titles are of Two kinds*

a. *Original title*: Original titles create rights for the first time *i.e.* a right *de novo*.

b. *Derivative title:* Derivative titles are those that transfer an existing right to a new owner.

For example, catching a fish is an original title of the right of ownership. It is a new right created for the first time. Nobody else had the right before him. When the fisherman sells the fish the buyer acquires a derivative title. Note that in legal theory no new right is created. That right which the fisherman has lost by selling the fish is acquired by the purchaser by the purchase. Hence that which is lost is identical with that which is acquired. *The essence of title is that it determines the acquisition of rights whether old or new and that it is linked to facts. It may be said that title is the cause and rights is the effect. Right is to be understood in the wide sense.*

3. *Facts Establishing Title are of Three Kinds: Vestitive, Investitive and Divestitive*

- Vestitive fact is one which either creates or destroys or transfers rights.
- Facts which create title are investitive facts. Facts which destroy title or alienate title are divestitive facts.
- Investitive facts may result in original titles or derivative titles.
- Original titles create rights.
- Divestitive facts may be either alienative facts or extinctive facts.
- Alienative facts result in transfer of rights.
- Extinctive facts divest a right by destroying it. Alienative facts divest a right by transferring it to some other owner.
- Derivative titles and alienative facts result in transfer of rights. As such they are not different classes of facts but are merely the same facts looked at from different angles.

For example

- *A* makes a gift of his property to *B*. *A* loses his ownership and *B* becomes the owner. It is an extinctive fact (divestitive) for *A* and a derivative (investitive) title for *B*.
- *A* leases his property to *B* the lessee for 5 years. *B* surrenders the lease back to the lessor at the expiry of 4 years. The lessee is divested of his right by extinctive fact. It destroys the lease.
- *A* surrenders his right in the property in favour of his brother *B*. It is an extinctive fact for *A* and a derivative title for his brother *B*.

4. *Acts in the Law: Vestitive Facts may be Voluntary (Act of the Party) and Involuntary (Act of Law)*

Vestitive facts are divisible into two fundamental distinct classes – voluntary and involuntary. For example, when *A* sells his property it passes from him voluntarily known as *act of the party*. But when his property is sold in execution of a decree in satisfaction of the debt of Rs. Two lakhs which *A* owes *B* (*B's* debt) the transfer is an involuntary one known as the *act of law*. An act of law is the creation, extinction or transfer of right by the operation of law itself, independent of consent of the person concerned.

5. *Act of the Party are of Two Kinds – Unilateral and Bilateral*

Act of the party[1] (called acts in law by Sir Fredrick Pullock; some call it juristic acts) are of two kinds – unilateral and bilateral.

6. *Unilateral Acts are of Two Kinds: Notwithstanding Dissent & Subject to the Dissent*

Unilateral act are of two kinds – They may take effect not only without his consent but notwithstanding his dissent *e.g.* a right of re-entry by the landlord on breach of a condition by the tenant; It is the will of one party which is operative for example, a testamentary disposition *i.e.* a person disposing of his property by Will; exercise of power of appointment, rescinding of a voidable contract. In other cases it is subject to the dissent of the other affected by it, though it does not require his consent. For example, a Will involves only a unilateral intention and assent of the testator. The beneficiaries need not know anything about it; they need not even be in existence. But if they subsequently dissent and reject the rights so transferred the testament fails.

7. *Bilateral Acts: Agreement in Wide Sense*

Bilateral acts involves consenting Wills of two or more parties. For example, a contract, a mortgage etc,. bilateral acts on the law are called 'agreements' in the wide sense of term. In this wide sense- for the purpose of jurisprudential analysis – agreement also includes a contract, though as a student of contract law, we draw a distinction between an agreement and a contract for we learn that all contracts are agreements but all agreements are not contracts. In this wide sense, agreement also includes a mortgage and lease, though strictly speaking –they are not just agreements but contracts.

II. Agreements

1. *Bilateral Agreement Most Important. Consent Supports Title to Right*

Of all the vestitive facts acts in law are the most important. Amongst the acts in law, the bilateral agreements are most important. Of the great number of rights and duties possessed by an adult member in the society a great majority have their origin in bilateral agreements.

Consent supports title to right due to two reasons: Agreement is an evidence of right and also constitutive of it. Men are the best judge of their interests. Hence consent is the best evidence that there is justice in an arrangement. Consent is constitutive of right. Consent to an agreement means that each party has

---

1. Sir Fredrick Pollock refer to it as "acts in the law" as distinguished from "acts of the law". Some call it "juristic Act" P.J. Fitzgerald: Salmond on Jurisprudence, 12th Edn., p. 334.

reasonable expectations from the other. One of the leading principles of justice is to guarantee to men the fulfillment of their reasonable expectations.

2. *Classes of Agreements*

Agreements are divisible into 3 classes; they create; transfer or extinguish rights

- Those which *create rights.* They are of two classes – contracts and grants. A contract creates an obligation or a *right in personam* (against the particular person) as distinguished from one *in rem* (against the world at large). A grant is an agreement which creates a right of any other description e.g. grant of lease, easements, charges patents etc.
- An agreement which *transfers* a right is an *assignment.*
- One which *extinguishes* a right is a release, discharge or a surrender.

An agreement is a set of promises made with an intention to create a legal obligation. Promise must be to do the act as a matter of legal duty giving a legal right to the other party to demand the performance of the act promised.

An agreement may be of a mixed nature: An agreement may be of a mixed nature, e.g. sale of specific movable goods is both a contract and also an assignment because it also transfers the ownership of the goods. It is a contract because there is consent and obligation to pay the price.

The same agreement may have one effect in law and another in equity: The same agreement may have one effect in law and another in equity. For example, a written agreement of sale of land is in law only a contract imposing a personal obligation upon the seller to execute the conveyance. Of itself it does not transfer the ownership of the land. In equity such an agreement amounts to an assignment in England. But in India contract to sell does not create any equity in favour of the buyer[1]. Under Section 53A of the Transfer of Property Act, 1882 if in part performance of the contract to sell an immovable property the transferee is put in possession of the property and the transferee is ready and willing to perform his part of the contract even if the sale is not registered the seller cannot claim any more rights than which are given to him under the written contract.

3. *Objective Theory of Agreement*

According to the objective theory of agreement contract is not a subjective meeting of the minds as evidenced through consent but a series of external acts giving an appearance of agreement. For example, for a concluded contract there must be an offer which is accepted by the offeree. Now *A* makes an offer and then revokes the offer through a letter. *B* accepts the offer before the revocation comes to his notice. There is a valid contract even if there is no *consensus ad idem.* Both the subjective theory and the objective theory go too far. The truth is that there are some cases where the law takes a subjective view and some in which law takes an objective view according to the policy of the case.

III. Classification of Agreements Based on Efficacy: Valid, Void and Voidable

Agreements may be simple and formal. In simple agreements consenting will is enough. In formal agreements law requires some other formalities like writing, registration, delivery etc. for its enforcement.

---

1. Section 54 of the Transfer of Property Act.

A valid agreement is one which is fully operative in accordance with the intention of the parties. A void agreement is one which has not received any legal recognition and is *ab initio* void. Voidable agreement stands in between. It is liable to be cancelled at the option of one party but not at the option of the other.

Void contract is a contract which was valid when made and then becomes void due to some circumstance beyond the control of the parties to the contract.

Void and voidable agreement are classed as invalid. Those without a free consent (presence of coercion, undue influence, misrepresentation, fraud and mistake) are voidable. An agreement without consideration is void; an agreement with a minor is void.

a. *Causes of invalidity of the agreement:* Following are the six causes for the invalidity of the agreement:

(1) *Incapacity:* Competency to contract is an essential requirement. Minor's agreement is void. But a person normally of unsound mind can enter into an agreement during intervals of sanity.

(2) *Informality:* Agreements may be simple or formal. A simple agreement is one which requires – just a meeting of the mind consensus *ad idem* – by whatever means. Formal agreement requires the agreement to be effected in the manner prescribed by laws. For example under our Indian law, a mortgage where the Principal sum secured is more than Rs 100; a gift of an immovable property whatever be its value requires registration and attestation; a transfer which creates, declares, assigns, limits or extinguishes a right, title or interest in the property of the value of more than Rs. 100 requires compulsory registration; a Will requires attestation by two witnesses. Equitable mortgage is effected by merely depositing the original title deeds with an intention that the property comprised in the deeds shall operate as security for the loan advanced. No other formalities are prescribed under the Transfer of Property Act, 1882.

Such formalities serve two purposes. They are evidence of consent between the parties. Secondly, it ensures second thoughts over preliminary negotiations and adequate reflection; brings in more solemnity in the relations between the parties.

(3) *Illegality*: Agreement must be within the framework of law. Agreement whose object or consideration is unlawful is void agreement. Such limitations are necessary in the interest of the parties and the society in general. For example, to rob a Bank; agreement to run a prostitution centre are unlawful. Under our law there are some agreements which are declared to be void under the Indian Contract Act, 1882, like a wagering agreement, agreement in restraint of trade; in restraint of marriage; in restraint of legal proceedings etc. are declared to be void. They are void but not illegal. Hence the agreements collateral to these agreements are valid and can be enforced. For example, *A* and *B* take a bet for a sum of Rs. 10000 on the results of the election the loser to pay the winner Rs. 10000. *A* loses. *B* cannot recover the amount from *A*. but if *A* has borrowed 10000 from *D* to enter into this wagering

agreement, *D* can recover the amount from *A*, because as between *A* and *D* – the loan agreement is a collateral agreement which is not void. But if the amount has been lent in order to help *A* to murder another person or to purchase contraband goods like drugs, arms etc. – such a collateral agreement also is not binding because here the agreement is not just void but illegal.

(4) *Error/Mistake:* Error may be essential or an unessential error. If error is of such a nature as to nullify or prevent real consent – it is an error with respect to essential aspect in an agreement. For example, *A* agrees to sell his house to *B*. *A* has two houses bearing names – Pitru-Chhaya and Matru-Chhaya. *A* intends to sell Pitru-chayya but *B* mistakes it to be Matru-chhaya. Here there is no consensus *ad idem* – meeting of the minds between the parties. Hence there is no concluded agreement. There is only an external appearance of an agreement but no real agreement. But if the error is due to negligence of one of the parties and is not known to the other this rule is not applicable and the contract will have to be performed.

Unessential error is one which does not relate to the essential contents of the agreement. There is consensus of minds and hence agreement is binding. For example, *A* agrees to buy *B's* horse believing it to be sound. In reality it is unsound. It is not an essential error, because there is true consensus between then. But if the error is caused due to misrepresentation of the other party then the agreement be avoided.

(5) *No free consent:* Coercion, fraud, misrepresentation, mistake and undue influence make the agreement a voidable one at the option of the party whose consent is so obtained.

(6) *Want of consideration:* An agreement without consideration is void. However the legal system may provide exceptions. For example, the Indian Contract Act, 1872 lays down some exceptions like promise to pay for acts done voluntarily in the past – *i.e.* past consideration is valid; promises made out of natural love and affection between parties standing in near relation to each other are valid.

CHAPTER 21

PRINCIPLES OF LIABILITY

SYNOPSIS

I. The Nature and Kinds of Liability
  1. Liability: Bond of Necessity between the Wrong-doer and the Remedy
II. Theory of Remedial Liability
  Three Cases where Duties are not Specifically Enforceable
  1. Duties of Imperfect Obligation
  2. Duties Transitory in Nature
  3. Specific Performance Inexpedient
III. Theories of Penal Liability: *Actus non facit reum, nisi mens sit rea*
  Two Exceptions
  1. Mere Negligence Punishable
  2. Offences of Strict Liability
IV. The Concept of Acts
  1. No Precise Definition
  2. Act may be Positive or Negative
  3. Voluntary and Involuntary Act
  4. Intentional and Unintentional Act
  5. Two Classes of Wrongful Acts
V. *Damnum Sine Injuria*: Damage without Legal Wrong
  1. Harm Done to an Individual
  2. Harm Done to Community
VI. The Place and Time of an Act
  Two Cases which Require Consideration
  1. Act is Done Partly in One Place and Partly in Another
  2. When there is an Omission to do an Act
VII. Concept of Causation
  Man's Liability Only if Damage is the Result of his Own Act
VIII. *Mens rea*
  1. Guilty Mind of 3 Categories
    a. Intentional or Reckless Wrongs
    b. Wrongs of Negligence
    c. Wrongs of Strict Liability
  2. Criticisms of the Doctrine of *Mens rea*
    a. It has Outlived its Purpose
    b. In India Every Offence is Defined
  3. *Mens rea* when not Necessary (Exception to the *Mens rea* Rule)
    a. Statute Itself Imposes Strict Liability
    b. Where it is Difficult to Prove *Mens rea*
    c. Summary Mode of Enforcing Right
    d. Cases Relating to Public Nuisance
    e. Ignorance of Law is no Excuse

IX. Generic Intention (Transmigration of Malice)

X. Intention

1. Intention is the Purpose or Design

2. Unintentional Act is one without such Purpose or Design

3. Partly Intentional and Partly Unintentional: Liability Only in Case of Absolute Liability or for Recklessness or Negligent Act

4. Intended Consequences are Normally Expected

5. Intention and Desire are Different

6. Forseen Consequences and Probable Consequences

7. Test of a Reasonable Man

XI. Motive

1. Difference between Motive and Intention

(a) Desire for Benefit is Motive for the Act

(b) Intention Indicates Immediate Objectives

Motive Indicates Ultimate Objective

2. Relevance of Motive

3. Stages in Commission of Crime: (a) Intention; (b) Preparation; (c) Attempt; (d) Commission

XII. Malice (Evil Motive)

1. Jus Necessitas (Right of Necessity)

2. The Rationale behind the Theory of *Jus Necessitatis*

3. Practical Limitations of the Doctrine

XIII. Negligence

1. Absence of Care

2. Test of a Reasonable Man

3. Negligence can take Several Forms

4. Carelessness may Occur in Several Ways

5. The Duty to take Care

6. Standard of Care: Standard of a Reasonable Man

7. Theories of Negligence

a. Subjective Theory of Negligence (State of Mind Theory)

b. Objective Theory (Type of Conduct Theory)

XIV. The Theory of Strict Liability

1. Strict Liability an Exception in Civil Cases and not a Rule

Strict Liability under Three Heads

a. Mistake of Law

b. Mistake of Fact

c. Inevitable Accident

XV. Vicarious Liability

1. Jurisprudential Dilemmas in the Concept of Vicarious Liability

2. Master's Vicarious Liability on Following Grounds

a. *Qui facit per alium facit per se*

b. Respondeat Superior

c. Public Policy

d. Financial Considerations

3. Liability of the Legal Representatives

a. Effect of Death on Suits

XVI. Measure of Criminal Liability

1. Motive for the Crime

2. Magnitude of the Offence

INTRODUCTION

In the previous chapters we have seen that law confers rights and prescribes duties. The idea of liability is closely linked to the non-performance of duties. What is liability, for what acts or omissions is a person liable; what is the basis for liability; the purpose it serves etc are the points for consideration under this Chapter.

I. The Nature and Kinds of Liability

1. *Liability: Bond of necessity between the wrong-doer and the remedy:* Liability means responsibility for a wrongful act or a wrongful omission. According to Salmond, liability is the bond of necessity that exists between the wrong-doer and the remedy for the wrong. This remedy may be either civil remedy or criminal remedy. Liability may be civil or criminal liability. The purpose of penal liability is punishment and the purpose of remedial liability is to enforce the plaintiff's right. All criminal liability is penal and civil liability is sometimes penal and sometimes remedial.

II. Theory of Remedial Liability

When law creates a duty and the duty is not performed, it enforces the specific fulfilment of it. For example, if *A* fails to give the possession of land to *B* as promised, law enforces the promise through its direction. Following are the three cases where duties are not specifically enforceable:

1. *Duties of imperfect obligation:* The duty is of such a nature that its breach does not give rise to a cause of action and therefore creates no liability whether civil or criminal. For example, a debt barred by the Law of Limitation is a legal debt but its payment cannot be compelled through legal proceedings. Nothing prevents the debtor from voluntarily paying off the debt, but the creditor cannot file a suit for recovering the debt after a period of 3 years after the debt becomes due.
2. *Duties transitory in nature:* Essence of a transitory duty lies in its not being violated even once; and once violated it is beyond specific enforcement. For example libel already published; or an assault already committed. Such wrongs once committed belong to the irrevocable past. Transitory duty must be distinguished from continuing duty for example, duty not to create nuisance can be specifically enforced even after being violated on a previous occasion. For example, playing songs on loudspeakers in temples, churches and mosques so as to cause noise pollution can be prevented for the future by specific enforcement of the continuing duty not to create nuisance.
3. *Specific performance inexpedient:* For example, contracts of personal services; promise to marry cannot be specifically enforced for it depends totally on

the question of choice. But the defaulting party can be compelled to pay damages to the aggrieved party.

III. Theories of Penal Liability: *Actus non facit reum, nisi mens sit rea*

Of the three purposes of punishment, deterrence, prevention and reformation, deterrence is the primary purpose. The fundamental principle of Penal liability is indicated in the maxim *Actus non facit reum, nisi mens sit rea* doing of an act prohibited by law coupled with a guilty mind incurs penal liability. It is neither act alone nor intention alone which invites penal liability. No person can be punished *merely* because his act has led to a mischievous result prohibited by law. Likewise he cannot be punished merely because he had bad intentions. Did he commit the act with a guilty mind is a relevant question before fixing up his liability.

A man can be punished only for the wrongful act done by him whether *willfuly or recklessly;* and not for what other persons do or for events independent of human activity altogether.

To this maxim there *are two exceptions:*

1. Mere negligence even if inadvertent may be punishable by criminal law.
2. Offences of strict liability may be created where guilty intention, recklessness or even negligence are irrelevant factors to fix up the liability.

To understand the theories of penal liability let us analyse the concept of 'act' and the concept of '*mens rea* the guilty mind' in its manifestation of recklessness, intention, and negligence.

IV. The Concept of Acts

1. *No precise definition*: The term act is not capable of precise definition. It must be distinguished from natural occurrences like floods, and storms over which man has no control.
2. *Act may be positive or negative*: Acts may be either positive or negative. A wrong-doer *does* what he ought not to do; or else he omits to do what he ought to do. *i.e.* his act may consist of a *commission or an omission.*

   For omission to incur legal liability there must be a *duty* to act. In most legal systems such duties to act are an exception rather than a rule. Thus rights *in rem* (against the world at large) corresponds to 'duty not to do something' like not to harm the reputation of another person, not to kill another, not steal etc.
3. *Voluntary and involuntary act*: A distinction must be drawn between voluntary acts and involuntary acts. Involuntary acts are outside normal human control like beating of one's heart and sneezing and acts done in sleep or under hypnosis. Acts done involuntarily are a defense to a criminal charge. Difficulties arise when a man could have avoided falling into such a situation which made him do the involuntary act which is wrongful in nature.

   An act is made up of 3 distinct aspects:

   1. The act originates in some mental or bodily activity. *E.g.* the act of pulling the trigger.

2. Its circumstances; *e.g.* the victim being within the range of the revolver.
3. Its consequences; bullet entering the victim's body.

The act is voluntary if there is a willed muscular contraction which incurs moral or legal liability due to the circumstances in which it is committed or the consequences which it produces. In involuntary act muscular contraction is not willed. This theory has lot of difficulties. It rests on dubious psychology. It is not suited where omission to do an act required by law to be done incurs liability. For example, I may forget to file my tax returns. In addition an act is spoken of to include all the 3 aspects mentioned under the above paragraph and not just muscular contractions resulting in the act.

4. *Intentional and unintentional act*: An act may be intentional or unintentional. It is intentional when it is the result of the person's will directed towards that result. For example *A* administers poison to *B* with an intention to procure his death. He is aware *i.e.,* he forsees that administering poison will cause the death of *B* and he desires it. Thus the act prohibited by law must be *intentionally done, must be foreseen and desired by the doer*. It is unintentional if it is not desired and not by the will of the doer.

5. *Two classes of wrongful acts*: Every wrong is mischievous in the eyes of law. An act may be mischievous

1. In its actual result or
2. In its tendencies.

In the first kind of wrong – actual damage must be proved. Here there is no wrong without actual damage. In the second, it is enough if only the act is proved, even though there is no harm in consequence of the act.

Criminal liability is sufficiently established by proof of some act which law deems dangerous in its tendencies. Even an unsuccessful attempt attracts liability as it is a wrongful act. But this is not invariably so. In some cases criminal responsibility depends on the accident of the event. Any negligence in the use of fire arms resulting in death of someone make him criminally liable. If by good luck there is no such eventuality there is no criminal liability. Trespass and libel are wrongful in their tendencies; but slander is not actionable without proof of loss sustained by the plaintiff.

In civil cases generally proof of actual damage is necessary though in some cases liability is incurred even without proof of actual damage.

V. *Damnum sine injuria*: Damage without Legal Wrong

In legal theory, all wrongs are mischievous but all mischievous acts are not wrongs. This is what is depicted by the maxim *damnum sine injuria. Damnum* means damage or loss or harm caused to an individual or the society. *Injuria* is legal wrong. *Damnum sine injuria* means – damage without legal wrong. Hence it is not actionable in the courts of law.

Damnum sine injuria may fall under two categories:

1. *Harm done to an individual:* Harm done to an individual which does not result in legal wrong because it is not against the society at large, it may even be to the advantage of the society at large. Hence it is *damnum sine*

injuria. For example – competition in trade may cause damage to some traders, yet it is a gain to the society as a whole. Hence competitors do harm (*damnum*) each other but there is no *injuria* (legal wrong). Construction of a structure on my land may block the free supply of light and air to my neighbour's land; when I dig a bore well on my land I may drain away water from my neighbour's well. They are a natural incident of others exercising their own rights. These acts are harmful to an individual but serve public interest for they recognize the freedom of every member in the society to do as they please on their own land; they also recognize the freedom of others to carry on their own business or profession; incidentally they also recognize the law that no man's right or liberty is absolute; that it is subject to the rights and liberties of others and that if members of the society are to live together amicably with each other- each one has to compromise a bit on his own comforts and absolute rights.

2. *Harm done to community*: Harm done to community does not result in legal wrong because of the triviality of the harm or because it is difficult to prove or because it is inexpedient to attempt to prevent it. For example, under Section 95 of the Indian Penal Code an act is not an offence if the harm resulting from it is so slight or trifle that no reasonable person with ordinary common sense and temper would complain of it. *De minimis non curat lex.* A little push while getting inside the local train in Mumbai – will not result in assault or battery; smell of fishes carried by fisherwomen in the local trains while travelling from one station to another or even the smell of a scert put by another co-traveller in a train which is irritating – is not nuisance.

VI. The Place and Time of an Act

In the majority of the cases jurisdiction of the courts is determined in terms of the territorial limits of the court. For example, suits regarding immovable property shall be filed within the territorial limits of the court where the property is situated; if it is situated within the jurisdiction of different courts it can be filed in either of the courts within whose jurisdiction the property is situated.[1] This inquiry generally does not present any difficulty. There are two cases which require some consideration:

1. *Act is done partly in one place and partly in another:* For example, a man standing on Indian soil kills another on the Pakistan territory. Is the murder committed in India or Pakistan? In fact and logically speaking it is neither in India nor in Pakistan. But such an answer serves no purpose.

Logically there can be 3 possible answers: it may be said that the act is committed in both places; or solely where it has commenced or solely where it is completed. Law is free to choose from any of the three. The last one is the most accepted. Murder is committed where death occurs and not where poison is purchased or the trigger pulled or from where the threatening e-mail sent or bombs dispatched. But a contract is made where the offer is accepted or the last necessary signature to the document is affixed

1. Under the Code of Civil Procedure, 1908, Sections 15 to 21 deal with the place of suing.

2. *When there is an omission to do an act:* When there is an omission to do an act legally required to be done which is the place where the negative act is done? In what place does a man omit to pay the debt or perform the contract? The answer is that the negative act takes place where the positive act ought to have taken place. Omission to pay a debt occurs in the place where the debt is payable.

The time of the act for most purposes is the date of the completion of the act.

VII. Concept of Causation

Man's liability only if damage is the result of his own act

When a man is guilty of doing an act, which has actually caused a damage his liability arises only if the damage, has resulted from his act. If there is no causal connection between the damage or loss caused to another person and his own behaviour, he will not incur liability. Hence causation is an important concept in determining liability.

The concept of causation is a complex one as can be seen from the following examples:

- If I shoot at *X* and he falls dead but if it is found that his death was caused by a shot fired at the very same instant by *Y* or that he died due to a heart attack just before I shot him I cannot be held liable.
- My travelling agents load my luggage on the wrong train, the train is derailed and my luggage lost. Who is responsible for my loss whether my agents or the railway?
- *An investigation into causation involves explanatory and attributive sides.* For example you throw a stone into the college kitchen and the whole college is burnt down. On *an explanatory inquiry* it is found that the kitchen was full of inflammable gas that was leaking out of a gas burner; the impact of the stone produced a spark which led to the fire. Explanatory enquiry is complete when all the facts leading up to the incident are discovered. And then the *attributive* enquiry starts. On the attributive side the court has to conduct an enquiry and come to the conclusion whether it was the throwing of a stone which actually was the cause of the accident. Both these enquiries are taken up by the court if necessary by taking the help of the experts. Based on the evidence established the court has to decide whether it was the defendant's act which was the cause of the damage. The legal task becomes complex when there are several circumstances which have intervened; several factors which have contributed towards the loss or damage. When the event results from a combination of several factors we study them under the two categories: abnormal factors and human acts.
- *Novus actus interveniens:* A new act may intervene. *A* is stabbed by *B*. He is admitted to the hospital where he is injected with a large dose of medicine to which he is shown to be allergic and he dies. It may be shown that the injection was the *novus actus interveniens which severed the causal connection* between the stabbing by *B* and the death of *A*.

VIII. *Mens rea*

Mens rea means guilty mind. A man is held liable only if his *wrongful act* (actus reus) is coupled with the *mens rea* or *guilty mind* with which he does it. The form which *mens rea* assumes depends upon the particular legal system.

1. *Guilty Mind of 3 Categories*

The guilty mind involved in the wrongs may be of the following 3 categories:

a. *Intentional or reckless wrongs:* Here *mens rea* amounts to *purpose* or design with which the wrong act is done. It may amount to foresight. In such wrongs defenses like mistake nullify *mens rea.*

b. *Wrongs of negligence*: *Mens rea* assumes a lesser form- where a person behaves unreasonably, carelessly as opposed to wrongful intention or foresight. Defenses of mistake negative *mens rea* only if the mistake itself is not negligent.

c. *Wrongs of strict liability: Mens rea* is not at all required. Wrongful state of mind or negligence is immaterial. Defenses like mistake are of no use. It is *actus reus* alone which constitutes the wrong.

Mens rea must extend to the following 3 parts of the wrongful act (*actus reus*)

1. the physical doing or not doing of the act
2. the circumstances accompanying the act
3. the consequences of the act.

If *mens rea* does not extend to any part of the act, then there is no guilty mind behind the act.

2. *Criticisms of the Doctrine of mens rea*

a. *It has now outlived its purpose*

b. *In India every offence is defined*

The doctrine is misleading, according to Sir Stephens. The doctrine was evolved when the criminal law had not developed the way it has developed today. Today we have Penal laws in every civilized country which define offences and the penalties prescribed with meticulous detailing. But in the earlier days wrongs were named as murder, rape, theft etc. but the essential ingredients of the crime were not defined. Hence the doctrine laid down that it is neither act alone not guilty mind alone which constituted an offence. What was required was a combination of both the wrongful act and a guilty mind. The doctrine has served its purpose. It has now outlived its purpose.

Thus in India, the maxim is out of place because the Indian Penal Code and the other criminal laws are specific about the contents of the offence which are made punishable. As J.D. Mayne the celebrated author on Criminal Law in India has pointed out "every offence is defined, and the definition states not only what the accused must have done but the state of mind with regard to the act when he was doing it." For example, theft must be committed *dishonestly,* cheating must be committed *fraudulently,* murder must be committed *intentionally or knowingly in order to be an offence under the IPC.*

Likewise there are numerous laws in India which lay down that if the provisions of the statute are not followed it shall be an offence. They too lay down the exact nature of guilty mind that is required for an omission or commission of an act to be an offence. For example, under Section 16 of the Environment Protection Act, 1986 if the person (the Company official) who is deemed guilty of the offence proves that the offence was committed *without his knowledge* or that he had exercised *due diligence* to prevent the commission of the offence – such a person escapes punishment; likewise under Section 20 of the Right to Information Act, 2005 if the information is *malafidely denied; or incomplete or incorrect information is knowingly given – a heavy penalty is imposed.* Thus the nature of the guilty mind required to constitute legal wrong is laid down by the Statutes themselves. Hence the doctrine of *mens rea* has become redundant.

3. *Mens rea when not Necessary (Exception to the mens rea Rule)*

Cases of strict liability are cases where *mens rea* is not necessary to constitute wrong. Following are the 5 exceptional cases where *mens rea* is not required in criminal law:

a. *Statute itself imposes strict* liability. Cases where the Statute itself imposes strict liability. For example *in India* Section 92A of the Motor Vehicles Act, 1939[1] provides for no fault liability where the owner of the vehicle involved in the accident is liable to pay compensation of a fixed amount even without proof of negligence or fault if death or permanent disablement results. As Dean Roscoe Pound justifies such laws on the moral ground that "such statutes are not meant to punish the vicious Will but to put pressure on the thoughtless and inefficient to do their whole duty in the interest of public health, safety or morals"[2]. However the Statute must clearly indicate expressly or by necessary implication that the Parliament intended to create a strict liability because the fundamental principle is that an offence cannot be made out without the existence of *mens rea*. The Supreme Court has held that under the Prevention of Food Adulteration Act, 1954, the prosecution need not prove that the employer or the employee has guilty intention or knowledge that the article was adulterated. The Act was enacted in the larger interest of the maintenance of public health.[3]

b. *Where it is difficult to prove mens rea:* Where it is difficult to prove *mens rea* and the penalties prescribed are petty fines. The Sea Customs Act, 1878 prohibits vessels and ships which have arrangements for concealing goods from entering the Indian Ports. For breach of this prohibition law imposes strict liability because it is difficult to prove the existence of *mens rea* against the owners or the master of the ship.[4]

However it is common to find statutes concerning public health, safety and morals to provide severe penalties for offences of strict liability.

c. *Summary mode of enforcing right*: Where the proceedings may be criminal in form but they are really only a summary mode of enforcing a civil right.[5]

---

1. 1982 Amendment.
2. J.G.P. Singh, Principles of Statutory interpretation, Wadhwa & Co., Nagpur, 6th Edn., p. 554
3. *Sarjoo Prasad* v. *State of U.P.*, AIR 1961 SC 631 (632-33).
4. *Indo China Steam Navigation Co.* v. *Jasjit Singh*, AIR 1964 SC 1140 (1149-50).
5. G.P. Singh, Principles of Statutory Interpretation, 6th Edn., p. 556.

d. *Cases relating to public nuisance – mens rea* is not necessary.

e. *Ignorance of law is no excuse i.e.* The wrongdoer cannot take the defense that he has no knowledge of the law and hence he committed the wrongful act without an intention to commit it.

IX. Generic Intention (Transmigration of Malice)

In criminal law it is the generic intention which is important. For example, if *A* intends to kill *X* and so fires at him. *Y* intervenes to prevent *A* from firing and the bullet hits *Y* and he dies. *A* is guilty of murder. His specific intention is to kill *X* but his generic intention is to kill a human being. But if *A* intends to kill a beast and instead kills a man, there is no murder as the injury inflicted and one intended are of different kinds.

If *A* without any reason or excuse fires into a crowd of persons and kills one of them, he is guilty of murder. This is a case of transmigration of malice.[1]

X. Intention

It is the *actus reus* plus *mens rea* which constitutes the wrong. *Mens rea i.e.* guilty mind may manifest in several forms. It may appear as intention or object to do a wrongful act; it may appear as knowledge that what he is doing is wrong; or just negligence and recklessness not caring for what will be the consequences.

1. *Intention is the purpose or design:* An intention is the purpose or design with which the act is done. Holmes defines intention as consisting of the foresight of consequences together with a desire of such consequences. When a person plants bombs in busy market areas so that they will explode during peak hours when the area is crowded to its brim, the obvious intention is to kill the people, to scare the public. X throws acid on the girl who has refused to marry him- intention is to take a revenge and to disfigure and ruin her.

2. *Unintentional act is one without such purpose or design:* An unintentional act is one without such purpose or design. In the above example, X does not throw the acid but it accidentally slips from his hands when a third person dashes against him by mistake and the bottle falls on her legs and she suffers injuries. The act is without the purpose of harming her. Through inadvertence I may disregard a traffic signal not because my purpose is to violate the traffic laws but may be because I have a patient with me to be taken to the hospital. In the process I may hit at another vehicle and thus commit the wrong. Here I fail to foresee the consequences. Even killing may be accidental and without an intention to bring about the consequences. I may kill X thinking it to be a beast as it happened in our ancient epic Ramayana where King Dashratha unintentionally kills Shravankumar mistaking the sound of the water in the pond to be that of a beast which had come for drinking water. He was ignorant of the existing circumstances.

Whether an act is intentional or unintentional depends partly on the description of the act itself. When *X* 'shoots' at *Y* it is intentional. When Dashratha 'killed' Shravankumar it was not intentional.

3. *Partly intentional and partly unintentional: Liability only in case of absolute liability or for recklessness or negligent act:* Many acts are partly intentional and partly unintentional. For example, X marries again during the lifetime of her

1. Section 301, IPC.

husband *Y* thinking him to be dead in a train accident. She does not commit bigamy. Here she intends to marry again but she did not intend to marry again during her husband's life-time. Where the act is partly intentional and partly unintentional liability arises only in cases of absolute liability or on grounds of recklessness or negligence

4. *Intended consequences are normally expected:* For example, I intend to kill X with a knife it means that I forsee the result of using a knife and also expect that it will result in death. But as an exception, expected consequences may not always be intended. The doctor performing a complicated operation may expect and fear that death may result; he may not be sure of 100% success in the operation but he does not intend the death of the patient. In fact he intends the recovery of the patient.

5. *Intention and desire are different*: For example, I desire to shoot down all the corrupt and unscrupulous politicians who according to me are doing a disservice to our nation. I cannot be said to intend a wrongful act unless I do something in furtherance of my desire. Conversely I may intend something without desiring it. X may enter Y's house with an intention to rob him and he may end up killing him. His desire is not to kill him. His intention is only to rob him.

6. *Forseen consequences and probable consequences:* In a given system of law a man can be held liable for consequences which are forseen as certain or highly probable whether intended or not. This has two advantages: firstly inquiries into the state of mind which is difficult and intricate can be avoided. Secondly, it will forbid people from doing acts which they forsee will result in harmful consequences to others, they will be prevented from taking up the defense that they had no intention to cause the consequences. But at times, the harmful consequences could be forseen or probable, yet justified in order to avoid a larger harm or if it is for a social good. The Indian Penal Code lays down the ingredients of offence and also the general exceptions.

7. *Test of a reasonable man*: To find out whether certain consequences are forseeable or not the test of a reasonable man is applied. Thus, if I intentionally do some unlawful act and I do not realize that it will result in the death of *B* but a reasonable man does so realize it is enough to render me guilty of murder. But mere knowledge of statistical probability will not impute liability in every case.

XI. Motive

1. Differences between Motive and Intention

a. *Desire for benefit is the motive for the act:* A person very rarely commits a wrongful act just for the sake of committing it. He has an object or some purpose or end in mind with which he commits it. For example, *X* robs *B* of Rs. 50,000. He may want to use the money for purchase of prohibited drugs or because he badly needs the money for the operation of his wife who would die if not operated immediately or he wants to feed the poor out of the money. Here the intention is to dishonestly and without the consent of *B* to rob him. This is his immediate purpose. His ultimate desire is his motive. Motive behind the wrongful act in one case was one deserving sympathy and in another a bad one. In either case he desires a benefit either for himself or for another.

b. *Intention indicates the immediate objectives.*
Motive relates to the ultimate object of the act.

Intention indicates the immediate objectives of the wrongful act. Motive relates to the object or series of objects with which the act is done. *X* shoots at *Y*. His intention is to kill *Y*. But his motive may be to take a revenge on him as *Y* had been harassing and threatening him, making his life miserable. Thus the ultimate object is the motive for the act. The immediate objectives are the intention.

- A man's intention helps to find out what the wrongdoer is trying to achieve; a man's motive helps to find out what is the personal advantage he tries to get. The advantage need not be only in terms of money; it may be a revenge; it may be to secure an ideology; it may be greed; it may be to settle a dispute over property or pertaining to illicit relations.
- A man's motives can be described in general or specific terms like saying that the motive is to take revenge, greed or curiosity all of which lead to some benefit in future. Intention cannot be described in such general terms.
- The answers to the following two questions bring out the difference between motive and intention.
    - "Did *X* kill *A* purposely, or was it by mistake?" if it was purposely it is intentional. If it was by mistake then it is an accident.
    - Why did *X* kill *A*? the answer to the question provides the motive for the crime. It may be revenge, to settle a row over property matter, over political rivalry, over love affairs etc.
- The ulterior intention may be complex and not simple. While *A* is killing *B* as *B* is his business rival *X* sees him and so to wipe out the only eye witness *A* kills *X* also.
- The object of doing one wrongful act may be to do another wrongful act. *X* makes a die with an intention to make counterfeit notes. He makes counterfeit notes in order to circulate it in another country. He circulates it in another country in order to ruin its economy. Here each of these acts is a distinct criminal offence. The intention of each act is immediate to that act itself. But the ulterior motive is with respect to all that goes before it in a series.

2. *Relevance of Motive*

Motive of the wrongdoer is generally irrelevant. It is the intention which is relevant. A good motive does not make an illegal act a legal one. Conversely a legal act done with a malicious motive will not make the act illegal. Thus if *A* poisons *B* to relieve *B* of his pain and suffering his motive is a good one but his act remains an illegal one in a legal system which has not legalised euthanasia *i.e.* mercy killing.

Motive is relevant in the following cases:

1. In cases of attempt to commit crimes. As the act has not taken place the motive is relevant for assessing the liability of the wrongdoer.
2. Though proof of motive is not necessary motive when proved is an evidence of guilty intention and is relevant to show that the person who had the motive had the reason to commit crime.

3. Where a particular intention forms a part of the definition of crime. *E.g.*, theft consists in intending to take dishonestly any movable property out of the possession of any person without that person's consent.
4. *Jus necessitatis*: It is an act done in necessity. When one has to opt between two acts one more harmful than the other the latter must be opted.
5. Motive is relevant in determining the quantum of punishment. If motive is good, punishment may be reduced at the discretion of the court.
6. In civil liability, motive is not relevant except in very few cases like in malicious prosecution.

3. *Stages in the Commission of Crime*

There are 4 stages in the commission of the crime:

a. *Intention* to commit crime followed by some act in furtherance of the intention. Mere intention will not incur liability. Motive is not relevant except for the purposes mentioned above. This stage has been dealt at length above
b. *Preparation:* It means taking steps for committing the crime. For example, if intention is to rob a Bank, secretly meeting with conspirators to discuss the plan; purchase of a suitcase, gun, chloroform to make people unconscious etc. is preparation. Under Section 511 of the Indian Penal Code acts done in preparation stages is not punishable. Thus when a person starts making preparations to commit crime but on second thoughts repents and decides not to go ahead with his plans, he is excused on the ground of *locus poenitentiae* (repentance). There are a few exceptions where preparations to commit crime are punishable: when preparation is to wage war against the State[1]; or to commit dacoity[2] or possessor of certain unauthorized arms[3] like bombs, dynamite capable of mass destruction or biological or chemical substances of warfare in any area, comes within the perview of POTA and is punishable; persons can be charged for possessing things with no legitimate records.[4]
c. *Attempt*: It is the direct movement towards the commission after the preparations are made. When the attempt is successful, it is the commission of the crime. It is an intentional act done towards committing the crime but it fails because he is caught by the police before the crime can be committed or due to some technical reason the attempt fails; it may also be because the crime cannot be committed because the pick pocketor finds the pocket of his victim empty. Thus the reason for the failure of the attempt to commit crime must not be the independent Will of the wrongdoer for that would come under *locus poenitentiae*. For example, *X* purchases a gun to kill *Y* and loads it.

---

1. Section 122, IPC.
2. Section 399, IPC.
3. Section 4, Prevention of Terrorist Activities Act.
4. Section 41(1)D, IPC.

He has not committed the offence. The moment he pulls the trigger the offence is committed even if the bullet does not kill *Y*. Preparation is arranging for the means to commit crime. Attempt is the direct movement towards committing the crime. Attempt is punishable because whether it fails or succeeds it creates alarm. Even attempt to commit suicide is punishable under the IPC.

d. *Commission*: When the crime is successfully completed it is commission of the crime.

XII. Malice (Evil Motive)

- In its popular meaning it means ill will.
- In law it means wrongful intention or recklessness.
- We have seen the differences between intention and motive. The term malice is applied to both intention and motive and hence it has to be understood carefully.
- An evil motive is malice. Take the phrase 'malicious injury to property' and 'malicious homicide'. The term 'malicious' is used merely as a collective term for motive and intention. But malicious prosecution does not mean just intentional prosecution. It means something more serious and vicious. For example a prosecution is malicious if its ulterior intention is extortion of money from the accused.
- I act fraudulently when the motive of my wrongdoing is to derive some material gain for myself whether by deception force or otherwise. But I act maliciously when my motive is the pleasure of doing harm to another rather than the acquisition of any material advantage for myself.

1. Jus Necessitas (Right of Necessity)

Necessitas non habet legem, necessity knows no law. An act which is necessary is not wrongful though done with full and deliberate intention. The maxim means that when an act is done under dire necessity in circumstances where the fear of punishment would be no deterrent he should not be punished severely or not punished at all. For example, throwing goods overboard to lighten the ship and prevent it from drowning; selling away the goods in the ships to save them from being totally spoilt without the consent of the owner of the goods; pulling down the house on fire to prevent it from spreading to the other surrounding houses.

Take the case of two men drowning and they have a single plank which will support only one but not both of them; the stronger one pushes the weaker one and he drowns. Law does not intervene to say that it is the moral duty of the one with no dependants to sacrifice himself for the sake of another who has kids, wife and parents to be looked after. This is not a crime because the weaker one is not killed but left to find another plank and continue swimming till then. The second case is where the ship has wrecked, they have run out of their food stocks; so to preserve themselves they have to murder one amongst themselves and eat his flesh or else all would die. Here it amounts to the crime of murder.

Sacrificing the unborn for the sake of the mother is another instance of the right of necessity. The concept of abortion can be justified on this basis.

2. *The Rationale Behind the Theory of Jus Necessitatis*[1]

The so-called Right of Necessity (*Jus necessitatis*) is the supposed right available in case of the danger of losing my own life, to take away the life of another who has, in fact, done me no harm. Viewed as a Right, this involves a contradiction. For this is not the case of a *wrongful* aggressor making an unjust assault upon my life. It is a question of allowing me to use violence against one who has used none against me.

Such a right is not to be understood objectively as what a Law would prescribe, but merely subjectively, as how the court would look at it and what sentence would be pronounced by a Court in such a case. The question is what penalty can law impose on a man whose ship has wrecked and is in extreme danger for his life, and so to save himself he may push aside another person who is trying to cling to the same plank. The threat of punishment could not be greater than the fear of the loss of life in the case in question. Such a Penal Law would serve no purpose. What fear could he have of an evil which is still *uncertain* such as death by a judicial sentence in the presence of an imminent fear of an Evil which is *certain*, as Drowning is, in this case. This does not mean that an act of violent self-preservation should not be condemned, but it is only to be regarded as exempt from punishment. Yet this *subjective* condition of impunity, by a strange confusion of ideas, has been regarded by Jurists as equivalent to *objective* lawfulness.

3. *Practical Limitations of the Doctrine*

- All crimes have the tempting motives behind them. The fear of punishment is needed to counteract the motive of temptation. It can never be argued that when the motive for commiting crime is greater than the fear of punishment law should take a back seat and allow the wrongdoer to go unpunished.
- Hence English law and the Indian law does not accept this doctrine as well as the doctrine of self preservation which would absolve a person of a serious crime like murder. Thus in *Dudley and Stephens*[2] three sailors on a wrecked ship were without food for 7 days. Two of them together killed a third boy and ate his flesh or else they would have died out of starvation. They were held guilty of murder. This was inspite of the fact that the boy had grown so weak due to starvation that left for a day or two more he would have in any case died.
- It is submitted that the doctrine of *jus necessitatis* as of now concerns a case where it is the physical life which is in imminent danger of being destroyed. What if the same analogy is extended to other crimes with respect to property etc because after the liberal interpretation in *Maneka Gandhi* v. *Union of India*[3] right to life includes practically every right under the sun. Hence the doctrine has to be applied very sparingly.

---

1. The Philosophy of Law/Introduction to The Philosophy of Law *by Immanuel Kant* Prolegomena First Section—General Introduction to the Metaphysic of Morals: From Wikisource
2. (1884) 14 QBD 173.
3. AIR 1978 SC 597.

XIII. Negligence[1]

Injuries are divisible into 3 categories; those which are intentional and wilful; those which arise out of carelessness; and those which arise out of strict liability. The first category has been dealt with above. We now deal with negligence.

1. *Absence of care i.e. culpable carelessness:* Negligence is the *absence of care.* It is not an act done intentionally as under the first category of injury. Negligence and intentional causing of injury cannot exist at the same time. If an injury is caused intentionally it cannot be said to be negligent and if it is negligent it cannot be said to be intentional. Negligence is *culpable carelessness.*

2. *Test of a reasonable man:* A man is said to be negligent if he fails or omits to do something which a reasonable man would do or does something which a reasonable would not do, guided by those considerations which ordinarily regulate human behaviour.

3. *Negligence can take several forms:* Negligence can take several forms. It may be thoughtlessness or inadvertence. This is the most common form of negligence. Suppose, I drive a car furiously along a crowded road conscious of the risk that others are being exposed to but not intending to injure anyone. Here I do not intend to injure anyone, but I am fully aware that there is a likelihood of someone coming under the wheels of my car. So, what if there is no intention to cause injury to anyone. I am intentionally and knowingly exposing the whole public to the risk of suffering an injury. It is only a chance that any of them escape from being injured. So if an accident does happen and results in death of a passerby, I will be guilty not of committing murder but of negligent homicide. *i.e.* it is an injury caused not intentionally and willfully but with the knowledge that my conduct has the potential of causing the injury and is likely to cause the injury.

Thus a person acting negligently—

- Consciously exposes another to the risk of wrongful harm
- There is no wish/desire/intention to harm him. [No score to be settled, no revenge to be taken, no greed, no bad motive he would not even be knowing the personal details of his probable victim].
- He has the foresight that injury is possible or even probable. [When the required foresight is there, there should arise a duty to take care].
- When harm actually occurs he is judged as negligent.

4. *Carelessness may occur in several ways:* Carelessness resulting in negligence may occur in several ways like he may fail to notice what is happening and the probable consequences; he may miscalculate his speed; he may be too confident of his driving skills; he may miscalculate the width of the road; there may be poor vision; he may miscalculate the speed of the other vehicles; or he may simply appreciate the risks involved and decide to take them. When injury results due to such carelessness and when taking of such risk is considered wrong under the circumstances he is judged to be negligent.

1. In Roman Law negligence is signified by the terms *culpa* and *negligentia* as distinguished from *dolus* meaning wrongful intention. Absence of *negligentia* is *diligentia* (care). Word diligence is obsolete in modern English but it is still used as an archaism of legal diction. In ordinary usage, diligence is opposed to idleness and not to carelessness.

5. *The duty to take care:* Mere carelessness is not culpable, it is not blameworthy. Man is free to be indifferent to others without bothering about them except in cases where there is a duty to take care imposed by law. According to Salmond, it is left to the particular legal system to lay down details regarding the circumstances when the duty to take care would arise.

L. Macmillan has observed in *Donoghue* v. *Stevenson,*[1] "law takes no cognizance of carelessness in the abstract. It concerns itself with carelessness only when there is a duty to take care and where failure in that duty has resulted in damage. In such a case carelessness assumes the quality of negligence and entails the consequences in law of negligence."

So if the question is whether *A* is liable to *B* for driving carelessly–following cardinal principles of liability must be taken note of:

- *A* must owe a legal duty towards *B* to take care
- *A* must have committed a breach of duty
- *B* must have suffered a consequential damage

In general, crimes are wilful wrongs and alternative lesser forms of *mens rea* like carelessness are deemed as insufficient to attract the rigours of criminal justice. But this is not an absolute rule. Negligent homicide is a criminal offence.

For example, Sections 88, 92 and 93 of the IPC pertaining to doctors are provisions which offer protection for acts not intended to cause death, done by consent or without consent in good faith for person's benefit. (like operations) However, protection under any of these three Sections is available only if the act is done in "good faith". Section 52 of the Penal Code lays down, "Nothing is said to be done or believed in 'good faith' which is done or believed without due care and attention". Thus a doctor who has not taken due care and attention and is negligent would not get any protection under these provisions and the provisions in no way supports special treatment for doctors in criminal law.[2]

In civil law no such distinction is drawn between the two forms of *mens rea.* This means – whenever an act would be a civil wrong if done intentionally it is also a civil wrong if done negligently. When there is legal duty not to do an act purposely there is also a legal duty not to do it accidentally and carelessly.

6. Standard of Care

Standard of a reasonable man

Intention simply exists or does not exist. Carelessness may exist in various degrees. The degree of carelessness varies directly with the degree of risk to which other persons are exposed by the act in question. Greater the risk to which others may be exposed greater is the care required to be taken. So the question

1. (1932) AC 562 (618-19).
2. The Supreme Court judgment of August 2, 2005 in the *Dr. Jacob Mathew* case: One Jiwan Lal Sharma had difficulty in breathing. The judgment itself notes, "An oxygen cylinder was brought and connected to the mouth of the patient but the breathing problem increased further. The patient tried to get up but the medical staff asked him to remain in the bed. The oxygen cylinder was found to be empty. There was no other gas cylinder in the room. Vijay Sharma (the son of the patient) went to the adjoining room and brought a gas cylinder therefrom. However, there was no arrangement to make the gas cylinder functional and in-between 5 and 7 minutes were wasted. By this time, another doctor came who declared that the patient was dead."

is what degree of carelessness would constitute culpable negligence. Law neither demands the highest degree of carefulness nor does it permit total carelessness.

The test is:

- has the defendant behaved as a man of ordinary prudence under the given circumstances?
- *Has he* done *what a reasonable man* would not do *under the circumstances? Or has he* failed to do *what a reasonable* man would do *under the circumstances?*[1]
- 'reasonableness' is the standard which judge thinks ought to have been observed in the particular case. It does not refer to the average standard.

The court scrutinizes the importance of the object to be achieved in terms of the risk factor involved. If the social gain is negligible risk factor cannot be of great magnitude.

Want of professional skill and professional competence amounts to negligence. Thus negligence in performing an operation would render the doctor liable. In India Doctors come within the perview of Consumer Protection Act and carelessness resulting in injury will mean deficiency in service.

Some examples

- a towel was left inside the woman's peritoneal cavity while she was operated for sterilization resulting in her death. Held by the Supreme Court that it was negligence of the doctors.[2]
- The requirement that the plaintiff had to prove negligence to succeed in a suit against railways was causing hardship in many cases. Section 82A was inserted in the Railways Act in 1943 which makes the Railway administration liable to pay compensation upto a fixed amount whether or not the accident or injury was caused by neglect, default or wrongful act.

Degrees of negligence: Negligence may be slight, ordinary or gross. In civil cases it may impose ordinary or heavy damages. Gross negligence may be taken as intention itself.

7. *Theories of Negligence*

Following are the two theories of negligence

a. *Subjective theory of negligence (state of mind theory)* – According to Sir John Salmond negligence essentially consists in the mental attitude of undue indifference with respect to one's conduct and its consequences. According to this theory negligence is a state of mind

b. *Objective theory (type of conduct theory)* – According to Sir Fredrick Pullock negligence is not a state of mind but a type of conduct. It is a *breach of duty to take care.* To take care means to take precautions against the harmful results of one's action and to refrain from unreasonably dangerous kinds of act. To drive at night without lights is negligence because a prudent man would be careful enough to drive with lights on

---

1. *Blyth* v. *Birmingham Water Works Co.,* (1856) 25 LJ Ex 213.
2. *Indian Medical Assn.* v. *V.P. Shanta,* AIR 1996 SC 550.

at nights. A careful surgeon would ensure that the nurse counts the instruments and other things taken on the operation table at the end of the operation to ensure that no instrument has been left inside the body of the patient during operation. Hence to find out whether a person is careful or not, one looks at the standard of conduct of the person and not his mental attitude.

Hence according to this theory negligence is not to be found in the state of mind but in the conduct of the person which is manifested by his external behaviour and not internal attitude. This theory derives support from the Law of Torts where it is clearly settled that negligence means a failure to achieve the objective standard of the reasonable man.

The subjective theory has the merit of bringing out the difference between intention and negligence. Cases which on the face of it are cases of innocent negligence may turn out to be those of willful carelessness. For example, poison may be deliberately left unlabelled so that it may be consumed as a soft drink and the person may die. That is his external conduct which is regulated by his internal attitude of mind and his desire for certain consequences.

Negligence is the result of faulty behaviour arising out of a lethargy of the mind or out of faulty thinking. It is both subjective and objective.

XIV. The Theory of Strict Liability

Normally liability arises when there is a wrongful act coupled with guilty mind. Under the theory of strict liability it is wrongful act alone which makes a person liable; guilty mind or an innocent mind or a negligent mind is immaterial. The wrong may have resulted in spite of all the care and caution exercised yet the person is held liable. Such wrongs result when there is a breach of an absolute duty. Thus absolute duty means a duty which renders a man liable without any fault of his and irrespective of any intention or negligence on his part.

1. Why is Strict Liability an Exception in Civil Cases and not a Rule

The answer may be arrived at with the following analysis:

- In criminal cases, as a rule no man is punished for a crime unless he has a guilty mind. It is only in exceptional cases that without a guilty mind a person is punished for an offence.
- It may be argued that in civil cases strict liability must be a rule and not an exception. Suppose due to my act *B* is put to loss or suffers harm. What does it matter to *B* whether I did the act intentionally or negligently or whether I had taken all the care and yet the wrong was committed inadvertently. The fact remains that *B* is put to loss due to my action or inaction. Law states that purpose of civil proceedings is to compensate for wrong and the purpose of criminal proceedings is to punish. *So why should strict liability not be made a rule in civil proceedings is a relevant question for a student of Jurisprudence.*
- To this there are two answers: Firstly, there is no way of undoing the wrong that has been done. If I burn down *B's* house due to my negligence I pay him say Rs. 5 lakhs as compensation. What has happened is the loss is transferred from *B* to me. But the mischief (burning of the house) remains, and it will always remain. The mischief is not abated. *Secondly*

idea of compensation is related to fault. Due to fault a balance is disturbed and it has to be set right by the wrongdoer. So when I am at fault I pay Rs. 5,00,000 to *B* and put him in a position as he would have been if he had suffered no loss at all. But if there is no fault on my part what is there to be balanced? Why should I insure *B* for harm he suffers for no fault of mine? Unless some definite gain is to be derived by transferring loss from one head to another, sound reason as well as the law requires that the loss should lie where it falls. This is the reason why even in civil cases liability is linked to intention and negligence; and strict liability remains as an exception and not a rule.

Strictly speaking doctrine of strict liability must not be made applicable to criminal law. *i.e.* without proof of guilty mind punishment must not be imposed. But then there are genuine difficulties in procuring adequate proof of intention or negligence. In cases where the strict doctrine of *mens rea* interferes with the smooth administration of justice the doctrine of strict liability is applied.

The cases of strict liability fall under the following heads:

a. Mistake of law
b. Mistake of fact
c. Inevitable accident.

a. Mistake of Law

Ignorantia juris neminem excusat – Ignorance of law is no excuse. The presumption is that every one knows the law. The presumption is irrebuttable. That is no person can take a defence that he had no knowledge of the law and hence he must not be made liable.

There are three reasons for the rule: (1) it is the duty of every person to know the law which governs him. Law is knowable and definite. (2) In fact the reality is that people do not have knowledge of the plethora of laws in our legal system[1]. Yet, if ignorance of law were to be an excuse it could provide an easy way out for every guilty person to escape liability. It is extremely difficult to find out whether in fact a person has the knowledge of law or not because it has problems of evidentiality. Hence the doctrine of *ignorantia juris non excusat*.

A mistake as to law in force in India does not make the contract voidable. *E.g.*, *A* and *B* make a contract grounded on the erroneous belief that the debt is barred by the law of limitation. The contract cannot be avoided. For example, *B* owes *A* Rs. 2000. *A* agrees to accept Rs. 1000 instead of Rs. 2000 from *B* thinking that the debt is barred by the Limitation Act. In fact the debt was not barred by the Limitation Act. *A* now cannot rescind the contract on the ground that he had made a mistake regarding the law of Limitation.

b. Mistake of Fact

Ignorantia facit excusat – Ignorance of fact is an excuse. The statement is generally understood to mean that a person is not liable for a wrongful act if

1. In order to assist the people in knowing laws, in India creating law awareness is one of the functions of the Bar Council of India and of the States under the Advocates Act, 1961. The High Courts and the Law Colleges are regularly conducting legal awareness camps which are helping in disseminating legal awareness amongst those who are illiterate. It is also a part of the mandate under Article 39A of the Constitution.

done under a mistake of fact. But under the English law mistake of fact is an excuse only within the criminal law while in the civil law responsibility is strict. For example if I trespass on your land believing in good faith that it belongs to me, it is no defence to say that I believed it to be my own. If in absolute good faith I meddle with the goods of another person I am liable for the loss incurred by the other.[1] Intending to arrest *A* if I arrest *B* by mistake I am liable to him inspite of all the care taken by me.

Contrast between 'mistake of fact' and 'mistake of law' finds its true application in the criminal law. Absolute criminal responsibility for a mistake of fact is quite exceptional for example. If *A* abducts *B* who is under the age of giving legal consent it is no defense that he had made a genuine mistake as to her age because the act was *mala fide per se*.[2]

In India, as far as contractual liability (civil liability) is concerned, when there is a mistake of fact following are the legal provisions:

- Where both the parties are under a mistake of fact the contract cannot be enforced. *E.g.*, *A* agrees to sell a horse to *B* unknown to both of them it is already dead. Contract is not enforceable.[3]
- A contract is not voidable merely because it was caused by one of the parties to the contract being under a mistake of fact.[4]
- Mistake of foreign law has the same effect as a mistake of fact.

c. Inevitable Accident

Inevitable accident is commonly recognized as a ground of exemption from liability. According to Salmond

- *Unintentional act: A mistake*: Every act not done intentionally is either done accidentally or by mistake. Accident is done by mistake when the consequences are intended but the actor is *ignorant* of some *material circumstances*. For example, I arrest *A* mistaking him to be *B*. I injure him not accidentally but by mistake. If I run over a man in the dark because I did not know that he was on the road. I injure him accidentally because I did not intend the consequences.
- *Unintentional act, Accident:* It is done *accidentally* when the consequences are not intended. It is one which could possibly not be prevented even with due care caution and skill. Accident is either culpable or inevitable. It is culpable when it is due to negligence (want of care). It is an inevitable accident when the degree of care required to avoid it exceeds the standard required by law. Calpable accident is no defence but inevitable accident is a defence.
- *Inevitable accident a good defence:* Inevitable accident is commonly a good defence both in civil and criminal law. But in civil law there are exceptions. If I desire to keep wild beasts or accumulate upon my land any substance which will do damage to my neighbours if it escapes I

1. *Consolidated Co.* v. *Curtis*, (1892) 1 QB 495.
2. *Rights* v. *Prince*, (1875) LR 2 CC 154.
3. Section 20, Indian Contract Act, 1872.
4. Section 22, Indian Contract Act, 1872.

will do these things at my peril though none of these acts are *per se* wrongful and will incur liability.

- *Examples*: In *Hundson* v. *Roberts,*[1] the owner of a bull knew of its tendency to attack anything which was red in colour. He was held liable when the bull attacked a person wearing red.

A man is not liable for damage caused by domestic fire *i.e.* a fire which began in his house if it originated by accident and not negligence.

Loaded firearms are highly dangerous and more than ordinary care must be taken in handling them. In *Dixon* v. *Bell*, (1816) 5 M and S 198, a young girl was sent by the defendant to get a loaded gun from another man; thinking that the gun would not go off she pointed it at the plaintiff's child and pulled the trigger. The child suffered injuries. Defendant was held liable though he had sent a message to the man in custody of the loaded gun as to the manner in which the gun must be sent with the girl, but the man had not followed the instructions properly.

Gas companies must exercise the greatest care. In *M.C. Mehta* v. *Union of India,*[2] the Supreme Court held that there is absolute liability in all cases where there is injury on account of escape of gas.

Rylands v. *Fletcher,*[3] is a landmark case on strict liability. Fletcher was working in a coal mine under a lease. On the neighbouring wall Rylands started erecting a reservoir for storing water and employed a competent independent contractor to do the work. After the construction of the reservoir, when it was half filled with water the shafts gave way and water flooded the plaintiff's mine. The plaintiff sued for damages but he was not able to prove negligence. It was held that under the circumstances negligence was immaterial. When dangerous things are artificially brought in one's land, there is a positive duty to protect and guard neighbours so that they do not suffer harm by reason of such dangerous things. Such duty is absolute and a positive duty.

XV. Vicarious Liability

Normally and naturally he who does the wrongful act must be liable at law, but when *A* is made answerable for the wrongful acts of *B* it is an instance of vicarious liability. In the primitive systems man was made answerable for the acts of his kin. It was such a normal feature in the society that in the Mosaic legislation it was felt necessary to lay down that fathers shall not be put to death for the fault of their children and the children shall not be put to death for the fault of their fathers[4]. When punishment is conceived as expiative, retributive or vindictive rather than as deterrent and reformative, there seemed no reason why a guilty man should not provide a substitute to bear his penalty and thus meet the requirements of law. This was the argument put forth in the primitive days for justifying vicarious liability in criminal cases.[5]

---

1. (1851) 6 Ex 697.
2. (1987) 1 SCC 395.
3. (1863) LR 3 HL 330.
4. Deut xxiv 16.
5. Jurisprudence by Sir John Salmond by Glanville Williams, 10th Edn., p. 413.

1. *Jurisprudential Dilemmas in the Concept of Vicarious Liability*

While dealing with the theories of punishment we have seen that infliction of pain by way of punishment is justified when it is proportional to the offence and when it serves as a greater good to the society by way of deterrence or for his own good by way of reformation. But when *A* is punished for the *B's* wrongful acts under the concept of vicarious liability, he is being sacrificed for the greater good of the others. *A's* conduct is not in question. There is no question of his reformation. This means that he is treated as less than a person – as a thing. So when law is in harmony with morality, vicarious liability is avoided. So the only justification can be that law treats the victim *A* as a mere means to an end. In English law vicarious liability in criminal law is exceptional.

Modern civil law recognizes vicarious liability in two main classes:

2. *Master's Liability*

Masters are liable for the acts of their servants done in the course of their employment. The legal basis is that a servant carries on the business of his master with the master's express or implied authority, a servant is a person who voluntarily agrees to work for wages or not and agrees to abide by the lawful orders and directions of the master in respect of certain work to be done. Master is a person who is legally entitled to give such orders and to have them obeyed. Master is held liable for the acts of his servants on the following grounds:

a. *Qui facit per alium facit per se:* That is he who does an act through another is deemed in law to do it himself. A servant is engaged by the master under a contract of service. What distinguishes a servant from an independent contractor is that the master tells the servant not only what to do but also how to do it; he supervises and controls the execution of the work. This is the *prima facie* test of a servant.[1] Master will not be liable for the unauthorized acts and acts done out of whims and fancies of the servant. *E.g.* the *A* lets out their crane along with the driver to *B* under a contract providing that the driver shall be the servant of *B*. The driver through negligence injures a person. It was held that *A* was vicariously liable and that there was no transfer of the servant along with the crane.[2]

b. *Respondeat superior*: Is the same as *qui facit per alium facit per se*. The maxim respondeat superior states the rule baldly and *qui facit per alium facit per se* gives a fictional explanation of it.[3]

c. *Public policy*: The master's vicarious liability rests on public policy that there ought to be a remedy against someone who can pay the damages and the master is in a better position to pay than the servant[4]. These days master is a firm or a company or even when he is an individual the liability is taken care of through insurance covers.

---

1. *Gopal Rao* v. *Public Prosecutor, A.P.*, (1969) 1 SCC 704; employers in relation to the *Reserve Bank of India* v. *Their Workmen*, 1996 (2) SCALE 708 (712).
2. *Mersy Docks and Harbour Board* v. *Coggins and Griffith (Liverpool) Ltd.*, (1946) 2 All ER 345 (HL) cited in the Ratan Lal and Dhiraj Lal's Law of Torts, 27th Edn., p. 132.
3. L. Reid quoted in *ibid.*, p. 135.
4. Holmes Common law p. 9.

d. *Financial considerations*: The master is in a better financial position to meet the liability than the servant.

3. *Liability of the Legal Representatives*

Representatives of the dead are liable for the acts of the deceased whom they represent.

Actio personalis moritur cum persona a man cannot be punished in his grave. Hence all actions for penal redress must be brought against the living offender and must die with him. A personal action did not survive either on the death of the offender or the person who sustained the wrong.

Present opinion: maxim rejected: The Law Reform (Miscellaneous Provisions) Act, 1934 has virtually abolished the maxim. Modern opinion rejects this conclusion on two grounds. *Firstly,* it is argued that once the liability has come into existence though the wrong doer has died and hence it is impossible to subject him to punishment, yet from the point of view of the person wronged, it is a valuable right because if the offence is proved he is entitled to compensation for the injury suffered. Why should his right to compensation be extinguished because his wrongdoer happens to die?

Secondly, A further argument to justify extension of liability even after the death of the wrongdoer is that punishment is *effective* not at the time it is inflicted but *at the time it is threatened.* Hence a threat that an evil will be inflicted on the descendant's of the wrongdoer by way of compensation to be realized from the property of the wrongdoer operates as a deterrent influence on him. The descendants will inherit the property subject to the charges on the property including the charge of paying the compensation to the person who has suffered injury due to the act of the wrongdoer.

a. *Effect of death on suits*: In India in civil cases following are the provisions regarding the effect of death on the suit:

1. The death of the plaintiff or the defendant shall not cause the suit to abate if the right to sue survives.[1] Right to sue means right to bring a suit asserting a right to the same relief which the deceased plaintiff asserted at the time of his death.[2]
2. Right to sue survives under the Indian Contract Act, 1872 unless the contract is of such a nature that it involves special skill or special personal confidence. In such exceptional cases contracts do not bind the representatives of the dead promisor. *E.g. A* promises to paint a picture for *B* but dies before that day. The contract does not bind *A's* representatives because the right to sue does not survive.
3. Under the Indian Succession Act, 1925 right to initiate an action or to defend an action existing in the deceased person pass over to his executors or administrators.

   But an action for (a) defamation, assault as defined in the Indian Penal Code, or (b) a personal action not resulting in death, or (c) if the relief cannot be enjoyed after the death of a party as in the case of restitution for conjugal rights does not survive upon the executors or the administrator.

---

1. Order 22, Rule 1 of the Code of Civil Procedure, 1872.
2. *Sarat Chandra* v. *Nani Mohan,* (1909) 36 Cal 799 (801).

4. Under the Code of Criminal Procedure an appeal by the State Government against a sentence or an appeal against the acquittal finally abates on the death of the accused. But when appeal is against conviction and death sentence or of imprisonment and the appellant dies during the pendency of the appeal his near relatives may continue the appeal after obtaining leave within 30 days of the death.

XVI. Measure of Criminal Liability

Measure of criminal liability is different from that of civil liability. We have dealt with several theories of punishment and the purposes of punishment. But the practical question is: what is the quantum of punishment to be awarded and what are the principles by which to determine the quantum of punishment. While analyzing the measure of punishment we mainly concentrate on 'deterrence' as the purpose of punishment.

If punishment were to operate surely and certainly as a deterrent that law would be the most efficient, which would extinguish crime altogether by imposing the *same severest* punishment for all crimes from murder to petty theft. But the deterrent theory is not hundred per cent effective. Man's actions are not always guided by the thought of the consequence or the thought of long term good and bad. Most of the time he acts on the impulse of the moment. Hence even with severest punishment it operates only to diminish crime and not extinguish it. This means deterrence as a purpose of punishment is partly effective and partly not effective. When deterrence operates to prevent crime it culminates in a sum total of good. When it fails to prevent crime there is a sum total of evil. The perfect law is one where the sum total of the good is more than the sum total of evil to its maximum extent. The measure for criminal liability are the rules for attaining this maximum. Merely going on increasing the severity of punishment for petty offences will not reduce the crime rate.

Following are the three elements to be taken into consideration for determining the measure of punishment:

1. *Motive for the crime:* The object of punishment is to provide artificial and contrary motives to counter the natural motive which leads to crime. In other words, punishment must be of such a measure that the offender will suffer more loss due to punishment than the gain he may earn by committing crime. In simple words *motive for not committing crime must be made larger than motive for committing crime.* For example, compare two set of laws in one theft, is punished with a penalty of Rs. 50 in another theft is punished with Rs. 1 lakh; motive for committing crime would be larger in the first case rather than the second one. Greater the temptation to commit the crime greater should be the punishment.
2. *Magnitude of the offence:* Greater the offence greater will be the evil consequences and so greater must be the punishment. Punishment cannot be measured solely by the profit derived by the offender, evil caused to the other persons also is to be considered. It also cannot be said that simply because the two crimes are equal in point of motive they should be equal in point of punishment. This is because suppose the motive for theft and murder are the same to punish both murder and theft with death penalty would not be reasonable because theft is comparatively

trivial in nature. Another reason why there should be less punishment for a lesser offence is that when the offender wants to choose between two offenses (say murder and theft he will choose the one for which the punishment is less.

3. *Character of the offender:* People abstain from committing crime due to various reasons may be the fear of punishment; religious beliefs; own pride and self respect; love for a good image in the public; fear of criticism by the public etc. If these urges are dominant it means that his temperament or his disposition is good and normal. But if he has anti social passions like anger, hatred, malice, revengeful attitude his disposition is not good.

If he responds to normal temptation with abnormal force law has to impose penal discipline with double measure. Following are the examples where bad disposition of mind is indicated: (a) person already punished once commits the same crime again it means punishment adopted for normal men does not work in his case. (b) his mischief quantum is disproportionate to the gain he anticipates *e.g.* murdering the victim as a revenge for an insult (c) disgusting to normal human behaviour *e.g.* killing one's father, mother; raping a child of 3 years etc.

XVII. Measure of Civil Liability

It is mainly based on the principle of compensation rather than of fault. It depends on the quantum of loss. At times higher damages are awarded due to malice, etc. civil liability takes no account of the character of the offender, motives. It takes no account of the probable or intended consequences.

The measure of contractual liability is determined by the Indian Contract Act, 1872. Following are the relevant provisions:

1. *Ordinary damages*: When there is a breach of contract, the aggrieved party can recover from the defaulting party such damages which naturally arose in the usual course of the things from such breach. These are known as *ordinary damages* arising in the usual course of the things. This means that the damages must be the proximate consequence of the breach of contract. It must not be remote or indirect loss or damage.

   For example, *A* contracts to sell to *B* 100 quintals of coconut oil for Rs. 5000 per quintal. *A* fails to deliver the same. The price of oil rises to Rs. 5500 per quintal. *B* can claim damages at the rate of Rs. 500 per quintal. He is thus placed in a position as though the contract was in fact performed by *A*.

2. *Special damages:* Damages other than those arising in the ordinary course of the breach which the parties knew to be likely to result from the breach are special damages and can be recovered from the defaulting party. For example, in *Simpson* v. *London & N.W. Rail Co.*, (1876) 1 QBD 274. *S* sent some agricultural implements for agricultural show to be delivered straight to the Exhibition Ground at New Castle. The consignment note mentioned "Must reach New Castle on Monday certain." The samples arrived later only after the show was over. It was held that it was within the contemplation of the railways that additional loss would occur if there was a default. *S* was awarded compensation.

3. *Exemplary or vindictive damages* : Exemplary damages have no place in the law of contract because they are punitive by nature/yet for breach of a promise to marry and for dishonour of a cheque by the banker wrongfully when he possesses sufficient funds to the credit of the customer-exemplary damages are awarded.
4. *Nominal damages*: are awarded in recognition of the violation of the right even if no damage has resulted.

Following are the cases in India where compensation is awarded even if no loss has actually occurred

1. Section 74 Indian Contract Act, 1872 provides for penal liability in case of breach of contracts in cases where penalty is stipulated for in the contract in case breach occurs. In such a case an amount not exceeding the amount mentioned is awarded whether or not actual damage or loss is proved to have been caused.
2. Even where the plaintiff suffers no loss the court may still award him nominal damages in recognition of his right.

CHAPTER 22
THE LAW OF PROPERTY

SYNOPSIS

Introduction

I. Nature of Proprietary Rights *in rem*
   1. Property in its Wide Sense
   2. Property in its Narrow Sense
   3. Proprietary Rights
   4. Corporeal Property

II. 5 Kinds of Property
   1. Corporeal and Incorporeal
      a. Incorporeal
      (i) *Jura in re aliena and*
      (ii) *Jura in re propria*
      b. Corporeal Property – Ownership in Material Things
      (i) General use and Specific use
      (ii) Absolute or Unlimited use not Known to Law
      (iii) Limitations on Owner's use
         For the Benefit of Public
         Arising out of Encumbrances
      (iv) Permanency of Right of Ownership
      (v) Right of Ownership – Inheritable
   2. Movable and Immovable Property
   3. Real and Personal Property
   4. Rights *in re propria* in Immaterial Things
      a. Patents
      b. Literary Copyright
      c. Artistic Copyright
      d. Musical and Dramatic Copyright
      e. Commercial Goodwill, Trade Marks and Trade Names
   5. Rights *in re* Aliena or Encumbrances
      a. Lease
      b. Servitude
      c. Securities
      d. Trust

III. Modes of Acquisition of Proprietary Rights
   1. Possession
      a. Occupation
      b. Possessory Ownership
   2. Prescription
      a. Positive or Acquisitive Prescription
      b. Negative or Extinctive Prescription
      (i) Perfect
      (ii) Imperfect
   3. Agreement

a. **Agreement is of Two Kinds: Grant & Assignment**
b. **Agreement: Formal or Informal**
c. **Assignor/Grantor cannot Assign/Grant more than what he has**
d. **Exceptions to Above Rule Arising Out of**
   (i) **Separation of Legal from Equitable Ownership**
   (ii) **Separation of Ownership from Possession**

4. **Inheritance**

INTRODUCTION

Laws may be substantive laws or procedural laws. Broadly spoken substantive laws lay down the rights and the obligations and the Procedural laws lay down the procedures for their enforcement.

Substantive Civil laws are divided into three categories:

- The law of property deals with the proprietary rights *in rem i.e.* rights available against the world at large.
- The law of obligations deals with proprietary rights *in personam i.e.* rights available against particular persons.
- Law of status deals with personal or non proprietary rights whether *in rem* or *in personam.*

I. Nature of Proprietary Rights *in rem*

The term property in the sense of proprietary rights *in rem* have different applications having different degrees of generality:

1. ***Property in its wide sense*** – In its widest sense, property includes all the legal rights of a person of whatever description. Master's rights over his servant[1]; man's right to his own life and limb[2]; right to his own person[3] But this sense is obsolete today.
2. ***Property in its narrow sense*** – *Proprietary rights: (dominium and status)* In the narrow sense it includes rights to his estate or property. His lands, chattels *i.e.* movable property; his shares and the debts due to him are his property. They are known as proprietary rights as opposed to personal rights. This is the most popular sense and the one in which it is used today.
3. ***Proprietary rights*** **in rem** *(dominium and obligation)*: It means only the proprietary rights which are available against the world at large, *e.g.* freehold or leasehold estate in land, a patent or a copyright; it has to be distinguished from proprietary rights *in personam* which are available only against particular person *e.g.* debt or a benefit of contract.
4. ***Corporeal property:*** *(dominium corporis and dominium juris).* In its narrowest sense it includes only the rights of ownership in material objects or that object itself. This is known as corporeal property. Bentham does not favour extension of the term to anything other than material things.

---

1. Blackstone.
2. Hobbes.
3. Locke.

In India, right to property was a fundamental right under Article 19(1)(f) of the Constitution. It was deleted from the list of fundamental rights and inserted as a constitutional right under Article 300A. The Supreme Court has held[1] that the word property must be given a liberal meaning and should be extended to all those well recognized interests which have the characteristics of property right. It includes both corporeal and incorporeal right.[2] It includes money,[3] contract, interest in property *e.g.* interest of an allottee, licensee, mortgagee or a lessee. The Mahantship of a Hindu temple. The right to receive pension is property.[4]

II. Kinds of Property

There are 5 kinds of property.

1. *Corporeal and Incorporeal Property*

All property is either corporeal or incorporeal. Corporeal property is the right of ownership in material things. Incorporeal property is any other proprietary right *in rem*. Property is incorporeal if any right in the bundle of rights constituting such property satisfies the test of acquisition, holding and disposal separately from the corpus.[5]

a. *Incorporeal property is of two kinds.*

  (i) *Jura in re aliena (encumbrance)* may be over material things or immaterial things, and

  (ii) *Jura in re propria* over immaterial things. For example, patents, copyrights and trademarks.

b. *Corporeal property: i.e. ownership of material things*: Owner of the material object is one who owns a right to the aggregate of its uses. If he has a limited right to it he is not the owner of the thing. For example, I own a house. House is the material object. I have a right to the sum total of its uses. For example, I can stay in the house myself; I can rent it out, I can mortgage it; sell it; Exchange it etc. If I mortgage (say a usufructory mortgage) it to *B* to secure a loan of Rs. one lakh, in effect I am transferring specific interests in the house to *B* as security for the loan he has given me. *B* has a limited right to the use of the house and to enjoy the income arising there from until the debt is paid off.

  (i) *General use and specific use*: All lawful use is either general (*i.e.* residuary) or specific. General use means ownership and specific use means encumbrance.

  (ii) *Absolute or unlimited use not known to Law:* Ownership is the right of general use and not absolute or unlimited or unregulated use. Law does not know of any absolute or unlimited use.

  (iii) *Limitations on owner's use:* Following are two kinds of limitation upon the owners' residuary use of the property:

---

1. *Commissioner, Hindu Religious Endowments* v. *Swamiar*, AIR 1954 SC 282.
2. *Dwarka Das Shrinivas* v. *Sholapur Spg. and Wvg. Co. Ltd.*, AIR 1954 SC 328.
3. *Bombay Dying Co.* v. *State of Bombay*, AIR 1958 SC 328.
4. *Deokinandan Prasad* v. *State of Bihar*, AIR 1971 SC 1409.
5. *Manathunainatta* v. *Sundarlingam*, AIR 1971 Mad 1.

- *For the benefit of the public*: Limitations *for the benefit of the public* or the neighbours. For example, I own a land in a residential area. I will not be allowed to start an industry on the land because areas are divided into residential and industrial areas for efficient management and administration and for the benefit of the public and the inhabitants at large.
- *Arising out of encumbrances:* Limitations arising out of encumbrances: For example, I mortgage my house to B to secure the repayment of a loan of Rs. One lakh. It means now *B* has a specific interest in my house; under certain circumstances he can cause my house to be sold in order to realize the debt. This operates as a restriction upon my right to general use of my property. But I am still the owner of the house. I have only transferred a specific interest in the house to *B*. By virtue of the remaining interests I am still the owner. When I pay back the mortgage debt and thereby exercise my right of redemption the restriction is removed and I can once again exercise my right of general use of the property (also known as residuary use). Likewise when I lease my house for 5 years there is a restriction upon my right of general use up to 5 years. At the expiry of 5 years my residuary right gains full momentum. Such specific uses are known as encumbrances. Encumbrances restrict the right of general use of the owner. When the restriction is removed right of general use revives fully.

Right of ownership remains in spite of any number of encumbrances. In the above example I may create a second mortgage in favour of *C* and lease the house to *D*. I am still the owner even if some encumbrancers like *B, C, D* may have more valuable rights than mine.

(iv) *Permanency of Right of ownership:* Right of ownership is permanent. A person having a temporary right to use the thing cannot be the owner of a thing. This permanent right lasts only as long as the thing lasts. If the thing is destroyed the right of ownership is lost. We may add that in cases where the thing is insured the right of ownership becomes a basis for claiming the amount for which the thing is insured.

(v) *Right of ownership inheritable:* Permanence involves the right of inheritance. A man can own only those permanent rights which can pass over to his successors after his death. All others are temporary rights.

Thus right of ownership is a right to general, permanent and inheritable right to the uses of that thing.

2. *Movable and Immovable Property (Chattels and Lands; or Bona Mobilla and Bona Immobilla)*

Among material things difference between movable and immovable is the most important. Each legal system has its own rules to govern them. Property may be movable or immovable depending on its capacity to suffer alteration in relation to place.

Immovable property includes the following elements:

- A determinate portion of the earth's surface.
- The ground below the surface down to the centre of the world.
- Column of space above the surface *ad infinitum*. Laws may recognize no right of ownership in the airspace at all, or at least no right of exclusive use. In England it is expressly provided by the statute that the flight of aircraft at a reasonable height above the ground is not actionable at the suit of the owner or occupier of the land below.
- All objects which are on or under the surface in the natural state like minerals and natural vegetation. Stones lying lose upon the surface are in the same category as the stone in the quarry.
- Objects placed by human agency on or under the surface with an intention of annexing it permanently. They become a part of the land and lose their identity as movables. For example, buildings, walls, the stones, the bricks, the nuts and bolts etc. If the intention to annex permanently is present, physical attachment to the surface is not required. Likewise mere physical attachment without the requisite intention also is not sufficient. Carpets and ornaments nailed to the wall or floor of the house are not immovable property and part of the house. Money buried in the ground is movable property just like moneys in the pocket.
- Distinction between movable and immovable is in fact applicable only to material objects. But where a property is immovable every right and every interest in it whether a *jura in re aliena* or *in re propria* is also immovable. For example, right of way; right to collect rents from immovable property; office of hereditary priest of a temple; a Hindu widow's life interest in the immovable property of her deceased husband; right to fishery; right to collect juice from the trees. Similarly if a thing is movable every right and interest in it is movable. The concept of treating such interests as movable or immovable property is regarded as illogical but it is a concept established in law.
- Under the General Clauses Act, 1897 immovable property includes land, benefit to arise out of land such as rent and things attached to the earth like trees and buildings but not standing timber, growing crops and grass.
- The local situation of an incorporeal right is difficult to fix. A debt is situated where the debtor resides; a patent, a copyright are situated where they are exercised or enjoyed. The goodwill of the business is situated where the business is carried on.

3. Real and Personal Property

In India the difference between real and personal laws is not there. Real property comprises rights over immovable property and all other proprietary property come within personal property.

Three meanings are given to the term chattel under English law:

- Movable physical object like a book;
- Movable property whether corporeal or incorporeal furniture, debts, shares contracts, patents, copyrights etc.;

- Personal property whether movable or immovable as opposed to real property, like leaseholds;

4. *Rights* in re Propria *in Immaterial Things*

A material object is a physical object. An immaterial thing is anything else which may be the subject-matter of a right. There are five kinds of immaterial things:

a. *Patents*: The subject-matter of a patent right is an invention. Patent right is a privilege granted by the State to the first inventor of any new product or invention that he and his licensees will have the sole right of making and selling such product or invention during a particular period of time. Patent Act in India has been amended in 2005 in order to make it compatible with Trade Related Intellectual Property Rights. It now provides for both process and product patents. Person who has registered the patent gets an exclusive right to sell, use or make the patented invention for 14 years.
b. *Literary copyright*: The subject-matter of this right is the literary expression of facts or thoughts. It is the exclusive liberty of printing or multiplying the copies of the books. *E.g.* copyrights in books, letters, dramatic work, musical works, and works of art.
c. *Artistic copyright*: Artistic designs in various forms like drawing, painting, etc. is the subject-matter of a right of exclusive use analogous to literary copyright. The material, the paint and the canvas belongs to the purchaser but the picture in the abstract form belongs to the person who made it.
d. *Musical and dramatic copyright:* Any unauthorized performance of musical and dramatic performance is an infringement of the exclusive use of proprietary right.
e. *Commercial goodwill, trade marks and trade names:* Goodwill is something that is earned in a business through hard work, integrity, honesty and it can be sold and purchased like any other property. Under the Indian Contract Act, 1882, goodwill of the business is recognized as a property and restrictions can be imposed on the seller of the goodwill that he shall not carry on a similar business within the specified limits for a specified time.

5. *Rights* in re aliena *or Encumbrances: Leases, Servitudes, Securities and Trusts*

Leases

The four important rights in *re aliena* are leases, servitudes, securities and Trusts. Generally speaking lease is associated with immovable property mainly land; and bailment is associated with chattels and movables. Yet for the sake of orderly classification the term lease is used to include both tenancy of land and also all kinds of bailments of chattels and all encumbrances of incorporeal property which possess the same essential nature as a tenancy of land.

Encumbrance may be on the material object or a servitude: In this generic sense lease is an encumbrance consisting of a right to possession and use of property owned by some other person. It results out of separation of ownership and possession. This separation may be rightful or wrongful. If rightful it is an encumbrance of the owner's title. *E.g.* A leases his house to *B* for a certain rent for 5 years. *A* the lessor is still the owner though *B* – the lessee is in possession of the house. The house is *encumbered* for 5 years as the separation between ownership and possession is lawful.

The right which is encumbered by the lease is the ownership of the house which *A* has. But then encumbrance need not always be on the right of ownership of a material object like the house in this example. *All rights which can be possessed and can be continuously exercised can be leased and consequently encumbered. But rights which cannot be possessed cannot be leased.*

Continuing the above illustration suppose *A* also owns a land adjoining the house he has leased to *B*. *A* may lease the right of way over the land to *B* along with the house. *B* may further sublease the house to *C* along with the right of way. Here it is the right of way which is encumbered by *B* the lessee who is the owner of a lease. Right of way is a servitude appurtenant to land. It is not a material object. Hence the law that encumbrance need not always be on the material object. Even obligations like annuities, shares can be encumbered.

Term of years: Generally a lease would be for a *term of years* but in legal theory there can be a perpetual lease also. The essence of a lease is the separation of the ownership from possession. I may exercise a permanent right to possess a thing without owning it. Ownership may remain dormant in the hands of the lessor.

Under Section 105 of the Transfer of Property Act, 1882, lease of immovable property has the following essential ingredients: Transfer of a right to enjoy the property for a duration *i.e.* a term of years or in perpetuity; price paid or promised; rent in the form of money or a share of crops or any other thing of value to be rendered periodically; acceptance by the transferee.

b. *Servitude*: If lease is possession without ownership; a servitude is a limited use of a piece of land without possession. It is also an encumbrance.

Servitudes may be either private where it vests in a determinate individual. It may vest in public for example, right of the public to a highway over my land. Servitudes may be appurtenant or gross. An appurtenant servitude consists of a dominant and a servient tenement. For example.

A is the owner *of two lands X and Y*.

A sells *Land X* to *B* and *B* also has a right of way over *Land Y* to reach a public road. This right of way is a servitude.

Now if *A* sells *land Y* to Z, Z takes it with a burden to allow *B* the right of way over land *Y*.

Likewise if *B* sells *land* X to *C*, *C* takes it with the benefit of the right of way over *land Y*. Hence both the benefit and the burden run with the land.

c. *Security: Security for enjoyment of some other right: mortgage and lien*

Security is an encumbrance and its purpose is to make sure or to facilitate the fulfillment or enjoyment of some other right (usually but not always, a debt) vested in the same person.

For example, *A* mortgages his house to *B* to secure a repayment of a loan of Rs. One lakh to be repaid within 5 years. What it means is:

- *B* has a basic right to recover Rs. One lakh from *A* within 5 yrs;
- In order to facilitate *B* in recovering the debt, an encumbrance is created over *A's* house and he is given the right to cause the house to be sold in order to realize the debt;

- Here encumbrance is on *A's* house; *A's* house is the security for repayment of loan;
- And the right to recover the debt and the right to the security vests in the *same person B*; and;
- It's purpose is to assist *B* in recovering the debt. (the same example will be followed to study the difference between mortgage and lien);

Thus a security is an encumbrance vested in the creditor over the property of his debtor for the purpose of securing the recovery of the debt.

Securities are of two kinds. Mortgages and liens. Security on immovable property is called mortgages and security on movable property is called pledge.

Mortgage does not necessarily involve transfer of the property to the creditor. In India under the Transfer of Property Act, 1882 it is defined as a transfer of an interest in a specific immovable property to secure the repayment of a loan advanced or to be advanced or an existing or a future debt or the performance of an engagement giving rise to a pecuniary liability.

	Mortgage	Lien
1.	It is not just a security. It is an independent and a principal right by itself. (refer the example given above. We will continue with the same example to note the other points of differences).	It is only a right to retain possession of a movable property until payment or a right to receive payment out of a certain fund. E.g. *A* finds a gold ring belonging to *B*. *A* can retain the ring until he is paid the expenses say Rs. 2000 that he has incurred in finding out the true owner, and the reward of Rs. 10,000 which has been declared by *B* to anyone finding and returning the ring. Other examples are pledge, vendor's lien, equitable charge on a fund.
2.	It can be created by transfer on an interest in the property to the mortgagee or by encumbrance.	It is created only by encumbrance.
3.	Right of mortgage is vested in the mortgagee as a *conditional right* and only as a security. For ex. In the above example, B can exercise his right to sell the property to realize Rs. One lakh *only if A* fails to pay the debt. Hence *B's* right to sell the property is only a security.	Right of lien is vested in the lienee absolutely and as a *primary right* and not as a mere security. In the above example, retaining the gold ring is a primary right.
4.	The right of security which the mortgagee has over the mortgagor's property remains outstanding even after the debt is paid off. Hence those rights have to be retransferred to the mortgagor. Right of the mortgagor to this reassignment or to recall the	A lien cannot survive the debt secured. In the above example, on payment of Rs. 12000 the lien ceases *ipso jure*. There is no right of redemption as in the case of mortgage because there is nothing to redeem.

Mortgage	Lien
rights that he has transferred to the mortgagee is called the right of redemption. Existence of the right of redemption is the test of mortgage. In England right of redemption is described as an equitable right of redemption. In India it is also a statutory right of redemption under the Transfer of Property Act.	
5. The debt is extinguished at the end of the period specified, yet the right of security continues. In the above example, when Rs. One lakh is paid off within 5 yrs the debt is over but the rights which have been transferred to the mortgagee still remain with him. The mortgagor has to call them back by exercising his right of redemption.	Duration depends on the debt that is secured. In the above example lien remains alive until the Rs. 12000 is realized. The moment it is paid or realized by sale of the gold ring the lien is extinguished.
6. In a mortgage, though some interests in the property are transferred to the mortgagee, the mortgagor (debtor) still remains the equitable owner of the property. On repayment of debt the mortgagee (*B*) holds the property in trust for the mortgagor (*A*). *i.e.* he (*B*) will be accountable to the mortgagor (*A*) for the income etc received on the property; to take care of the property etc.	Legal and equitable ownership vests in the debtor and the creditor has only such limited rights which give sufficient protection to recover the debt.

In India, there are 6 kinds of mortgage simple, usufructory, English mortgage, mortgage by conditional sale, equitable mortgage, anamolous mortgage.

Liens are of 5 kinds:

Possessory liens: Right to retain possession until debt is paid off.; pledge of the chattels, lien of the inn keeper and of the sellers.

Right of distress or seizure: Right to take possession of the debtor's property

Powers of sale: It is incidental to right of possession.

Powers of forfeiture: *e.g.* landlord's right of re-entry upon his tenant.

Charges: Right of the creditor to receive payment out of some specific fund.

(d) *Trusts:* Trust is an obligation annexed to the ownership of the property. There are 3 parties – the owner, the trustee and the beneficiary. The owner transfers property to the trustee – who is treated 'as' the owner, but is not the beneficial owner of the property. He uses the property for the benefit of the beneficiary.

III. Modes of Acquisition: There are 4 Modes

1. Possession 2. Prescription 3. Agreement 4. Inheritance

1. Possession

The possession of a material object is a title to the ownership of it. He who claims a piece of land as his own and makes good its claim *in fact* by possession makes it good *in law* also by ownership. *E.g.* if I *possess* a fountain pen *in fact* and also show that I own it say by showing that I have purchased it or that it has been gifted to me, my claim to my pen is now supported by *the fact of possession and in law by ownership*. In other words by possessing a material object, the owner may acquire a legal title to it in two ways: by occupation and by possessory ownership.

a. *By occupation*: When the claimant takes the possession of a property which did not belong to anyone before- the possessor acquires a good title against the whole world. Things which do not belong to anyone are known as *res nullius.* They are things which cannot be possessed exclusively by anybody like fishes in the sea. This mode of acquisition is known as *occupatio* in Roman law. Occupation is taking possession of a *res nullius* in order to own it. The title so acquired is good against the whole world.

b. *By possessory ownership*: The thing of which possession is taken may be already the property of someone else. Here I take possessory ownership not by agreement but only by possession. The title so acquired is good against the whole world except the true owner who shows a prior better title in himself. This is the position even if my possession is consciously wrongful. I can effectually transfer it, sell it, bequeath it but whoever takes it from me takes only my title which is imperfect and limited because no man can transfer more than what he has. If I am wrongfully deprived of my possession by X, I can recover it back. X cannot set-up the defense of the right of the true owner *i.e. jus tertii.* He cannot refuse to deliver back the property on the ground that it is not me but some third person – who is the true owner of the property.

2. Prescription

Property may be acquired by prescription. Prescription may be defined as the effect of lapse of time in creating and destroying rights. Prescriptions are of two kinds:

a. *Positive or acquisitive prescription*: By prescription a right is created. For example right of way acquired by the *de facto* use of it for 20 years. Positive prescription is possible only in the case of rights which admit of continuing exercise and enjoyment. Most of such rights are rights *in rem.* It is the investitive operation of lapse of time with possession.

b. *Negative or extinctive prescription*: The right is extinguished by prescription. *E.g.* right to sue for recovery of money is extinguished after 3 yrs from the date on which it becomes due. They are common to the law of property and cbligations. It is the divestitive operation of lapse of time without possession. Negative prescriptions are of two kinds:

(i) *Perfect prescription* – It destroys the principal right itself. *E.g. A* dispossesses *B* of his property for 12 years. *B* becomes the owner by adverse possession.

(i) *Imperfect prescription* – The principal right remains and the accessory right is destroyed. Example, Time-barred debt. The debt remains but the remedy is barred.

The rational basis for the rule of prescription is that: if a thing is possessed in fact it is a *de facto evidence that it is owned de jure*. Conversely if it is not possessed *de facto* it means that it is not owned *de jure*. Hence possession is evidence of title and want of possession is evidence of no title. The point is: all proof of title may be lost. Witnesses may die; documents may wear out and be lost; memory may fade. Long possession may be an effective substitute.

Acquisition by prescription is not limited to rights *in rem*. It is extended to the sphere of obligation and also property.

Section 26 of the Limitation Act, 1963 lays down the law as to acquisition of easements by prescription. Where access to light and air and water course is enjoyed peaceably and without interruption for 20 yrs and in case of Government property for 60 yrs such right shall be absolute.

3. *Agreement*

Agreements include not merely contracts but all other bilateral acts in the law, *i.e.* all expressions of consenting wills of two or more persons directed towards alterations of their legal relations. According to Paton, agreement is an expression of two or more persons communicated to each other, of a common intention to affect the legal relations between each other.

a. *Agreement is of two kinds:*

- *Grant* – New rights are created by encumbrance upon the existing right of the grantor. For example, when *A* leases his land to *B* it is a *grant* created by an *agreement* between *A* and *B*. *A* is the grantor; *B* is the grantee. Leasehold is vested in the grantee *B*; and an encumbrance is created on the right vested in *A*, the grantor.
- *Assignment* – Existing rights are transferred from one owner to another. In the above example, B assigns his leasehold to *C*. *B* is the assignor and *C* is the assignee.

b. *Agreement: Formal or informal*: Agreement is either formal or informal. Formal agreements must satisfy all the requirements prescribed like that of registration, writing, attestation etc. Informal agreements are verbal and no formalities are needed to be fulfilled. Under the Roman law agreement had to be accompanied with delivery of possession. In England, it is only after 1845 conveyance of land could be effected without delivery of possession. Until 1845, land could be conveyed by no other method then by delivery of possesion.[1] In India, transfer of property means an act by which one living person conveys property to another living person or to himself and to transfer property is to perform such act. Thus the manner of conveyance depends upon the mode prescribed by the Act.

1. P.J. Fitzgerald: Salmond on Jurisprudence, 12th Edn., p. 440.

c. *Assignor/Grantor cannot assign/grant more than what he has*: The leading principle is that the grantor or the assignor cannot grant or assign more than what he has. The maxim is *Nemo plus juris ad alium transferee potest, quam ipse haberet.*

d. *Exceptions.*

There are two exceptions:

- *Separation of legal from equitable ownership*: Those arising from separation of legal from equitable ownership. Under the English law where legal ownership is in one person and the equitable ownership in another the legal owner is the trustee for the equitable owner. He holds the property on behalf of that other. The obligation of this trusteeship is an encumbrance upon his title. Yet he may give an unencumbered title to a third person provided the third person has taken the property for value and without notice. Note that the Indian law does not recognise the distinction between legal and equitable owner. For example, *A* contracts to sell his Sultanpur estate to *B*. While the contract is still alive he sells it to *C* who takes it for value and without notice of the contract. Under our law,[1] the contract of sale gives rise only to an obligation on the part of *A* to sell Sultanpur to *B* and does not create any interest legal or equitable in the property in favour of *B*.
- *Separation of ownership from possession*: Those arising due to separation of ownership from possession. Law allows people to act on presumption that the possessor of the thing is the owner of it and he who honestly acts on this presumption gets a valid title in all events. For example, possessor of a bank note may not have title to it because he may have found it but he can give a good title to anyone who takes it from him for value and in good faith.

4. *Inheritance*

On the death of a person his rights in the property get divided into two classes: heritable or uninheritable rights. A right is heritable if it survives its owner. It is uninheritable if it dies with him. Personal rights are in general uninheritable. For example, right to conjugal rights in the spouse; right to enforce a contract to paint a picture are uninheritable. They are not merely divested but are totally extinguished.

Proprietary rights are inheritable. In respect of them death is a divestitve fact and not extinctive fact. There are exceptions to this rule. *A* lease for the life of a lessee is extinguished on the death of the lessee. *A* and *B* jointly own a property – A dies. His right in the property is extinguished and *B* acquires an exclusive title by the right of survivorship (*jus accrescendi*). On the death of a coparcener property devolves according to the right of survivorship under the Hindu law subject to exceptions laid down under Section 6 of the Hindu Succession Act, 1956.

Law has given an option to a person to decide who shall be the owner of his property after his death by executing a Will. If he does not exercise the option then law of the land determines in whom the property shall vest after his death

1. Section 40 of the Transfer of Property Act, 1882.

by the law of intestate succession. In either case such persons are referred to as his representatives. They may be the legatees and the executors in case of a Will executed by the deceased person; or the heirs and the administrators in case he has left no Will. Thus the rights of a deceased person vest in his representatives appointed by him or appointed by law on his behalf. This representative bears the person of the deceased and hence all the heritable rights and the inheritable liabilities vest in them. This representative need not be the beneficial owner of the property. He may hold it for the benefit of two categories of persons the creditors of the deceased and the beneficiaries of the estate. He himself may or may not be a creditor or a beneficiary. The representatives take the benefits and also the liabilities. They are liable only to the extent of the property of the deceased that has passed into hands. *i.e.* if *A* has inherited Rs. 1,00,000 from *B* and the debts of *B* are 1,10,000. *A* is liable only to the extent of 1,00,000.

The beneficiaries who are entitled to the residue of the property left by the deceased after paying off the creditors are:

- Those nominated by the last Will of the deceased. The succession is known as testamentary succession.
- And if no Will is executed then those appointed under the law of intestate succession. The succession is known as intestate succession. In India we have the Hindu Succession Act, 1956 for the Hindus and the Muslims are governed by their personal laws. Parsis and Christians are governed by the Indian Succession Act, 1925.

As far as a Will is concerned there are three limitations on the power of a person while disposing of his property by Will:

1. It is only during a limited period after his death that he can impose directions regarding disposition of his property. He cannot prevent the vesting of the estate in perpetuity.
2. Limitation upon the amount: Most legal systems impose a pecuniary limit on the portion that can be disposed of by Will. The rest is allotted by law to those whom he owes a duty to support like the wife and children. For example, in India, Hindus can dispose of even the whole of the property by Will to the total exclusion of wife and children but under the Muslim law they cannot dispose of more than one third unless the heirs consent to it after the death of the testator.

CHAPTER 23
OBLIGATIONS

SYNOPSIS

I. Nature of Obligation

Obligation in its popular sense is synonym with duty. But in its *legal sense* there are several differences and it should be understood in the following senses:

1. *Correlatives of rights in* personam *and not rights* in rem: Obligations are the correlatives of rights in personam[1] as distinguished from rights *in rem*.[2] An obligation is the *vinculum juris* or the bond of legal necessity, which binds together two or more determinate individuals. For example, duty to pay a debt, to perform a contract or to pay damages

1. Available against a particular person.
2. Available against the world at large.

for tort. But not a duty to refrain from interfering with person, property or reputation of others because they pertain to rights *in rem*. Take *A's* obligation to pay *B* Rs. 2000. *A's* obligation is a correlative of *B's* legal right to recover Rs. 2000 from *B*. The obligation creates a *vinculum juris* between two determinate individuals *A* and *B*.

2. *Correlative of a duty & of a right:* The term obligation means not only a correlative of a duty but also correlative of a right. It denotes *vinculum juris* in its entirety. In the above example obligation has a holistic meaning. It means "*A's* duty to pay Rs. 2000 and B's right to receive the same". Putting it in a legal language we say '*B* (creditor) *owns an obligation* (right) to receive Rs. 2000 & that *A* (debtor) *incurs an obligation* to pay Rs. 2000.
3. *Relate to proprietary rights only:* All obligations pertain to sphere of proprietary rights. Rights relating to a person's status like those created by marriage, are not within the meaning of obligation even though they relate to rights *in personam*.
4. *Definition of obligation:* The obligation is defined as a proprietary right *in personam* or a duty corresponding to such right. In the broad sense of the term every obligation is described as belonging to the creditor and available against the debtor. In the narrow sense obligation means debts *i.e.* an obligation to pay a liquidated or a definite sum of money.

II. Chose-in Action and Chose-in Possession

A proprietary right *in personam* is a chose-in-action whereas a right to the thing which is in possession of the claimant is chose-in possession. For example, money in my purse is a chose-in possession. Money which you owe me as a debt is a chose-in-action. Note that the term chose-in possession is not in use. Chose in action and chose-in possession are peculiar features of English law arising out of difference between real and personal rights. The distinction is not so important in India.

In India the Transfer of Property Act defines an actionable claim under Section 3. It means.

1. Any unsecured debt to pay a liquidated sum of money. (That is where there is no mortgage or pledge as a security for loan advanced). *E.g.* right to recover damages for a breach of contract is not an actionable claim; but a claim for rent is an actionable claim.
2. Any beneficial interest in movable property which is not in the possession of the claimant whether actual or constructive. For example, the benefit of an executory contract[1] for purchase of goods is an actionable claim and it can be assigned.

III. Solidary Obligation

Two or more persons owing the same thing to the same creditor.

A normal type of obligation is one where there is one creditor and one debtor. A solidary obligation is one where two or more persons owe the same thing to the same creditor. For example, a partnership firm consisting of two partners *A* and *B* owe me Rs. 2000. It is a single debt owed to me from *A* and

1. Contract to be executed in future.

B taken together. It is not like I can recover Rs. 2000 from *A* and again Rs. 2000 from *B;* nor is it that I can recover 1000 from *A* and 1000 from *B*. I can proceed against either of them or both of them and recover Rs. 2000 from any of them. On payment of Rs. 2000 by any one of them the debt is discharged. Such obligations are known as solidary obligations since each of the debtors is bound *in solidum* (for the whole) and not for the proportional part (pro parte).

Solidary obligation are of 3 kinds: several; joint and joint and several.

1. Several: There are as many number of distinct obligations as the number of debtors. There is a distinct *vinculum juris* with each debtor and in each case the subject matter of the obligation is the same. Each debtor is liable for the full amount. Payment by one discharges the other.

2. Joint: Even if there are two or more debtors there is a single *vinculum juris* which binds several debtors to the same creditor. The main effect is that all the debtors are discharged by anything which discharges any of them. If the *vinculum juris* is severed with respect to one it is discharged with respect to the others also.

3. Joint and Several: Each debtor is separately liable for the full debt and all the debtors are also jointly liable for the full debt. For example, joint promisors are jointly and severally liable unless there is an agreement to the contrary. If the creditor discharges any one of the debtors the other debtors are not automatically discharged. Joint tort-feasors are jointly and severally liable.

Basis for determining the class to which the solidary obligation belongs depends on whether the source is the same or different.

- *Obligations are several: Solidary obligations are several:* When they are distinct in their origin though they have the same subject matter. They are joint when they have the same subject matter and also the same origin. For example, *P*, the Principal debtor owes *C* the creditor Rs. 2000, for which *S* is the surety. If the suretyship is subsequent to the creation of the debt the obligation is several. Because they are distinct in their source or origin. But if *P* and *S* have signed a joint bond then it is a case of joint obligation because the origin and the subject matter are the same.
- *Joint and several obligations:* Joint and several obligations are those joint obligations which law chooses to treat as if they were several for special reasons.

4. Provisions under the Indian Contract Act, 1872 Regarding Joint, Several and Joint and Several Obligations: When two or more persons have made a joint promise, they are known as joint promisors. They must jointly fulfil the promise unless a contrary intention appears in the Contract. If any of them dies, his legal representatives must jointly with the surviving promisors fulfil the promise. If all of them die the legal representatives of all of them must fulfil the promise. Section 43 lays down three rules regarding the performance of joint promises:

a. Any of the joint promisors may be compelled to perform- which means that the obligation is joint and several. For example, *A, B, and C* jointly promise to pay *D* Rs. 3000. *D* may compel all or any of them to pay him Rs. 3000.

b. A joint promisor compelled to perform may claim contribution from others. To continue the above example- *D* compels *A* to pay the whole of Rs. 3000. *A* may recover Rs. 1000 each from *B* and *C*.

c. A release by the promise of any of the joint promisors does not discharge the other joint promisors from their obligation. In the above example, suppose *D* releases *A* from his obligation to pay; *B* and *C* are not released from their liability towards *A;* nor is *A* released from his obligation towards *B* and *C* for contribution.

IV. Sources of Obligation

Sources of obligation are 4:

Contractual; Delictal; Quasi-contractual; Innominate.

1. ***Contractual***: Contract is an agreement which creates rights *in personam* between the parties to it. These rights are generally proprietary *i.e.*. Concerning property. But at times they may be otherwise as in the case of a contract to marry.
2. ***Delictal:*** *i.e.* Those arising from torts: Tort is a civil wrong for which the remedy is pecuniary compensation. There are 4 kinds of wrongs which are *excluded* from thė sphere of torts:
   a. *Some Crimes and Torts coincide*: Torts are a civil wrong. Crimes are wrongs but not torts. At times they coincide as in the case of trespass, defamation which are both a crime and a tort.
   b. *Every civil wrong is not tort*. What is important is that there must be a remedy in damages. If the wrong gives rise to *exclusive* remedies like injunction, restitution of property then it is not a tort.
   c. *Civil wrong which is exclusively a breach of contract is not a tort:* No civil wrong is a tort if it is exclusively a breach of contract. At times the same act is both a tort and a breach of contract. This is so in two cases:

- A man enters into a contract to do something which he is already under a duty to perform. For example, if I fail to return the vacuum cleaner as promised that I have borrowed from you there is a breach of contract and also a liability for conversion in tort for detaining another man's property.
- In certain cases breach of a contract with one person creates liability towards another person who is not a party to contract. The fundamental principle is that a person who is not a party to the contract cannot sue on the contract. But then whether he can sue *ex delicto* for a tort depends on the particular legal system. For example, a mother takes a ticket for herself in a train and thereby enters into a contract with the railways. Due to negligence there is an accident in which her 2-year old child suffers injuries. Whether there is a cause of action depends upon the details of the legal system concerned.

d. *Breaches of trust and other equitable obligations* form a class of wrongs which are not torts. They were wrongs handled by the courts of equity (Chancery courts) and not known to the common law courts. Yet even after thė law and equity were administered by the same court, contracts, torts and trusts are treated differently and with different principles.

3. Quasi-*contractual Obligation (Obligations ex contractu)*

There are certain obligations which are not contractual as they do not rest on any agreement but law treats them as though they were contractual obligations. It is a contract implied in law. According to Dr. Winfield it is an obligation imposed on a person to pay money to another person on the ground of unjust benefit.

Meritorious obligations are *quasi*-contracts. They are services rendered voluntarily, even without the consent of the owner who may not be present when the voluntary service was rendered. For example, *A* by mistake leaves a box of oranges in *B's* house without any intention of giving it as a gift. *B* consumes the same. He is bound to pay for the value of the oranges.

Under the Indian Contract Act there are 5 kinds of *quasi*-contractual obligations:

(a) *Claim for necessaries:* Claim for necessaries supplied to person incapable of contracting or on his account. *E.g. A* supplies to the wife and children of a lunatic the necessaries suited to their station in life. *A* is entitled to be reimbursed from *B's* property.

(b) *Reimbursement of payment in which interested:* Reimbursement to person who pays money due by another in payment of which he is interested. For example, *A*, a tenant of *B* pays the revenue to the Government in order to avoid the property from being sold in auction by the Government. He can recover the amount from *B*.

(c) *Non gratuitous act*: Obligation of person enjoying benefit of a non gratuitous act. It is the same as meritorious obligation seen above.

(d) *Payment by mistake:* Liability of a person to whom money is paid by mistake or thing delivered by mistake or under coercion. For example, the Bank pays an extra amount to the customer by mistake, he must return it.

(e) *Finder of the goods:* Rights and liability of the finder of the goods. The finder is treated as a bailee in respect of the goods found. He must return them and he can claim compensation for it.

4. Innominate Obligations

It is a residuary class of obligations. Those not coming within the above category are called innominate obligations. *E.g.* obligation of trustees towards their beneficiaries and other equitable obligations.

CHAPTER 24
PROCEDURE

SYNOPSIS

I. Substantive and Procedural Law

Substantive law defines rights and procedural law determines the remedy

Salmond's alternative definition based on process of litigation

Statute law is either substantive or procedural. *Substantive law defines rights and procedural law determines the remedy.* For example, Indian Penal Code is the substantive law. Code of Criminal Procedure, 1973 is the procedural law. Indian Contract Act is the substantive law. Code of Civil Procedure, 1908 is the procedural law. But then rights and procedures cannot be put in tight compartments as pointed out by Salmond. There are rights which belong to the area of procedures, for example, the right of appeal; right to examine oneself and to cross examine your opponent is not just a procedure but it is a right. Likewise there are procedures which belong to the sphere of rights, for example, abolition of capital punishment is not just an alteration in law of procedure but it deals with the valuable right to life and liberty. Similarly The Indian Penal Code deals not only with crimes but also punishments. It defines the crime and then lays down the punishment for it. Some sections of the Indian Contract Act[1] dealing with measure of damages pertain to procedures. Sections in The Code of Civil Procedure deals with substantive law whereas the Orders and the Rules under the Code deal with procedural law. The Right to Information Act, 2005 lays down both the substantive rights and also the remedies.

II. Differences between Substantive Law and Procedural Law: Salmond gives an alternative definition and the *differences between substantive law and procedural law which* are as follows:

Substantive law	Procedural law
1. What is not procedural law is substantive law and relates not to the process of litigation but to its purpose and subject matter. *i.e.* what remains after taking away the procedural laws the *residue is substantive laws.*	Law of procedure is defined as that branch of the law which *governs the process of litigation*. Salmond calls it the law of actions[2] which includes all legal proceedings civil and criminal.
2. It deals with the ends or *goals of administration of justice.*	It deals with the *means* and instruments to attain those goals.
3. It determines the conduct and relations in respect of the matters litigated.	It regulates the conduct and relations of the courts and litigants in respect of the litigation.
4. Determination of the question whether I have a right to recover certain property is a question of substantive law because it is towards the ends of justice.	In which court I must institute the case; within what time; how to institute it whether by an application or an affidavit etc. is a procedural law.
5. What facts *constitute wrong* is a substantive question because it relates to the subject matter of litigation.	What facts *constitute proof of wrong* is a procedural question because it only relates to procedure.
6. Abolition of capital punishment would be an alteration in the substantive law because punishment is one of the ends of criminal justice.	Abolition of imprisonment for non-payment of debt was only an alteration in the law of procedure because imprisonment was only an instrument for enforcing the debt.
7. In case of conflict between the substantive law and the procedural law the substantive law prevails because it deals with the substance or spirit and not the form as in the case of procedural law.	

1. Sections 73 & 74.
2. *Jus quod ad actions pertinent.*

III. Areas where Substantive Law and Procedural Laws Coincide

In spite of the differences mentioned above there are areas where substantive law and procedural laws coincide. Following are the 3 areas:

1. *Evidential fact corresponds to the title of the right:* An exclusive evidential fact corresponds to an essential ingredient in the title of the right to be proved. For example, the rule of evidence is that a mortgage can be proved only by writing and registration corresponds to the substantive law under the Transfer of Property Act that a mortgage must be in writing and registered where the principal sum secured is more than Rs. 100 or else it is void.
2. *Conclusive presumptions*: All conclusive presumptions pertain in form to procedure but in effect to the substantive law. for example the rule of evidence is that under section 82 of the Indian Penal Code a child under seven years of age is *doli in capax i.e.* incapable of criminal intention. The substantive law is that no child under seven years of age is punishable for a crime. The procedural law and the substantive law differ only in form.
3. *Time severs the bond between right and remedy:* The law of limitations like the Indian Limitation Act is the procedural equivalent of the prescriptions of rights which are given under several laws and Statutes. The Limitation Act lays down that if the remedy is not sought within the time prescribed under the Limitation Act the remedy is lost. In effect time prescribed by the Limitation Act destroys the remedy. That is operation of time under the Procedural law severs the bond between right and remedy. The procedural law leaves an imperfect right subsisting; the substantive law leaves no right at all. Take for example, the Indian Limitation Act prescribes three years for initiating an action in the court of law to recover the debt. At the expiry of 3 years the remedy is lost but an imperfect right remains.[1]

IV. 5 Elements of Pleading: Normally there are *5 Elements of Pleading*

1. *Summons*: Notices are issued to all the parties so that no person is condemned unheard and the principles of natural justice[2] are complied with.
2. *Pleadings*: Under the Code of Civil Procedure pleadings include plaint (given by the plaintiff) and the Written Statement (reply by the defendant). The pleadings set out claims, counter-claims of the parties. The pleadings help the court in framing the material propositions of law and fact alleged by one party and denied by the other party known as 'issues'. Based on the issues, evidences are led and arguments offered in support of one's own contention or to defeat the contentions of the opponent.
3. *Proof*: The contentions urged by the parties are required to be proved. Proof may be by oral evidence, documentary evidence or production of

1. "Imperfect" – because you cannot file a suit to recover it. But if the debtor voluntarily pays off the debt he cannot recover it back saying that he was not bound to pay it and that it was paid on the basis of ignorance of law of limitation.
2. Two basic principles of natural justice are: *audi alterem partem* – no person shall be condemned unheard and bias- no person shall be a judge in his own cause.

witnesses etc. This constitute the data necessary for the decision of the questions or issues raised.

4. *Judgment*: It is the decision of the judge. It is in the form of a statement given by the judge about the grounds of a decree or order.
5. *Execution*: This is the last step in the proceeding. It is the use of physical force to compel the compliance with the judgment in cases where it is not complied with voluntarily. It may involve sale or attachment of property or arrest or detention of the defendant or appointment of the receiver for the property. A decree may be executed by the court which passed it or by the court to which it is sent for execution.

Of the 5 elements of judicial procedure 'proof' requires a jurisprudential consideration.

V. Evidence

1. *Evidential fact & principal fact:* According to Salmond, fact *A* is the evidence of fact *B* when it tends to render the existence of fact *B* probable. The quality by virtue of which fact *A* has such an effect is called its probative force. Evidence is therefore defined as any fact which has a probative force. Probative force may be of varying degree. When the probative force is great enough to form a rational basis to infer that the fact evidenced really exists the evidence possessing it is said to constitute proof. Thus if fact *A* is of such a force that the inference is that fact *B* really existed then fact *A* is the proof of fact B. Fact *A* is known as the *evidential fact* and fact *A* is the *principal fact*. Taylor has defined evidence as 'all the legal means exclusive of mere argument which tend to prove or disprove any fact the truth of which is submitted to judicial investigation."[1] Thus it is after judicial investigation that a fact becomes a proof.

2. *Under the Indian Evidence Act, 1872:* Under section 3 of the Indian Evidence Act, 1872 'evidence means and includes (1) all statements which the court permits or requires to be made before it by witnesses in relation to matters of fact under inquiry, and (2) all documents produced for the inspection of the court." Section 3 has been amended to include electronic documents also.

VI. 5 Kinds of Evidence

1. Judicial and Extra-judicial Evidence

- Judicial evidence is that which is brought to the personal and direct knowledge and observation of the courts. Extra-judicial evidence is that which does not come to the direct knowledge of the courts but it forms an intermediate *link* between *judicial evidence and the principal fact.*
- *Judicial evidence includes*: Testimony given by witnesses in the court; documentary evidences produced and read by the court; all things personally examined by the court for the purpose of proof. Extra-judicial evidence includes those evidential facts known to the court through inference from some judicial evidence.
- Confession of guilt is judicial evidence if made to the court itself but extra judicial if made elsewhere and proved to the court through judicial evidence. Document is judicial evidence if produced to the

1. Taylor: Treatise on the Law of Evidence.

court but extra-judicial if known to the court through a copy or through evidence of a witness.

- In every process of proof some form of judicial evidence is an essential element; extra-judicial evidence may or may not exist.

2. *Personal and real evidence*: Personal evidence is also known as testimony. It includes oral or written statements, judicial or extra judicial so far as they are possessed of probative force. Real evidence includes all the residue of evidential facts. It is the evidence supplied by material objects other than the documents produced for inspection of the court.
3. *Primary or secondary evidence*: Often, there is a chain of evidence of the principal fact. For example, *A* is the evidence of *B*; *B* of *C*; *C* of *D* and so on. Each intermediate fact is 'evidential fact' in respect of all that follow it and principal fact in respect of all that precedes it. Thus *A* is the evidential fact for *B* which is the principal fact; *B* is the evidential fact for *C*; for principal fact *D*- *A, B, C* are all evidential facts. Longer the chain of evidence less is its probative value because with each successive inference the risk of error grows. Lesser the intermediate links more is it the proof of truth of the principal fact. Primary evidence is evidence viewed in comparison with any available and less immediate instrument of proof. Secondary evidence is that which is compared with any available and more immediate instrument of proof. For example, primary evidence that *A* assaulted *B* is the judicial testimony of *C* that he saw the assault. Secondary evidence is the judicial testimony of *D* that *C* told him that he saw the assault. Secondary evidence must not be used when primary evidence is available.
4. *Direct and circumstantial evidence (positive evidence and presumptive evidence):* Direct evidence is testimony relating immediately to the principal fact. All other evidence is circumstantial. For example, if *A* saw *B* killing *C* it is direct evidence. If *A* saw *B* coming out of *C*'s house with a blood stained knife and with a scared and a nervous look it is circumstantial evidence; or if it is found that C was killed by a knife belonging to *B* and that there was a financial transaction between them which had led to enmity and that on earlier occasions *B* had threatened to wipe C out during an altercation is circumstantial evidence.
5. *Original and hearsay:* Evidence which is seen or heard by the witness' own senses is original evidence; that which is not perceived by a witness with his own sense but it is that which is told to him by a third person is hearsay evidence.

VII. Valuation of Evidence

1. *Rules Determining the Probative Force of Evidence* (2) *Rules for the Production of Evidence*

Rules of evidence comprises two parts: *Rules determining the probative force of evidence and the rules for the production of evidence.* The two are intimately connected yet they are distinct in theory.

Note the following to understand the differences properly:

- Evidence is defined as any fact which has a probative force. That is a force which will lead us to conclude that the principal fact is proved.

- Thus, if fact *A* is produced as evidence of fact *B* under the rules of evidence we have to *measure the probative force of fact A* and find out the rules for producing the evidence.

Following are the differences:

Rules for probative force of evidence	*Rules for production of evidence*
1. They determine the probative force of the evidence.	They determine the modes and conditions of the production of evidence.
2. It deals with the *effect* of evidence when produced.	It deals with the manner in which the evidence must be produced.
3. It is concerned with evidence in all its forms whether judicial or extra-judicial.	It is concerned with judicial evidence only.

2. Weighing of Evidence—5 Rules

In some aspects law has made the weighing of evidence a matter of inflexible rule and in effect taken away the judicial discretion. Following are the 5 rules:

a. *Conclusive proof (presumptio juris et de jure):* It raises a conclusive presumption. Law regards the fact as having been proved beyond doubt and the party is not allowed to adduce contradictory evidence. A child below 7 years of age is incapable of guilty intention is a conclusive proof under section 82 of the Indian Evidence Act. A judgment is a conclusive evidence of the matters heard and decided by a court of competent jurisdiction and is binding between the parties and their privies and at times against the world at large. Though the court may have made a mistake, the matter cannot be raised again in the interest of giving finality to the dispute.

b. *Conditional presumptions (presumption juris et de jure):* They are rebuttable presumptions. For example a person not heard of for 7 years by persons who would normally have heard of him if he were alive is presumed to be dead[1]. Negotiable instrument[2] is presumed to be given for value. These presumptions can be rebutted by contrary evidence.

These presumptions are not based on any real estimate of probability. But they are based on the principle that the party which is best capable of proving the facts must prove them by rebuttal evidence. For example, an accused is presumed to be innocent until proved guilty. The presumption puts the burden of proving the guilt on the prosecution which is in a superior position to find out the truth and present them to the court than the accused.

c. *Insufficient evidence:* Where the law prescribes a certain amount or a particular nature of evidence- but the evidence adduced is not upto the prescribed standard it is said to be insufficient evidence and it is not permissible for the courts to act upon it. For example, a Will or a gift of immovable property requires a minimum of two attesting witnesses. If it is attested by only one witness it is insufficient evidence.

---

1. Known as civil death.
2. Cheques, promissory note and Bills of Exchange under the Negotiable Instruments Act.

d. *Exclusive evidence:* Certain facts are exclusive evidence. No other facts are admissible as evidence. For example, an execution of a document can be proved in no other way than by testimony of the attesting witness. A written contract can be proved by the production of the contract deed itself.

e. *Facts which are not evidence:* Certain facts are no evidence at all because they have no probative force. For example, hearsay evidence is no evidence. The general bad character of a person is no evidence that he is guilty of a particular offence though his good character is an evidence of his innocence.

3. The Production of Evidence

The second part of the law of evidence consists of rules for the production of evidence. It concerns the manner in which the witnesses are to be examined and cross examined; the process of adducing evidence; and not with its effect or the weight to be given to the evidence.

Some of those rules are:

1. Consideration of expense, delay, vexations, and public interest require certain evidence to be excluded even though it may be of evidentiary value.
2. No public servant can be compelled to give evidence as to the affairs of the State. Right to Information Act, 2005 in India[1] has considerably narrowed down this restriction. There has been a transition from an era of secrecy into an era of transparency.
3. No person can be compelled to give a self incriminatory statement *i.e.* answers which would tend to prove him guilty of the offence which gives the accused a right of silence.[2]
4. Legal advisor cannot be compelled to disclose confidential communication made by his client. Indian Evidence Act, 1872.
5. No Magistrate or any police officer shall be compelled to disclose communications made to him in official confidence.
6. All evidences are taken on oath or affirmation. Those who believe in God give evidence in the name of God; others give it of affirmation. This is to invoke an awe in the name of God. But the question always has been: how should a lying witness be detected? Today in the 21st Century we are trying to find out an answer in forensic Science.
7. A major breakthrough in the area of evidence is due to forensic science where science is applied for law purposes. "Information stored in the brain of the accused is retrieved through brain mapping. Investigators and law court are focusing towards higher probative values of evidence and the source for the same could be the brain of the individuals who have participated in the commission of crime. The fundamental difference between an innocent and the guilty person in the crime scenario is that a guilty person has committed a crime and has the

1. More than 60 countries in the world have passed the Right to Information Act.
2. Article 20 of our Constitution. Justice Malimath has questioned this provision while considering the Criminal Law Reforms.

record of crime stored in the brain and no information is present in the innocent's brain."[1] Likewise Narco analysis has emerged as a scientific tool for interrogations and criminal investigations.[2] Narco analysis means analysis of the knowledge of the individual in drug induced sleep like state.

4. Innovative Procedure under the Concept of Public Interest Litigation (PIL)

Under the concept of Public Interest Litigation in India, *locus standi* concept has been liberalized;[3] procedures are relaxed, letters have been treated as writ petitions when the petition is filed by a public spirited person without any ulterior motive in the interest of the people who are illiterate and poor. It requires no plaint, no written statement etc. proof is sought by the court by appointing *amicus curie* (friend of the court); etc commissioners are appointed by the court as fact finding body; courts play the role not of umpires but take an active part in the whole process. Yet the traditional method of litigation occupies major space in the courts of law.

In ordinary cases litigations are governed by the rules laid down in Code of Civil Procedure. Ordinarily when a dispute arises between two parties they hire the services of the advocates; plaint is prepared laying down the facts of the case; the jurisdiction of the court and the relief claimed. The case is filed in the appropriate court, court fees are paid. Court issues summons to the defendants; the defendant files his written statement answering the allegations of the plaintiff; issues are framed by the court; evidences are adduced; examination and cross examination is done by the advocates. After the arguments the judges give their decision. Judges thus play the role of an umpire. This is known as adversarial procedure.

In public interest litigation cases, the court is pro-active. It is more assertive and assumes a positive attitude in determining facts. The procedure is of a non-adversarial nature. It is known as inquisitorial procedure. The Supreme Court disapproves the adversarial procedure for PIL matters because it sometimes leads to injustice as where the parties are not evenly balanced in social and economic strength. There is also difficulty in getting competent legal representation and a difficulty in producing relevant evidence before the court because a PIL can be filed by any public spirited person with a *bona fide* intention. He need not be a law graduate. He can be as illiterate as a person who does not know to sign his name also. But he may be driven by the public spirit to fight injustice.

Nevertheless one thing is certain. The procedure may be relaxed in PIL cases, but not given a go-bye. Hence the court requires evidence of the facts and proof of the allegations before any judgment is passed and the sound principles of natural justice have to be followed. Hence, some procedure had to be evolved by

1. Brain mapping: a non-invasive Technology – by Dr. S. Malini and Dr. B.M. Mohan –Asst. Director and Director Forensic Science Laboratory, Bangalore. Paper presented at the One Day National Level Seminar on 'Forensic Science In The Administration Of Justice: Perspectives, Challenges And Agenda For The Future' conducted by the J.S.S. Sakri Law College and KILPAR, Bangalore at Hubli on 12th April, 2008.
2. *Ibid.* Paper titled "Narco Analyisis."
3. Under the traditional *locus standi* concept only the person aggrieved could approach the court..

the Judiciary to handle PIL cases. Procedures evolved include appointment of Commissions to investigate and ascertain the facts; courts have appointed advocates as *amicus curie* to help them in PIL matters. At times the judges have themselves visited the places like jails to ascertain the truth. The commission's report furnishes *prima facie* evidence of facts gathered by the Commissioner. In *Bandhua Mukti Morcha* v. *Union of India* the court has held that it is not correct to say that the Commissioner's report has no evidentiary value because the statements are not tested by cross examination. When the Commissioner holds enquiry, considers facts and circumstances; makes local inspection and discusses the matters with the parties and submits a report with its findings and reasons, *prima facie* it constitutes evidence and the courts can act upon it. The court will not ordinarily interfere with its findings. Only when reliable contradictory evidence is available it may interfere with its findings.

This innovative procedure is judge-made and judge-induced and its jurisprudence is developed by the courts in the sense we have no statute to deal specifically with public interest litigations enacted by the Legislature.

CHAPTER 25

THE EVOLUTION OF LAW

SYNOPSIS

I. The Primitive Community
II. Primitive Law: Before the Era of the Courts
III. Primitive Law: Courts
IV. Primitive Law: Codes
V. Middle Law
VI. Middle Law: Equity
VII. Classical Law
VIII. Post-Classical Law

I. The Primitive Community

Speculation has invented simple lines of human evolution. Thus it was said that men lived first in the stone age, then in the bronze age and finally in the iron age; that in marriage promiscuity came first, then one wife with many husbands, then one husband with many wives and finally monogamy. In economic activity there is a simple advance from hunting to pastoralism, to agriculture and then to the machine age. Anthropological research has shown that this is a misleading simplification of the problem which in reality is much more complex. All races have not followed the same lines of evolution. Thus if economic means of obtaining a livelihood influence a social structure, social doctrines also influence economic forces.

Hence it is not possible to lay down a definite a correlation between law and the culture of a society. Law is a result of all forces which make up a society. There is definitely a relationship between the law and the culture of the society. But there is a time lag between the creation of new material culture – such as machine of the industrial age and the development of new social methods of control. Law adapts itself slowly to the new conditions, so a violent revolution is necessary. At times there are rapid jumps in legal revolution because of direct borrowing of modern commercial codes (laws) without passing through intermediate stages. India and Pakistan have taken rapid jumps in legal revolution.

Societies may be classified on the basis of the methods employed in earning a living. Primitive Law covers communities in the following categories; Lower Hunters, Higher Hunters, Pastoralists, Advanced Pastoralists, First Agricultural Grade, Second, Agricultural Grade and Third Agricultural Grade. The most ambitious attempt to discover the correlation between the economic stage which a tribe has reached and its culture and legal institutions is that of Hobhouse, Wheeler and Ginsberg.

Some striking features in the evolution of law are[1]

1. Primitive law
2. Middle law
3. Classical law
4. Post classical law

II. Primitive Law: Before the Era of the Courts

It was once thought that there was no need of a system of law in the primitive society because it was automatically law-abiding. The traditions of a tribe were regarded as a confused mass of usage, custom and religion; it was said that there was no law, no individual property, no real means of enforcing any right which an individual thought he possessed- except self-help. What kept the community together was the fear of the unknown, of th estrange spirits that may punish man. Early law, therefore springs from a religious sanction, the fear of the unknown, of te spirits that dwell everywhere.

Modern research shows that this view needs correction. It is true that public opinion is more powerful in a tiny village than in a world capital. Yet all customs are not on the same level- some are followed because men choose to follow them either as a matter of convenience or because they have never dreamt of doing otherwise, but others cut across human desires and passions and hence require an effective machinery of enforcement. If harmless, innocent ways of life are altered the society would not bother. But rules concerning adultery or rape may need a powerful sanction. Malinowski considers this as the germ of primitive law. There is no sanction in the Austinian sense (that law is the command of the Sovereign). There is no penalty imposed by a determinate body- but the law does rest on a greater force than the vague pressure of public opinion. The very organization of community protects the law, ultimate sanction for the primitive man was expulsion or death- a sentence imposed not by a predetermined tribunal but by some members with the active approval of the rest. Later even when courts were fully developed there were sentences of death pronounced by a community which had no police constables or professional hangmen. Economic sanctions were enforced by the threat of the 'stop list' – that is, if a person refused to make the customary payment, no other member would help such a defaulter.

At a very early stage there was a distinction between a payment made out of an obligation and a payment made out of generosity. This was undoubtedly the germ of law.

Before the advent of courts – the sphere of pre-law was very small. There were few rules concerning property, marriage, inheritance on death. Private wrongs were settled in some cases by the victim taking revenge and in some cases through payment of compensation. There were a few offences which were regarded as an outrage on the community as a whole, such as incest, witchcraft, and general incompatibility of temperament.

As far as India is concerned-even during the pre-civilization days the Hindu legal system was quite comprehensive though intermingled with religion. The

1. G.W. Paton: a Text Book of Jurisprudence, p. 42.

Vedas, the Smritis, the Shrutis, the Bhagwad Gita all speak of a duty-based society and contain

III. Primitive Law: Courts

About the end of the First Agricultural grade, institutions emerged which performed several functions including the functions performed by the courts. With the starting of the courts the sphere of law became more definite and the rules became more precise. Yet it was a long and a slow evolution before there were institutions with the effective powers of the courts, legislatures, and the police mechanism of the modern State.

The orthodox theory is that the first task of the court was to moderate the blood feud[1] and regulate self-help. The *lex talionis* permits the aggressor to inflict an injury similar to that which he received. Then the doctrine was that the victim could accept compensation, and if that was not paid, physical violence may be inflicted. As courts became more powerful, acceptance of compensation was made compulsory, except for offences which were regarded as an outrage against the community and deserving punishment. Courts existed but the methods of enforcement were still primitive *e.g.* a claimant must himself secure the attendance of his opponent – even by violence as a last resort. In Assyria the State benefited by the forced labour imposed on the criminals, and a compensation was given to the injured party and desire for revenge was satisfied by infliction of beatings.

This orthodox theory of legal evolution needs correction. The distinction between civil and criminal law appears to be there much before it was suggested. That depends on what is the test of criminal law. If the test of criminal law is the that the wrong is regarded as a wrong against the community at large and not just the individual- the distinction between civil and criminal law was there much prior in point of time during the primitive law period. But if the test of criminal law is the sentence passed by the court and execution of the sentence by the State- then the distinction between civil and criminal law was a late development. In some primitive societies definite rules of criminal law were enforced by superstitious practices-sorcery or the supernatural consequences of taboo (prohibition).

In the beginning, the concept was more of *physical liability than of legal duty;* it was more *of community responsibility than of individual responsibility.* A debtor gives a hostage as security; if the debtor defaults, it is the hostage who is liable and not the debtor. Liability for debt meant physical liability of the hostage to be cut in pieces or sold into slavery and not execution against goods as we understand today. The law of contract was not yet born. The debtor was regarded as one who wrongfully detains the creditor's property.

In the law of delict, we notice a similar concept as 'thing liability'. *Deodand*[2] illustrates this tendency. If Paul took John's sword and killed Peter with it, the sword was forfeited. Later in English law, instead of losing the *res* (*the thing, the property*), the owner could pay its value to the Crown. In 1842, in England, a railway company was forced to pay deodand because of deaths resulting from

1. Old quarrel amongst groups resulting in murder on both sides.
2. It is a thing forfeited or given to God, specially in law, an object which becomes forfeit because it has caused a person's death.

a locomotive accident. In deodand- liability was attached to the inanimate thing (*res*).

There has been a gradual change from liability of the person to the liability of the goods possessed by the person. In the beginning when the court began to grant execution against the property- the tendency was to seize *all* the property of the defendant even for a small sum of money owed to the creditor. To take only sufficient property as to cover the debt amount was a slow development. Today imprisonment for debt is restricted- liability is limited to man's property. It may be noted that in India, under the Code of Civil Procedure, 1908 – we still have a provision for civil imprisonment under section 51-A though Justice J.V.R. Krishna Iyer has condemned the same in *Jolly Verghese* case.[1]

Primitive law is not rigid and inelastic not is it largely concerned with procedural details. It is in the middle period that excessive formality develops. Law begins with vague and elastic rules. Technicality is the result of a long period of development. When technicalities appear in commercial transactions, in property or in legal procedure, they mark the end of he period of primitive law. for example, the law of contract begins in a simple way and it is only in the middle period that it becomes technical and relatively fixed.

IV. Primitive Law: Codes

Codes begin to appear somewhere after the third agricultural grade. Classified according to degree of internal development – early codes may be represented by the *Salic Law*; middle codes extend from the *Leges Barbarorum* of the reign of Charlemagne to the more developed laws of the *Pentateuch* and the *Twelve Tables*; as an example of a late code we have that of *Hammurabi* (which is very early historically).

Maine emphasized the influence of religion on early codes. The codes of Hammurabi and of the Assyrians are predominantly secular in character. In the Hebrew Pentateuch in the Hindu Code of Manu, and in the Roman Twelve Tables- religious sanctions are to be found. Diamond submits the Hebrew code to precise analysis and shows that the early code was secular but there were priestly additions made at a later date. His theory is that there was a clear-cut division between jurisdiction of the priest and the ruler. When the priest became more powerful – they not only acquired more secular powers but also made priestly additions in the secular code.

During this period punishments were imposed on the religious idea that the community is polluted by the crime and the "land can be cleaned only by the blood of him that shed it."[2] Driver and Miles conclude that the Assyrian theory of punishment had no such religious basis. In primitive times religion was undoubtedly one of the forces which created society and therefore the law. in all probability the codes did not create much that was new and were largely the result of a consolidation of scattered legislation. The much accepted view is that all primitive law was the work of one person for example, Hebrew law was traced to Moses. However it is inconceivable that it could be one man's job.

1. AIR 1980 SC 470.
2. Hebrew text.

The use of writing has an important influence because law becomes more definite and generates a new professional class which is more diverse, numerous and active than when the custody of law was with the oral tradition of the law.

V. Middle Law

In this period we notice a gradual growth of rigidity and technicality in the sphere of law. Formalism is a relic of traditional ceremonies of religious ritual, that parties desire a religious sanction or that some ceremony is considered necessary to create a binding sense of obligation in the minds of the parties.

Maine writes that "when primitive law has once been embodied in a code, there is an end to its spontaneous development". Thereafter law is brought into harmony with society by three instrumentalities – legal fiction, equity and legislation.[1]

The use of fictions and equity is not confined to any one period. The fiction is useful at a time when legal stability is desired, but a change in the applicability of law is felt to be imperative. Fictions are in use even on this date – for example, quasi-contract is a legal fiction. Fiction is an assumption which conceals the fact that a rule of law has undergone an alteration. But it is not meant to deceive. It is partly 'economy of thought' – the desire to use old devices that have worked well instead of running the risk of innovation.

VI. Middle Law: Equity

Every legal system has a conflict between two types of judicial mind- upholding the logical elegance of law even at the cost of injustice and inconvenience on one hand; and that law exists for men and not men for law and hence rules must be so adapted that injustice is avoided. It is a difference between *strictum ius and aequitas*. Once the era of formalism and technicality begins we see the commencement of strife. Legal technique may become so absorbing that the game is played for its own sake as in the hay days of the formalistic rules of English pleading.

In England there were separate courts of law and courts of equity. Chancery courts were the courts of equity where judgments were rendered in accordance with the dictates of one's conscience based on what is just and reasonable to do justice to the case on hand. Hence the English lawyers exaggerated the opposition between *strictum ius and aequitas*. (strict law and perfect justice) Yet the increasing technicality of the common law rendered the existence of the equity powers of the Chancellors a real necessity.

In Rome the work of the praetor in modernizing the law, enforcing the requirement of good faith, emphasizing the intention of the parties rather than the form of the agreement – is similar to that of the Chancery courts of equity. Interference of equity with the law is more 'open and avowed' than in the case of a fiction which pretends to leave the letter of the law unchanged. In most continental countries the same word is used for law and justice. Equity is a force working through law and not in opposition to law.

VII. Classical Law

The classical stage is marked by a sudden flowering of legal genius. The community is economically well established but rapid social developments have

1. H.J.S. Maine: Ancient Law (ed. F. Pullock), 26, 29.

left the law far behind. There was a danger that law may become a mere chaos of specific precedents for, although, rules are many; principles are few. There is a need for classification, analysis and synthesis (blend). The dead law of the past must be cut away in order to allow future growth to be unhampered.

The Roman jurists of the classical era and the English judges and writers of the nineteenth century analyzed the concepts which the law uses in order to achieve clarity; made a search for the general principles which explain the actual rules in force and provided a ground for future development. A law which has a proper theoretical basis is more easily understood, applied and extended than one which lacks such a foundation. Developed Jurisprudence begins in the classical age. For example the English law of Torts was greatly developed through the influence of the writings of Pollock and Salmond. Search for principles may be carried out by the court and also by an academic writer. Thus J. Blackburn explained several isolated rules of strict liability by a new principle which has shown great capacity for development. In our country the Judiciary has pooled its dexterity in several areas. To quote just a few examples- the Jurisprudence of Article 21 and Article 32 opened up a new vista of enforceable rights of the aggrieved citizens; the *locus standi* concept was liberalized resulting in entertaining Public Interest Litigations.

The classical period cannot hope to stabilize the law entirely. But if the search for the principle has been successful, the can be adapted and modified to suit new conditions.

VIII. Post-Classical Law

In this period, society becomes more complex, and rapid development of the law is inevitable. In Roman post-classical law there are certain definite characteristics: increasing reliance on equity at the cost of legal principle-the desire for attaining justice is understandable and commendable but there is too much of a tendency to take an intellectual short-cut; a desire to protect the weak at the expense of the strong.[1] This was due to in part to the influence of Christianity and a growing appreciation of the value of the human personality; increasing emphasis on intention at the expense of form. These characteristics are seen today also.

After the post-classical period Roman law has left its mark deep on the modern world. In mature systems- there is a tendency to deal with new situations by statutes designed for a particular mischief only. A flood of such remedies leaves the law in a somewhat incoherent state. Legal elegance is needed otherwise the system loses its underlying unity and it becomes hard to teach and difficult to apply. Hence there is need to study the basis of statutory law. Otherwise law may cease to be a system and become a collection of *ad hoc* rules.

After independence- we have been very much influenced by the western philosophy.

---

1. As in India today–where the laws giving effect to the directives principles have been upheld even when the fundamental rights of the few are adversely affected.

GLOSSARY OF IMPORTANT WORDS

Words	Meaning
Abstract	theoretical,
acting for the Crown	acting for the King/Queen
actionable in the courts of law	filing of Civil or criminal proceedings in the court of law
adaptation	alteration to suit the needs of the time or situation etc
alleviating	lessen, reduce
amenable	Agreeable, open to
amicably	kindly, harmoniously good naturedly
anomalous	strange, abnormal, irregular
antecedent	earlier, forerunner
archaic	old, outmoded
archaism	old
arid	dry
artifice	trick, pretence
ascertain	find out
at times predictability is more important	it means that even if the law laid down by the courts is –say- a bit unjust *i.e.* not ideal-
than approximation to an ideal	it is to be tolerated if there is predictability or certainty.
bequeath	gift by will
caliber	talent, ability
complies	observes or follows
conform	obey the rules
consequent.	result, effect
contingent-	conditional
co-ordinate	matching; on same footing
corresponding rights	equivalent rights
culpable	Blameworthy
cause of action	All those bundle of facts which a plaintiff must prove in order to be entitled to the relief claimed
de-novo	new; afresh
derecognizing the custom	custom recognized in the past is now not recognized by law

Words	Meaning
derivative	derived from someone
design	plan
determinate	identifiable
detrimental	harmful
diligence	care- (absence of negligence)
dissent	opposition
dissuade	discourage
divest	take away
dominion	control, authority
dubious	doubtful
enduring	lasting or stable
entity	body, unit, thing
ethical	moral, principled
exotic	foreign
extortion	obtain by threat
fallacy	error in belief
foresee	anticipate, hope for, to see in advance that certain results will follow from a certain act
functus officio	ceases to hold office
formalization	to put in a form extra judicial evidence: extra judicial evidence: *e.g.* hither to unwritten personal or conventional law is inserted in a statute which is formal in nature
genus	class or group
gulf	gap
garnishee order	an order to recover from your debtor's debtor. For example, *A* has a decree against *B* to recover Rs. 1000. *C* owes *B* Rs 1000. *A* can recover Rs. 1000 from C by obtaining Garnishee order from the Court, so that court directs *C* to pay Rs. 1000 to *A* instead of *B*.
Habeas Corpus petition	produce the body of the person before the court
hardly quoted any decisions	did not quote decisions or those quoted were negligible
identical	same, matching
idiosyncrasy	unconventional behaviour
immunity	protection
in spite of	notwithstanding; despite of; regardless of

Words	Meaning
inadequate	insufficient
inanimate	lifeless
incorrigible	incurable, irredeemable
indicative	pinpointing
inexpedient	Inconvenient, impractical
inherent	incurable, irredeemable
ipso jure	legal force
irrevocable	Irreversible
institutionalized imposition of penalties	as distinguished from personalised imposition of penalties. There is a whole set up of judiciary to try the case, give a hearing, listen to arguments of the parties and then penalties are imposed. Distinguish it from non institutionalised penalties as in the case where parent punished the child
legal diction	Legal speech
letters of administration	They are issued by the competent authority to the administrator who has to administer the property of the deceased person who has died without leaving a will *i.e.* died intestate
measure the probative force of fact-	weighing the evidence of facts that is given in a particular case
mortgage	Transfer of an interest in the immovable property to secure the repayment of loan One who transfers the interest is the mortgagor and in whose favour it is transferred is the mortgagee and the loan amount with its interest is the mortgage money.
matter in issue	All material propositions of law or fact alleged by one party and denied by the other are said to be in issue.
negligence	casual, inattention
obligatory	compulsory
obsolete	outdated
omnipotent-	all powerful
paradigm	example, model
per-se	by itself
perverted	misrepresented, changed
philosophical	truth seeking, thoughtful, idealistic

Words	Meaning
pledge	debtor deposits movable goods with the creditor to secure the repayment of loan
preceding	former, earlier
precise	clear cut
premise	foundation, hypothesis
previous	earlier
proprio vigore	of its own force
purpose	goal, target
purpose	goal, target
power of appointment	power given by one person to another to dispose of a property of which he is not the owner. *E.g.* by my will I authorize you to dispose of my property
patent right	A person invents something which is new, innovative. He can register the patent by following the prescribed procedure in the Indian Patents Act and get an exclusive use and control over his invention like he can assign it to some one else for a monetary consideration or use it himself for the prescribed number of years and then the invention falls into the public domain *i.e.* it becomes a public property. It protects, recognises and promotes research talent which ultimately benefits the society.
rationale	underlying principle or justification
recklessness	careless, irresponsible
redundant	Superfluous, outmoded
residue	remainder
resume	Restart, take up again
restitution for conjugal rights	Petitioner –say wife- seeks a direction from the court to her husband who has left her consortium (company) to join and perform the conjugal duties i.e. marital duties
right to redeem	in a mortgage the mortgagor transfers his interest in his immovable property to secure the repayment of a loan. Under the right of redemption the mortgagor pays off his debt to the mortgagee and gets back the interests that he has transferred to the mortgagee to secure the repayment of loan.

Words	Meaning
sanctions	penalties, punishments
severed	to cut off
static	motionless or inert
subsequent	later
synonym	same meaning word
synthesis	combination
suits for declaration	they are suits where the relief sought is only a declaration (without any consequential relief) that the plaintiff has a right to a particular thing/or a right or a share in a particular property/or that he is in possession of property/or it may be a declaration regarding the date of birth/or that the plaintiff is an adopted child etc.
taboo	forbidden
testimony	evidence
touchstone	criterion
title	originally it meant a mark, sign, or inscription. As now understood it means evidence of right or ownership.
vicious	cruel, inhuman
voidable contract	contract which can be rescinded (avoided) at the instance of one party but not at the instance of another

SUBJECT INDEX

•••